CROSS-CULTURAL
ADAPTATION

INTERNATIONAL AND INTERCULTURAL
COMMUNICATION ANNUAL

Volume XI   **1987**

Editor
Young Yun Kim
Governors State University

Coeditor
William B. Gudykunst
Arizona State University

Consulting Editors for Volume XI

John W. Berry
Queen's University, Canada

Richard W. Brislin
East-West Culture and Communication Institute

Amado M. Padilla
University of California at Los Angeles

W. Barnett Pearce
University of Massachusetts at Amherst

Stella Ting-Toomey
Arizona State University

Ingemar Torbiorn
University of Stockholm, Sweden

June O. Yum
State University of New York at Albany

INTERNATIONAL AND INTERCULTURAL COMMUNICATION ANNUAL
VOLUME XI   1987

CROSS–CULTURAL ADAPTATION

CURRENT APPROACHES

edited by

Young Yun KIM
William B. GUDYKUNST

Published in Cooperation with
The Speech Communication Association
Commission on International and Intercultural Communication

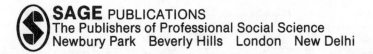

SAGE PUBLICATIONS
The Publishers of Professional Social Science
Newbury Park   Beverly Hills   London   New Delhi

For information address:

SAGE Publications, Inc.
2111 West Hillcrest Drive
Newbury Park, California 91320

SAGE Publications Inc.
275 South Beverly Drive
Beverly Hills
California 90212

SAGE Publications Ltd.
28 Banner Street
London EC1Y 8QE
England

SAGE PUBLICATIONS India Pvt. Ltd.
M-32 Market
Greater Kailash I
New Delhi 110 048 India

Printed in the United States of America

International Standard Book Number 0-8039-3037-2

International Standard Book Number 0-8039-3038-0 (pbk.)

International Standard Series Number 0270-6075

FIRST PRINTING

Contents

Preface

The flow of humans across national and cultural boundaries is more active than ever before. In a single year, millions around the world relocate from country to country. Among them are diplomats and other intergovernmental agency employees, business men and women on international assignments, researchers working in cultures other than their own, students attending academic institutions overseas, military personnel on foreign duty, and missionaries carrying out their religious services. Then there are refugees and immigrants who are on the move across societal boundaries—in search of freedom, security, and social, economic, or cultural betterment.

In this worldwide context of cross-cultural migration, the concept "adaptation" takes on a special social and academic significance, not only here in the United States but also in many other countries that receive immigrants, refugees, and sojourners. This volume presents current studies dealing with the cross cultural adaptation of individuals who are born and raised in one culture and find themselves in need of modifying their customary life patterns in a foreign culture.

The present volume is the eleventh of the *International and Intercultural Communication Annual*. This publication is sponsored by the Speech Communication Association Division of International and Intercultural Communication. Beginning with Volume VII, the *Annual* has focused on specific themes as captured in the volume titles: *Intercultural Communication Theory* (VII), *Methods for Intercultural Communication Research* (VIII), *Intercultural Communication in Organizations* (IX), and *Interethnic Communication: Current Approaches* (X). The guiding principle in preparing for this volume was to present theoretical and research studies that focus primarily on *individ-*

uals in examining the cross-cultural adaptation process. To maximize the representation of interdisciplinary approaches to the present theme, a call for papers was announced in newsletters of all major behavioral-social science associations in the United States. Additionally, a number of prominent individuals, both in the United States and in other countries, were invited to participate in this volume.

Thus we have brought together some of the most current conceptualizations and research findings on cross-cultural adaptation. The 14 chapters reflect the multidisciplinary and multi-societal approaches that exist today. The authors are from the disciplines of psychology, communication, and anthropology; they reside in Australia, Canada, England, Sweden, and the United States. Individually and collectively, they present ideas and research findings that contribute to the further development of our scientific understanding of the dynamics of cross-cultural adaptation.

THE THEME:
ADAPTATION OF CULTURAL STRANGERS

The international migrants who travel in both time and geographical space achieve an "existential alertness." International migration represents a situation in which the newly arrived individuals are required to cope with substantial cultural change. Although situations of migration vary in the degree to which the transition is abrupt or smooth, voluntary or involuntary, and temporary or permanent, all individuals in a new cultural milieu share common adaptation experiences. All are "strangers" in a foreign land, and no one can completely escape from the demands of the new life setting. Every stranger in a new culture must cope with a high level of uncertainty and unfamiliarity. The task of all cultural strangers is to acquire the necessary competence to function satisfactorily, at least at a minimal level.

Being at risk, moving into a new and unfamiliar land makes cultural strangers alert and quick to learn. Sooner or later, the cultural strangers come to structure, or better make sense of, a personally relevant situation in the host society. Handling the transactions of daily living necessitates detecting similarities and differences between the surrounding host society and the home culture. They gradually become acquainted with various aspects of living in any given environment; from maintaining basic survival necessities—physical safety and health—to working for their livelihood, developing relationships, and enjoying leisure activities. They become increasingly proficient in handling their daily activities in the new culture with improved skills to deal with the situations they encounter.

This process of cross-cultural adaptation is the theme of this volume. The term *cross-cultural adaptation* is used here in a broad and all-inclusive sense to refer to the complex process through which an individual acquires an increasing level of "fitness" or "compatibility" in the new cultural environment. The term is also intended to accommodate other similar terms such as *acculturation, assimilation,* and *adjustment.*

THE FIELD: A BACKGROUND

The study of cross-cultural adaptation has been active in the United States, a nation in which immigrants and ethnic diversity have always been a major reality and an issue of serious concern. Comparatively, immigrant adaptation studies have been more recent and less extensive in the academic traditions of European countries. Cross-cultural adaptation, because of its multiple facets and dimensions, has been viewed from many angles and measured in terms of various aspects and categories such as changes in economic condition, perception, attitude, behavior, linguistic proficiency, and ethnic/cultural identity. Each of these categories, in turn, has included diverse elements that could be examined separately with varying degrees of scientific legitimacy. Social scientists today are far from being homogeneous in intellectual orientations in studying the adaptation process.

The literature related to cross-cultural adaptation has accumulated since the turn of the century. Serious work began in cultural anthropology and sociology that focused primarily on the level of immigrant/cultural groups rather than on the level of individuals. Many anthropological studies have investigated cultures (primarily "primitive" cultures) that were going through changes as the result of continuous contact with another culture. The term *acculturation* has been used in anthropological literature to refer to "those phenomena which result when *groups* of individuals have different cultures and come into first-hand contact with subsequent changes in the original pattern of either or both *groups*" (Redfield, Linton, & Herskovits, 1936, p. 149; emphasis added).

As indicated in this definition, the discipline of anthropology has treated acculturation primarily as a group phenomenon. In examining the acculturation of various groups, anthropological studies have often observed the importance of the presence of kin, friends, and ethnic affiliates. These and other aspects of urban ethnic communities have been investigated in anthropological studies as a key agency facilitating the acculturation of new immigrants (Snyder, 1976; also Chapter 13 in this volume).

While the majority of anthropological studies have observed changes and activities in the culture of the target group itself, sociological studies have primarily focused on issues pertaining to social stratification, that is, hierarchical classification of ethnic groups based on the unequal distribution of resources, power, and prestige (see Parrillo, 1966, p. 80). In addition, many sociological studies have analyzed the patterns and processes by which immigrant (ethnic) groups are integrated into the political, social, and economic structure of the host society, and the dynamics of relationships within and among minority and majority groups (see Glazer & Moynihan, 1970, 1975; Gordon, 1964; Spiro, 1955). The terms *ethnicity* and *assimilation,* in addition to *acculturation,* have been frequently used in sociological literature.

More recently, an increasing amount of academic attention has been given to cross-cultural adaptation on the individual level. Numerous studies in psychology (or social psychology), psychiatry, communication, and other related disciplines have focused on individual immigrants and sojourners since the 1950s. While studies of immigrants' adaptation are a natural extension of the "older" group-level approaches, studies of short-term adaptation of sojourners were stimulated by the post-Second World War boom in student exchanges and by the Peace Corps movement. In the sojourn studies, psychological terms such as *culture shock, adjustment* and *social integration* have been used to refer to the sojourners experiences in the new environment.

One of the earlier views of long-term immigrant adaptation was presented by Taft (1957, and Chapter 7 in this volume). He delineated seven stages of "assimilation," progressively from the "cultural learning" stage to the "congruence" stage. These stages were based on a number of key psychological concepts (such as "attitude," "frame of reference," and "role behavior") that were considered to influence an individual's adaptation process. Another view was provided by Berry and his associates (1980, and Chapter 3 in this volume), who identified four types of "acculturation" ("integration," "assimilation," "rejection," and "marginality"). This fourfold model was proposed by Berry and his associates based on an immigrant's adherence to the original cultural identity and attitude toward the host society. In addition, Y. Kim (1979, in press) proposed a multidimensional, interactive theory of immigrant "acculturation." Kim's theory incorporates the psychological and social processes of immigrants in interacting with their host environment. In this approach, the individual immigrant's personal, interpersonal, and media communication activities are viewed as central to his or her acculturation.

Compared to approaches to immigrants' long-term adaptation, the studies of short-term adaptation have placed a greater emphasis on the psychological well-being and mental health of cultural strangers in encountering unfamiliar environmental demands. Such concern is based on the common recognition of the "problemetic" nature of the cross-cultural adaptation process. This problem orientation is reflected in the frequent reference in literature to "culture shock" and similar terms such as *transition shock* or *culture fatigue* (see Chapter 2 by Furnham and Chapter 8 by Torbiorn). Closely related to this orientation is the emphasis on the "U-curve" or "W-curve" process of change in the attitude and satisfaction level of sojourners (see Lysgaard, 1955; Gullahorn & Gullahorn, 1963).

Another group of studies has focused on the "effectiveness" of sojourners in foreign cultural environments. These studies have attempted to identify a set of "independent" variables that are considered to promote or deter the effectiveness of sojourners overseas. Different studies have, however, focused on different factors that influence the overseas effectiveness, as recently summarized by Kealey and Ruben (1983).

TOWARD AN INTEGRATION OF DIVERSE APPROACHES

Today, the serious scholar of cross-cultural adaptation has thousands of books and articles that must be studied for a complete understanding of work in this area. A wide variety of literature and data sources makes it difficult for any one individual to gain familiarity with all of the literature across the disciplinary boundaries. Although the field has benefited from the richness of the literature that reports information and insights regarding various aspects of the cross-cultural adaptation process, it has also suffered from increased specialization and complexity. Often, confusion has resulted from the application of divergent viewpoints, definitions, and methodologies peculiar to different disciplinary perspectives. The studies of immigrants and of sojourners have been more or less separate and independent from each other with little cross-fertilization, although many common features have been discussed in the respective areas of study.

Some of the diversity and complexity that characterizes the field is reflected in this volume. Within this diversity, however, this volume presents an integration between the theoretical and empirical research endeavors, between the psychological, communication, and anthropological approaches, and between the studies of long-term and short-term adaptation. Each of the six theoretical essays in Part I presents an effort to provide a synthesis of the relevant concepts and perspectives. In Chapter 1, Pearce and Kang lay a metatheoretical groundwork for theorists in interpreting cultural differences embedded in individuals' communication patterns—a key aspect of cross-cultural adaptation. The authors analyze the monocultural, ethnocentric perspective prevalent in the tradition of "objective" inquiries and propose the "new paradigm" that emphasizes the fundamental role played by culture in studying the communication behavior of individuals. Pearce and Kang also discuss an isomorphism between the experiences of immigrants adapting to cross-cultural differences and to the experiences of all individuals in contemporary societies adapting to their rapidly changing cultural milieu.

In Chapter 2, Furnham attempts to integrate the widely diffuse area of sojourner adaptation. The varied definitions and conceptualizations of "sojourners," "adjustment," and "culture shock" are critically examined. The author looks into the almost exclusive emphasis on the negative aspects in existing views of sojourner adaptation, and carefully evaluates eight possible theoretical explanations for culture shock. Taking a somewhat broader perspective, Berry, U. Kim, and Boski provide in Chapter 3 an overview of the various concepts associated with cross-cultural adaptation of individuals. The authors also present a model of "psychological acculturation," in which different adaptation patterns of five types of groups (immigrants, refugees, native peoples, ethnic groups, and sojourners) are identified.

The next two theoretical approaches in Chapter 4 and Chapter 5 are based on communication-oriented concepts. In Chapter 4, McGuire and McDermott introduce a communication-based model that explains the process of immigrant adaptation. This model focuses on the "assimilation" and the "alienation" states as two opposite end-states, and "deviance" as the intermediate state, of individual immigrants' communication in the host cultural environment. The key concept employed by McGuire and McDermott to explain these different communication states is the "communication denial" perceived by individual immigrants. The other communication-based theory, explicated by Gudykunst and Hammer in Chapter 5, focuses on the "uncertainty reduction" and the accompanying "anxiety" as two central theoretical concepts. This approach accommodates both immigrants and sojourners as cultural "strangers" in an unfamiliar cultural environment, and explicates axioms and theorems that relate the two central concepts with various other factors that accompany the adaptation process.

The theoretical perspective presented in Chapter 6 by Yoshikawa can be described as a humanistic-psychological-philosophical approach with a specific focus on the perceptual development in the process of cross-cultural adaptation. Yoshikawa views the cross-cultural adaptation process as a creative process that shares an analogous relationship with scientific discovery and religious enlightenment. Incorporating both the Western and Eastern traditions of idea, the author places a particular emphasis on the "double-swing" stage as an advanced stage of perceptual refinement.

Part II presents eight recent empirical studies dealing with cross-cultural adaptation that differ in their respective research foci and variables. Taft, in Chapter 7, presents his theoretical framework of immigrant adaptation. As described previously, Taft views immigrant adaptation in terms of five "facets" (such as "adjustment" "national and ethnic identity," "cultural competence," and "role acculturation"). Based on this perspective, Taft reports some of the findings (as well as measurements) from a study of Soviet immigrants in Australia.

While Taft's approach covers a wide range of adaptation-related ideas, Torbiorn concentrates on one important aspect: "cultural barriers" in Chapter 8. Torbiorn theorizes that the cultural barrier experienced by an individual sojourner varies according to "objective" cultural differences between the original culture and the host culture and reports some empirical support for this theory from a study of Swedish expatriates in 26 countries. Similarly, Yum's study reported in Chapter 9 focuses on the "locus of control" of individuals as the key concept that influences some of the communication patterns of immigrants. Yum tested this theoretical relationship among five ethnic groups in Hawaii, and reports a generally supportive empirical evidence for the hypothesized relationship.

In Chapter 10, Szalay and Inn investigate the "psychocultural meaning systems" of five Hispanic immigrant groups in the United States. Employing the Associative Group Analysis method to assess and compare the respective group's meaning system, the authors report findings that clearly suggest an adaptive change in the immigrants toward the mainstream American way of thinking. In Chapter 11, Mägiste reports a study of German and Polish immigrant groups in Sweden focusing on the developmental changes in the cerebral "lateralization" patterns. Employing various linguistic measures, Mägiste observed decreasing left hemisphere involvement with increasing proficiency in Swedish in the immigrants.

In Chapter 12, Punetha, Giles, and Young report a study of three immigrant groups (Sikhs, Hindus, and Muslims) in England, as well as the native Britons. The study explores the psychological distances between groups as assessed by their perceptions and evaluations of each other. These intergroup perceptions and evaluations are then linked to each group's collective self-esteem and satisfaction about prevailing societal conditions.

The next two studies by Zenner (Chapter 13) and by Mortland and Ledgerwood (Chapter 14) employ "qualitative" research methods in analyzing immigrant communities. Zenner presents a historical-cultural account of four Jewish immigrant groups in the United States in order to demonstrate the conflicts among them in spite of their common Jewish ethnic and religious identity. This analysis is presented as a case study to demonstrate the complex dynamics within an ethnic community in the host society and the influence of such an ethnic community on the individual in adapting to the larger American society. Similarly, Mortland and Ledgerwood analyze the ethnic communication network in a Southeast Asian refugee community in the United States. The authors argue that such an informal network serves the community as a vital "patronage" system, controlling the flow of information and resources between the host society, its service agencies and the refugee population.

All in all, the 14 chapters in this volume, individually and collectively, make a special contribution to the field of cross-cultural adaptation. Each chapter presents a perspective and emphasis in conceptualizing or researching the adaptation process. There exists some inconsistent use of terminologies as authors emphasize different aspects of cross-cultural adaptation and the related phenomena. Yet, each of these chapters offers unique knowledge and insight that contributes to moving the field toward a more complete and integrated understanding of the cross-cultural adaptation process.

ACKNOWLEDGMENTS

Many individuals have contributed substantially in the making of this volume. First, I would like to acknowledge the invaluable contribution of the members of the Consulting Editorial Board who generously gave their time and expertise reviewing the papers. I am also grateful to Sara McCune, President and Publisher of Sage Publications, and to William Work, Executive Director of Speech Communication Association, for their continuing enthusiasm and support for the annual series. My special thanks go to Gordon Craigo for his excellent assistance in proofreading and indexing. Most of all, I am proud to have worked with my co-editor, Bill Gudykunst, whose competent partnership has made the task of putting this volume together a pleasure.

Finally, this work owes its worth to the dedication and labor of the authors. On their behalf, I present this volume. I sincerely hope it will facilitate even greater interdisciplinary, international fertilization of academic talents. Together, we will be able to reach an integrated, comprehensive understanding of cross-cultural adaptation—one of the most socially relevant topics of inquiry today.

Young Yun Kim
Steger, Illinois

REFERENCES

Berry, J. W. (1980). Acculturation as varieties of adaptation. In A. M. Padilla (Ed.), *Acculturation: Theory, models and some new findings* (pp. 9-25). Washington, DC: Westview.

Glazer, N., & Moynihan, D. P. (1970). *Beyond the melting pot.* Cambridge: MIT Press.

Glazer, N., & Moynihan, D. P. (1975). *Ethnicity: Theory and experience.* Cambridge: Harvard University Press.

Gordon, M. (1964). *Assimilation in American life.* New York: Oxford University Press.

Gullahorn, J. T., & Gullahorn, J. E. (1963). An extension of the U-curve hypothesis. *Journal of Social Issues, 19*(3), 33-47.

Kealey, D., & Ruben, B. D. (1983). Cross-cultural personnel selection criteria, issues, and methods. In D. Landis & R. W. Brislin (Eds.), *Handbook of intercultural training: Vol. 1. Issues in theory and design* (pp. 155-175). Elmsford, NY: Pergamon.

Kim, Y. Y. (1979). Toward an interactive theory of communication-acculturation. In D. Nimmo (Ed.), *Communication yearbook 3*. New Brunswick, NJ: Transaction.

Kim, Y. Y. (in press). *Communication and cross-cultural adaptation: An interdisciplinary theory*. Clevendon, England: Multilingual Matters.

Lysgaard, S. (1955). Adjustment in a foreign society: Norwegian Fulbright grantees visiting the United States. *International Social Science Bulletin, 7*, 45-51.

Parrillo, V. N. (1966). *Strangers to these shores: Race and ethnic relations in the United States*. Boston: Houghton Mifflin.

Redfield, R., Linton, R., & Herskovits, M. J. (1936). Outline for the study of acculturation. *American Anthropologist, 38*, 149-152.

Snyder, P. Z. (1976). Neighborhood gatekeepers in the process of urban adaptation: Cross-ethnic commonalities. *Urban Anthropology, 5*(1), 35-52.

Spiro, M. E. (1955). The acculturation of American ethnic groups, *American Anthropologist, 57*, 1240-1252.

Taft, R. (1957). A psychological model for the study of social assimilation. *Human Relations, 10*(2), 141-156.

I

CURRENT THEORY

1

Conceptual Migrations
Understanding "Travelers' Tales" for Cross-Cultural Adaptation

W. BARNETT PEARCE ● *University of Massachusetts, Amherst*
KYUNG-WHA KANG ● *Yonsei University, Korea*

"Travelers' tales" of differences between cultures make up a form of data interpreted variously by social scientists. The "new paradigm" approach in social science allows for a sympathetic and rewarding "reading" of such tales, focusing on the fact of cultural differences, the problem of describing them, and the "necessity" and significance of these differences. An isomorphism is noted between the experience of immigrants and modernity, indicating that the process of acculturation is a model for life in contemporary society.

Travelers' tales of exotic customs, cultures, and peoples have been told since Herodotus. Marco Polo, Mark Twain, and Lowell Thomas gained their fame by giving accounts of what they saw—and imagined—on their travels. More recently, the primary sources of travelers' tales have been successive waves of migration. In the nineteenth and twentieth centuries, millions of people immigrated to new nations. Whatever the reason, and whatever the other consequences, these migrations required cross-cultural adaptation and spawned travelers' tales.

One function of travelers' tales is entertainment. They describe something that elicits a (direct or masked) wide-eyed exclamation ("Gosh! do they really do THAT?"). For those with a taste for the socially bizarre, tales of cross-cultural adaptation are particularly rich.

People in all cultures have some form of "greeting ritual," but these differ among cultures. In the United States, men extend their right hand, thumb up, with fingers pointing toward the other person, grasp the other's similarly extended hand, squeeze and "shake" it. In less formal contexts, a single hand may be raised in a "palm flash" or brief wave. In recent years, American Blacks have developed a variety of much more elaborate hand greetings:

clasping hands with fingers pointing upward or a reciprocated palm slap, sometimes accompanied by the imperative "Give me five!" Japanese greet each other by holding both arms at their sides and bowing from the waist. Competently performed, these cultural patterns are graceful and functional; however, a *mixture* of greeting behaviors appropriate to these two cultures is bizarre, carrying with it the potential not only for misunderstanding but for serious injury! A White American may extend his right hand, fingers pointing toward a Japanese, who bows politely from the waist and rams his eye into the American's thumb. Or a Japanese, understandably, may feel apprehensive if he bows and notices that the Black American whom he is greeting has raised his hand above his head preparing to slap downward with friendly gusto.

In addition to amusing us, travelers' tales should tell us something important about ourselves and about communication. We believe that contemporary communication theory already reflects the considerable impact of such tales. There is an untold story that an intellectual historian will someday relate showing the influence of cross-cultural adaptation on the development of communication theory. Rightly read, travelers' tales are the stuff on which a communication theory sufficient to explain cross-cultural adaptation can be built.

The problem, of course, is that of reading such tales "rightly"; this problem stems from a profound irony in the relation between "data" and "theory." The reading of any data depends on the theory that guides it. Yet the theory is the result of successive readings of data. The very questions that might be posed to travelers' tales differ depending on the theoretical commitments of those who hear them.

MONOCULTURAL AND ETHNOCENTRIC PERSPECTIVES

A *monocultural* perspective denies the differences of other cultures. From this perspective, travelers' tales are not very interesting and certainly irrelevant for communication theory. However, an examination of this perspective from the "other side"—one already informed by a careful reading of travelers' tales—is instructive. The "monocultural perspective" itself becomes an exotic culture, and its practices the content of amusing and edifying travelers' tales.

The monocultural perspective characterizes the "common sense" of persons who have lived all their lives within a single culture, or who have accepted some creed that claims to be universal. Either way, the "margins" of their own culture function as boundaries rather than as limits. The distinction between boundaries and limits is useful.

We are writing at the end of a long New England winter. If we knew only the geography of New England, the "margins" set by the Atlantic to the east, New York City to the south, the Berkshires to the west, and the St. Lawrence River to the north would appear to be the boundaries of the world. We would feel free if we could travel unrestricted within this area. The idea of "leaving" would never occur to us because we do not know of—or believe in—anything outside it. Travelers who tell us of warm sun on white beaches with sparkling blue water even in the winter (sigh!) seem to us to be telling fairy tales. If they insist on being taken literally, we may accuse them of being malicious or deluded. On the other hand, if we learn that there is a world outside New England, with deserts and rain forests and warm beaches and coral reefs, then the margins of the region function as limits rather than boundaries. Our sense of freedom vanishes unless we can travel outside the limits: Unrestricted regional travel, which gives us freedom within boundaries, is frustrating confinement within limits.

Those who believe that their own culture is the only one—or the only "real" one—treat communication patterns appropriate in other cultures, but not their own, as "mistakes" rather than "differences." The margins of their own culture function as boundaries rather than as limits. A well-known historical example of this perspective is that of the Christian missionaries to the South Pacific islands who insisted that the nearly nude natives of those balmy climates dress according to the fashions that seemed appropriate in chilly New England. For them, the margins of New England still set boundaries for thought even after they crossed the geographic limits of the region.

One need not look only to fashionable topics such as clothing;

even such basic moral values as telling the truth differ among cultures. If you ask persons from different cultures a question about a matter of "fact," you are likely to get very different responses. The answer given by a Bantu may have little or no relevance to "truth"; the Malagasy may answer so indirectly as to prevent an outsider from understanding what they mean; traditional Japanese may give the answer that best serves the "face" of all concerned; and members of collegiate debating teams at American universities may tell you far more about every potentially related topic than you ever cared to know. When persons encounter forms of communication not a part of their own cultural patterns, they often conclude that the people with whom they are talking are evil, uncivilized, or ignorant. These inferences are appropriate *if* one assumes the "monocultural" worldview, but are strikingly inappropriate inferences from others.

The great preponderance of scholarly treatment of travelers' tales has taken an *ethnocentric* perspective, in which a particular form of discourse was given a privileged status. This form of discourse was called "science." The people who figured in travelers' tales were not supposed to be able to use this form of discourse, but it was taken as a superior way of describing what the natives "really" meant and did. The natives' own accounts of the creation of the universe, their customs, their visions of the good life, their medicines, and so on, were treated as if inherently flawed, and those who used the scientific method had little or no reluctance to tell members of other cultures what they should do about everything.

This scientific approach is based on an assumption that the world can be known "objectively." From this perspective, the differences among cultures are artifacts that can be counted and compared as different ways people respond to a common physical environment. For example, it makes sense to sketch the geographic distribution of gestures, showing the differences in the ways various cultures position the fingers to "summon" another. Using the American "palm up, index finger extended then curling" summons in Malaysia is not a summons; it is a serious social insult. On the other hand, the Malaysian "palm down, all fingers extended then curling" summons is not a part of the message system in most of the United States. However, from this objectivist perspective, the different interpretations given to those gestures is a regrettable and unnecessary source of misunderstanding, since people in different cultures are doing "the same thing." Such misunderstandings could be prevented by the use of an intercultural dictionary or perhaps the acceptance of some standard code: a nonverbal Esperanto similar to the international traffic signs, which are supposedly culture-free.

THE NEW PARADIGM OF SCIENCE

In recent years, there has been increasing and severe criticism of both monocultural and ethnocentric perspectives. For example, the scientific perspective was applied to the "problem" of initiating "development" in the "underdeveloped" countries. A program of individual "modernization" and national capital-intensive investments was prescribed to help "backward" nations move more quickly along the same sequence of development that has produced the ideal—the industrialized states of Western Europe and North America. For many reasons, this project failed, and in failing it provided room for voices that argued that culture is not just an amusing or troublesome, exotic overlay over the "same" objective facts. Rather, culture is a socially constructed world in which development itself means different things; culture is a form of discourse *other* than science, not necessarily *inferior* to science. A scientific account of another culture may be a "translation," but is not an "explanation" of what that culture is about.

One outcome of this criticism of science as practiced by the international development community was the recognition that development always and necessarily occurred in the context of culture, and that the forms of development would be adapted by the institutions and signifying systems of that culture. Another consequence was a profound rethinking of science itself.

The twentieth century has witnessed great migrations not only of peoples across national boundaries, but of concepts across the boundaries of traditional paradigms. Travelers' tales have been a part of an energetic movement that has changed the nature of "science" itself. It is no longer accurate to identify science with objectivity as we did in the preceding paragraphs. A "new paradigm" is emerging in which the form of scientific discourse is radically changed, and this new paradigm is both informed by and enables "good readings" of travelers' tales.

The new paradigm approach to travelers' tales may be unpacked in these four questions:

(1) Are there actually differences among cultures in forms of communication?
(2) If so, how should the differences in forms of communication among cultures be described?
(3) Do these differences *have* to occur? What is the "necessity" of these differences?
(4) What difference do these differences make? What are the implications of these forms of communication?

The new paradigm treats knowledge as "edifying" the theorist rather than describing the world, and treats communication as the process by which social reality is created and managed rather than as a relatively unimportant means of achieving particular goals. This perspective yields quite a different, and richer, array of answers to the questions about culture and communication. It also makes some concepts problematic.

The central aspect of (our version of) the new paradigm is a model of persons as social agents, having particular "powers" because of their "natures" (see Harré & Madden, 1975). The primary and relevant power is that of *mediating* between patterns of *interpretive procedures* (the myths, stories, and typifications that constitute culture as a conceptual abstraction of ideology) and emerging, temporally and spatially situated sequences of *actions* (which constitute culture as an array of artifacts). *Communication* is the generic term for the processes of interpreting one's own and others' actions, *and* for performing actions that will be interpreted. Neither process is differentiable from the other except as a convenient fiction. Giddens (1981, p. 19) described this relation as "the duality of structure," in which "the structured properties of social systems are simultaneously the *medium and outcome of social acts.*"

It used to be thought that communication worked by pointing to events and objects that exist independently of the communicator. We now have good reason to believe that all communication acts are "intentional."

> In its very occurrence, then, human action, human being "in" action, implies or indicates something beyond itself. It posits a realm of other *possible* actions, a "world of meaning or reference" which seems to make its appearance even as an action occurs, and can thus function as *the context in which the sense of the action can be understood*. Simply to glance at someone is to posit a world in which recognition of like by like is possible, in which "recognition" is a possible activity. (Shotter, 1984, p. 276)

Normal adult communication is predicted on a reciprocated assumption that the messages produced by self and other will be taken as "intending" the appropriate meanings within the resources of the culture. That is, normal adult communication consists of treating each other as acting "like a native," using the same array of interpretive procedures to identify the intentions of particular messages.

Defined in this way, communication is not simply one form of action in contrast to others, but constitutes the cultures in which persons live. One cannot decide whether to eat, or sleep, or read, or run, rather than to communicate, because eating, sleeping, reading, or running are—in the sense of Shotter's quotation above—"intentional." That is, they are ways in which we communicate no less than by speaking or writing. To run away from a crime is a powerful message; reading on a bus communicates to potential conversationalists; sleeping through class is an explicit message with which we, as teachers, are all too familiar; and eating—particularly eating with other people—is a rich communication system in many cultures.

Cultures are not orderly. As Harris (1974) argued, each culture is made up of a variety of systems, and people find themselves enmeshed simultaneously in many of them. For example, a person may be at once daughter, student, wife, sister, employee, friend, and teammate, and the "social realities" of each of the systems in which these roles are constituted may impose quite different duties and offer quite different resources for the intentions of messages. In part, the meaning of any message is "forward-looking," constituted by its effect in shaping the direction of the ongoing communication. But a particular message may have different effects in the various systems in which the communicator holds social roles. To some extent, we are all one-armed jugglers, trying to keep our various "scripts" going simultaneously. Giddens (1981, p. 19) said that "all action consists of social practices, situated in time-space, and organized in skilled and knowledgeable fashion by human agents. But such knowledgeability is always 'bounded' by unacknowledged conditions of action on the one side, and unintended consequences of action on the other."

"Behaving as a native behaves" does not constitute "acting like a native." Harris (1974) showed that knowing all the "rules" a native knows cannot enable one to act as a native acts, because every rule that tells you to act in a certain way has exceptions, there are other rules that countermand it, and people often act in ways that violate the rules but are still perceived as acting as a native. Rather, "acting like a native" consists of *being perceived by natives as using the cultural resources* that contain the "moral order" or "language games" that are "intended" by particular acts. A "behavioral parroting" of acts without appropriate intent is not acting as a native. Even knowing the rules that describe the cultural resources does not constitute acting as a native. *Using* those resources to identify what is intended by one's actions, even if the act is revolutionary or deviant, is "acting like a native."

Obviously, when persons from different cultures interact, they usually do not treat each other as "acting like a native." The intentions of their acts are equivocal because that to which they "point" may be different in the cultures of each of the participants, and different yet again in the "culture" they have created by interacting with each other. That persons from different cultures often misunderstand each other is nothing new, but the perspective that the "new paradigm" gives on how communication works enables us to understand why this occurs with such obstinacy and answer the questions posed above.

(1) Are there actually differences among cultures in forms of communication? Yes, and the differences go far deeper than meets the eye. More significant than just differences in the way

communicative acts are performed, cultures differ in the array of meanings and motives to which those acts point and that provide the context from which acts derive their meaning. The variety of ways people communicate, from expressions to rituals, are not just different ways of doing the same things, because the "things" of cultures differ, and sometimes have no precise correspondence.

(2) *What are the differences among cultures in forms of communication?* From an ethnocentric, objective perspective, this question might well be answered by lists of behaviors differentiating among cultures, such as handshakes in the United States, bowing from the waist in Japan, and a two-hands-pressed bow in India. From a "new paradigm" perspective, however, the question becomes unexpectedly difficult to answer. The emphasis is on the intention of the act rather than (just) its surface form. This reveals that a "movement" does not even *become* a communicative act until it is located in the array of meanings within the culture.

(3) *Do the differences among cultures in forms of communication have to occur? What is the "necessity" of these differences?* Yes, they have to occur because of the characteristics of people and of cultures. Geertz (1965, pp. 36-37) said that "the diversity of custom across time and over space is not a mere matter of garb and appearance, of stage settings and comedic masques . . . humanity is as various in its essence as it is in its expression." This remarkable claim is based on the observation that culture functions as a "control mechanism," a set of rules that guide people to see the world in a certain way, to act in particular manners, and so on, and that a human being is precisely that animal that most needs and most uses such cultural controls.

> There is nothing as a human nature independent of culture. Men without culture would not be the clever savages of Golding's *Lord of the Flies* thrown back upon the cruel wisdom of their animal instincts; nor would they be the nature's noblemen of enlightenment primitivism or even, as classical anthropological theory would imply, intrinsically talented apes who had somehow failed to find themselves. They would be unworkable monstrosities with very few useful instincts, fewer recognizable sentiments, and no intellect; mental basket cases. As our central nervous system—and most particularly its crowning curse and glory, the neocortex—

> grew up in great part in interaction with culture, it is incapable of directing our behavior or organizing our experience without the guidance provided by systems of significant symbols. . . . Such symbols are thus not mere expressions, instrumentalities, or correlates of our biological, psychological, and social existence, they are prerequisites of it. Without men, no culture, certainly; but equally, and more significantly, without culture, no men. (Geertz, 1965, p. 49)

To be human is to have been enculturated, and not just enculturated to culture in general, but to some specific culture whose characteristics have been internalized. Geertz (1965, p. 35) argued, "There is, there can be, no backstage where we can go to catch a glimpse of Mascou's actors as 'real' persons' . . . disengaged from their profession, displaying with artless candor their spontaneous desires and unprompted passions." Desires and passions, no less than thoughts and characteristic forms of communication acts, are the result of culture. The preexisting code identifies what they are, how they are to be expressed, how much importance to give to them, and so on.

Because there is no human nature without culture, and because some people have become human by learning Lutheran concepts of truth-telling, it is necessary for them to "intend" different things as a way of understanding lies and factual statements than do persons who have learned to be Bantu. Forms of communication must differ among cultures because cultures differ, and communication is the process by which cultures are expressed and given substance.

(4) What difference do these differences make? Since communication is the process by which persons collectively create and manage social reality, the forms of communication action that express a culture—those that are required in order to "act like a native"—are the means by which cultures are perpetuated in their individuality.

If little Johnny runs into the house shouting, "There's a tiger in the backyard!" and his mother replies by scolding him for slamming the door and running indoors, Johnny has been told more than the rules about entering his home; he has also been told that he does not have the right to introduce his imaginary playmates with the same intensity that "the real thing" would permit; that his parents are not willing to play his games with him; and so on. If this happens once, Johnny is unlikely to be scarred by it, but if it happens 20 times a day for 20 years, then Johnny is likely to internalize some important learning about himself, his family, and his perceptions (Giffin, 1970).

Traditional Korean culture prizes persons who understand the Confucian virtue *li*, part of which consists of carefully adhering to traditional forms of speech, preventing rhetorical "mystification" as a means of political power, and avoiding the conceptual traps inherent in language. By contrast, Western cultures prize arguments and debates and honor those who present themselves invincibly in argument against all challengers. Koreans whose early learning features "reticent" persons honored as wise, internalize cultural resources quite dissimilar from those in the West, and by using them to interpret the "intentions" of talkative, argumentative people, perpetuate a culture conspicuously different from that of the West (Kang & Pearce, 1980).

NASA achieved spectacular success in building technological marvels, in part because their "culture" defined information-sharing as the means of demonstrating personal worth. Groups working on one project would receive a great deal of specific, often unsought information from other groups working on ostensibly different things. The significance of this communication style can be seen with a thought experiment. Assume that all NASA personnel were replaced by Malagasys, whose rules for sharing information legitimize hoarding information and prescribe circumlocution. There is no reason to think that the Malagasy have any less native intelligence than the staff of NASA, but their cultural communication patterns were developed in a situation quite unlike that of a research and development institution and in which open, precise, informative communication is not a survival skill. If the "culture" of NASA were made up of the Malagasy rules for meaning and action, it is likely that there would have been no manned space program in the United States. Or turn the thought experiment around: If the personnel of NASA were transplanted to Madagascar and lived in the environment of the Malagasy, they would not fit into the life-style of the Malagasy well at all. Our guess is that they would perpetuate their own culture if it meant changing their environment completely. They would "develop" their environment—perhaps draining swamps, damming streams, clearing the forest, and so on. These are characteristically "modern" things to do, and "modernity" is a kind of culture that imposes particular demands and opportunities on communicators.

THE STRUCTURE OF MODERNITY[1]

Modernity does not mean simply "historically recent"; it refers to a particular cluster of attitudes, values, institutions, and folkways. Consistent with Giddens's (1981) notion of "the duality of structure," modernity may be described equally well as the "performance demands" that this form of society places on individuals who live it, or as the myths by which it explains itself.

"Myths" have been told in every society, and have had an important place in them. LeGuin (1979, p. 31) noted:

> The story—from *Rumpelstiltskin* to *War and Peace*—is one of the basic tools invented by the mind of man for the purpose of gaining understanding. There have been great societies that did not use the wheel, but there have been no societies that did not tell stories.

Modern society depreciates the importance of stories, dismissing them as mere amusements or as outmoded surrogates for knowledge. This treatment is unfortunate, for, like travelers' tales of exotic customs, myths are stories that people tell to explain themselves to themselves. Even the story that stories are unimportant is an important story.

Campbell said the myths of every culture provide answers to four questions: Who am I? Who are we? What is the nature of the world in which we live? What is the nature of the answers to these questions? These questions correspond to the academic topics of psychology, sociology, cosmology (natural science), and epistemology, respectively, but the themes are common to the collective wisdom of all cultures. It does not take a certified genius to see that these four questions are not all alike: The fourth is fundamentally different from the first three and is reflexively related to them. Some interesting things can be seen by comparing

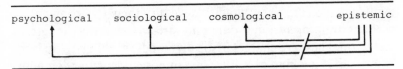

Figure 1.1   The Structure of Myths in Primitive and Traditional Societies

the ways various societies handled the strain between the epistemological and the other questions.

Primitive and traditional societies "solved" the problem in a similar manner, as shown in Figure 1.1. First, they effected a strict division of labor between those who dealt with the question of epistemology and those who did not. In primitive cultures, shamans were considered to have unique access to the source of power and were custodians of the myths and rituals that contained the answers to questions of personal and social identity and about the world. Their indispensable function was to sanctify the profane physical world and human actions. In traditional culture, this function was performed by priests or magicians—all of whom presaged the modern "specialist."

Second, the content of the myths in primitive and traditional societies explicitly assumed that whatever answers were given to the epistemological question would undergird and support the culturally sanctioned answers to the psychological, sociological, and cosmological questions. In primitive societies, this was done by sanctifying virtually all of life, and in European traditional societies, by locating the profane as inferior to the sacred in the "Great Chain of Being." Campbell (1959) shows some evidence that primitive shamans were often aware that their knowledge was, in important ways, incompatible with the content of the myths they held in stewardship for the tribe, but that they "protected" those who were not shamans from learning this disturbing fact. In traditional societies, the theology that is preached to the laity is often simpler than that discussed behind closed doors in monastery and seminary. For present purposes, the actual discrepancy between epistomology and the rest of the cultural wisdom is less important than the fact that cultural wisdom *represented itself* as fully compatible with its epistemology while ordinary persons were directed away from epistemic considerations by the division of labor that relegated this question to specialists.

The structure of primitive and traditional society is shown in Figure 1.1. The words indicate categories of questions raised and answered by the cultural myths; the vertical bars denote a division of labor; and the arcs represent the assumption that whatever is the content of the epistemic function of myths, it will undergird the others.

In terms of the structure of myth, modernity consists of a breakdown of the division of labor that shields epistemology from the rude hands of the uninitiated. Although modernity is now a pattern of institutions, values and folkways found throughout the world, it originated in the West and, necessarily, in the context of a particular set of events usually designated as the Protestant Reformation, the Renaissance, or the origin of modern science. The crucial revolutionary event was the development of tools of inquiry of unprecedented power and their application to the questions of psychology, sociology and cosmology. These tools were so powerful—and the nature of the object of their study so unexpectedly perverse—that the answers shifted categories. People who started to ask questions that were carefully limited to physics wound up talking about perception and sounding like Taoist monks (Capra, 1975). Western philosophers abandoned their 2,500-year-old quest to know the nature of the world, God, and the good in favor of Wittgenstein's agenda to make clear what we mean by what we say. The Church and scientists found themselves natural enemies because scientists invaded the domain that the Church had defined as its private preserve (Durant & Durant, 1965).

The *promise* of modern society is a mythology with a strikingly different structure, as shown in Figure 1.2. The absence of vertical bars indicates that concerns once carefully limited to particular domains now intrude into others. Note also that the arcs move from the first three questions to the fourth, describing the way the results of investigations in these areas have been used as a basis for constructing a secular epistemology.

The clear promise of modernity, articulated by Isaac Newton, Karl Marx, Sigmund Freud and others, is that the replacement of

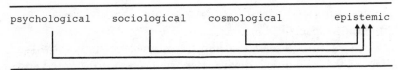

Figure 1.2   The Structure of Myth Promised by Modern Society

the illusions of traditional mythologies with confident knowledge was the path to peace and prosperity.

While it lasted, the promise of modernity was a bright one indeed.

> The Renaissance had gone back beyond Christianity to explore the pagan mind; the Reformation had broken the bonds of doctrinal authority, and almost despite itself, had let loose the play of reason. Now these two preludes to modernity could complete themselves. Man could at last liberate himself from medieval dogmas and Oriental myths; he could shrug off that bewildering, terrifying theology, and stand up free, free to doubt, to inquire, to think, to gather knowledge and spread it, free to build a new religion around the altar of reason and the service of mankind. It was a noble intoxication. (Durant & Durant, 1965, p. 607)

For the sake of that promise, governments have deliberately sown dissatisfaction with traditional ways of life, offering radios, tractors, and carbonated beverages in exchange for a mythology that provided an explanatory context for the terrors of history. Countless individuals have—often gladly, sometimes with great reluctance—given up traditional ways of thinking and action for modern ones.

MODERNITY MAKES IMMIGRANTS OF US ALL

And the promise is a hoax. Figure 1.3 presents the structure of modernity as we have come to know it. The lower part of the figure is identical to Figure 1.2, indicating that modernity does break down the "horizons" which had functioned as comforting boundaries in primitive and traditional societies. The upper part of the model, however, indicates that the content of what the first three functions of mythology produced in the fourth subverts rather than supports the content of the first three functions. This is a paradox, and has the precise form of the well-known two-step paradox:

> The following statement is true.
> The preceding statement is false.

If the first truly asserts the truth of the second, then the second truly asserts the falsity of the first, which then undercuts the reason for accepting the second as true . . . and so on, in what Hofstadter (1979) called a "strange loop."

Modernity is not just the substitution of one set of answers for another (for example, conversion from Christianity to Islam), but a change in the structure of the mythology from which answers are expected to come. Campbell (1972, pp. 16-17) best summarized the difference between the traditional and the promise of modern society:

> We don't know a thing, and not even our science can tell us sooth; for it is no more than, so to say, an eagerness for truths, no matter where their allure may lead . . . The old texts comforted us with horizons . . . According to our sciences, on the other hand, nobody knows . . . There is no 'Thou shalt!' any more. There is nothing one *has* to do.

One salient feature of this structure is that modernity institutionalizes change—as Campbell (1972, p. 16) said, it is "an eagerness for truths" coupled with techniques of inquiry sufficiently powerful to undermine the authority of *any* proposed "truth." The one thing that the natives of (modernistic) NASA could not do, if suddenly placed into the world of the (traditional) Malagasy, is leave things alone.

Modernity can be described as the eternal pursuit of the novel, fueled by a quest for individual value derived from effectiveness in changing the social world. The way modernity appears at the individual level may be "reported" in the diagram of a strange loop in Figure 1.4. The primary goal is to make the self worthwhile, which can be done only by making the self the initiating agent of external change. Follow the arrows in the figure: the strange loop is initiated by the perception that one has

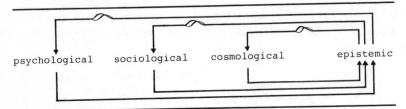

psychological   sociological   cosmological   epistemic

Figure 1.3   The Actual Structure of Myth in Modern Society

encountered something "not new," a state that impels (a) acts of "development" or change, which, if successful, may produce (b) novelty, an accomplishment worth celebrating and preserving; but (c) this celebration itself defines whatever is celebrated as "not new," and (d) the cycle starts all over again. In such a system, nothing is good or bad. "Change"—the replacement of something old with something new—is what is valued, and change is a relationship between events and objects, not an attribute of any given event or object; not a "thing" at all. So, no "thing"—"nothing"—is valued in modernity. As Berman (1982, p. 13) said, "To be modern is to live a life of paradox and contradiction."

THE PERFORMANCE DEMANDS OF MODERNITY

All cultures impose "performance demands" on those who would "act like a native." In primitive and traditional cultures, these performance demands consist of acting appropriately according to the content of the myths within the boundaries of the culture. Certainly there are changes within the culture, but—like unrestricted mobility *within* New England—these do not threaten the boundaries. The performance demands of traditional and primitive cultures consist of learning and using an array of resources, which—supported by the "epistemology" that is stipulated as unaffected by anything else that happens in the society—remains stable.

Modernity, on the other hand, makes all boundaries into limits, by depreciating the value of anything that is "not new" and providing powerful tools for the development of "new" things. The "performance demand" consists not of staying within

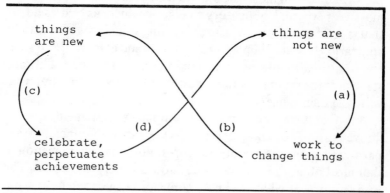

self is worthwhile only if it makes "progress" - where progress means change and effecting the social/physical world

Figure 1.4   The "Strange Loop" in Modern Society

comforting horizons, but of constantly destroying what *is* for what *might be.* Perhaps the clearest expression of modernity is the bargain Goethe's Faust made with Mephistopheles: Faust was to be given supernatural powers during his life, but his soul was immediately to be taken to Hell if he ever said that the passing moment was so sweet that he would like it to remain unchanged.

In primitive and traditional societies, the forms of "competent" communication consist of patterns sanctioned by the content of the myths. In modern societies, anyone who "merely" follows established patterns is incompetent. "Acting like a native" requires acting "creatively."

In a society in which the value of self derives from the ability to effect change on the external world, the primary fact of life is change, and there are no stable values. The threat is nihilism, a loss of all values. In this way, modernity imposes performance demands for which the social institutions and perhaps our genetic and cultural heritage is poorly adapted. For thousands of years, we have learned how to live in societies that set boundaries, within which the individual could be comforted and perhaps a little daring—that is, seeing some boundaries as limits; reaching a little beyond the conventional, but with the assurance of a stable social reality as a context and haven. Only within the last 250 years—

and much less in most countries of the world—modernity has created a very different type of culture, with very different performance demands. The individual is confronted with change; massive, perpetual, obligatory change, in which, as Marx said, all that is solid melts into air, and everything seems pregnant with its contrary. How are people to act in such a social reality? For sure, the traditional patterns of communication, and the traditional standards for evaluating those patterns, will not suffice, but what will take their place?

As a culture—alluding to Campbell's statement quoted above—we do not know. It is not that members of our culture are paralyzed with uncertainty or self-doubt. The phenomenon is that most of us, most of the time, know precisely how to act. The problem is that what we know contradicts the content of what others, equally confident, know, and is inconsistent with what we "knew" before (or will "know" after) our next "mid-life-crisis." As was said of a presidential candidate some years ago: "often in error; never in doubt." This description matches the usual condition of those in a strange loop: oscillating certainty about different things; an amazing amalgam of celebrating our triumphs and treating them as outmoded, a sufficient cause for additional innovation. In general, those who focus on modern technology are able to maintain the social reality of Figure 1.2, the promise of modernity, while those who attend more to the social effects of technology inhabit the social reality of Figure 1.3.

> Contrary to the confidence in our powers of technology and information, the prevailing image of man we find in modern art is one of impotence, uncertainty, and self-doubt. Perhaps at no time in history has there been so glaring a contrast between the different ideas of itself that this age has fashioned in the two parts of its culture. (Barrett, 1972, p. 6)

So how are we to act? To "act naturally" is to follow round and round the treadmill of the strange loop described in Figure 1.4. Maybe this is best; to celebrate the characteristic pattern of communication of this culture in much the same way that we are tolerantly respectful of the patterns in other cultures. Berman (1982, p. 345) seems to recommend just this response:

To be modern, I said, is to experience personal and social life as a maelstrom, to find one's world and oneself in perpetual disintegration and renewal, trouble and anguish, ambiguity and contradiction: to be part of a universe in which all that is solid melts into air. To be modern*ist* is to make oneself somehow at home in the maelstrom, to make its rhythms one's own, to move within its currents in search of the forms of reality, of beauty, of freedom, of justice, that its fervid and perilous flow allows.

If there were no travelers' tales of the strange customs of far-away peoples—and if we had no historical recollection of times in which our own ancestors were different—we could live comfortably enmeshed in the accelerating cycle of change within the strange loop of modernity. But we know that cultures differ and we have learned that these differences signify the human agency of cultures, including our own. This learning transmutes the margins of the strange loop of modernity from a boundary to limits. We do not have to remain enmeshed within this loop.

One alternative to staying enmeshed within the strange loop of modernity is to retreat from it, deliberately enmeshing oneself in a society having a different structure, and defending that society against the incursions of modernity as strongly as possible. Of this response, Campbell (1972, p. 17) rather acidly remarked:

> One can, of course, if one prefers, still choose to play at the old Middle Ages game or some Oriental game, or even some sort of primitive game. We are living in a difficult time, and whatever defends us from the madhouse can be applauded as good enough—for those without nerve.

A second alternative is to invent a new mythology that will serve the same functions as those in other societies, but that will be relevant to the conditions of modernity. This may be more difficult than it might seem. Campbell (1972, p. 275) states the problem clearly:

> What is—or what is to be—the new mythology? It is—and will forever be, as long as our human race exists—the old, everlasting perennial mythology, in its "subjective sense," poetically renewed in terms neither of a remembered past nor of a projected future, but of now: addressed, that is to say, not to the flattery of

"peoples," but to the waking of individuals in the knowledge of themselves, not simply as egos fighting for place on the surface of this beautiful planet, but equally as centers of Mind at Large— each in his own way at one with all, and with no horizons.

But if modernity constitutes a unique structure of myths, just changing the content from one to another will not work.

A third alternative to running around the strange loop is that of developing a new form of communication. The patterns of communication that have been taught by all cultures (until relatively recently, perhaps) are appropriate for monocultural and ethnocentric communication, but the powerful engines of perpetual change have made "immigrants" of us all.

In every traditional society, there have been unusual persons— shamans, artists, visionaries—whose typifications were at risk and who were inside and outside their cultures simultaneously. The performance demands of modernity are not unique; they are just applied to an unprecedented proportion of the population. The communicative skills demanded only of the atypical artists, leaders or priests in traditional societies are, in modern society, demanded of us all.

There is an unexpected source of help. The unprecedented movement of peoples among nations that has occurred in modern times has created a large population practiced in intercultural adaptation. The experience of those people who have confronted a novel culture and learned to cope with cultural pluralism in their own experience can serve as a basis for identifying the skills necessary for those whom modernity has made immigrants in their own homes.

There is a curious and somehow satisfying isomorphism between the experience of the theorist and ordinary citizen in modern society: For both, conceptual migration is a way of life. Rightly read, travelers' tales are the best basis for learning to cope with the performance demands of modernity and for developing communication theory. In the final analysis, these are two aspects of the same task.

NOTE

1. This section draws heavily from Pearce and Lannamann (1982).

REFERENCES

Barrett, W. (1972). *Time of need: Forms of imagination in the twentieth century*. New York: Harper & Row.

Berman, M. (1982). *All that is solid melts into air: The experience of modernity*. New York: Simon & Schuster.

Campbell, J. (1959). *The masks of God: Primitive mythology*. New York: Viking.

Campbell, J. (1972). *Myths to live by*. New York: Bantam.

Capra, F. (1975). *The Tao of physics*. New York: Bantam.

Durant, W., & Durant, A. (1965). *The age of Voltaire, Vol. IX. The story of civilization*. New York: Simon & Schuster.

Geertz, C. (1965). *The interpretation of cultures*. New York: Basic Books.

Giddens, A. (1981). *A contemporary critique of historical materialism*. Berkeley: University of California Press.

Giffin, K. (1970). Social alienation by communication denial. *Quarterly Journal of Speech, 56*, 348-358.

Harré, R., & Madden, E. H. (1975). *Causal powers*. Totowa, NJ: Rowland & Littlejohn.

Harris, M. (1974). Why a perfect knowledge of all the rules one must know to act like a native cannot lead to the knowledge of how natives act. *Journal of Anthropological Research, 30*, 242-251.

Hofstadter, D. (1979). *Gödel, Escher, and Bach: The eternal golden braid*. New York: Basic Books.

Kang, K. W., & Pearce, W. B. (1980). The place of transcultural concepts in communication research: A case study of reticence. *Communication, 9*, 79-96.

LeGuin, U. (1979). Introduction to *The left hand of darkness*. In S. Wood (Ed.), *The language of the night*. New York: Perigree.

Pearce, W. B., & Lannamann, J. W. (1982). Modernity makes immigrants of all. *Journal of Asian-Pacific and World Perspectives, 6*, 27-34.

Shotter, J. (1984). *Social accountability and selfhood*. Oxford: Basil Blackwell.

2

The Adjustment of Sojourners

ADRIAN FURNHAM • *University College, London*

This chapter presents a working, psychological definition of a sojourner and describes the various types and motives of sojourners. The concept of culture shock is discussed and criticized for putting exclusive emphasis on the negative aspects of geographic movement. The mental health of foreign students is examined in some detail as an example of sojourner adjustment. Finally, eight possible conceptualizations of culture shock derived from very different theoretical orientations are examined. These often overlapping, noncompeting theories are critically examined on a number of grounds.

For we are strangers before thee, and sojourners, as were all our fathers: our days on earth are as a shadow and there is none abiding. (1 Chronicles, 29:15)

A review of the extensive, diffuse literature on sojourner adjustment begs the question as to the definition of a sojourner. As usual the dictionary is of limited help. It defines *sojourn* as a temporary stay at a place and offers various synonyms: a delay or digression; to tarry, lodge, rest, or quarter. The word *sojourner* usually has been used to denote a traveler and a sojourn is often thought to be an unspecified period of time in a new (different, unfamiliar) environment. What is missing from the dictionary and necessary to begin any analysis of sojourner adjustment are (1) a clear distinction between sojourners and other types of travelers such as tourists, migrants, and refugees; (2) some idea of the motives of sojourners for traveling; (3) a taxonomy of the different types of sojourners and how they are related to each other; and (4) some idea (albeit imprecise and subjective) of the temporal extremes distinguishing, for instance, tourists and migrants from sojourners. Of course these questions are mutually dependent and are all part of the need for a clear conceptual definition of the term *sojourner*.

In order to get a useful working definition of *sojourner,* it is important to identify those dimensions that are useful (discriminatory) and to specify the independent variables that define *sojourn*. Various dimensions have been proposed, including the nature of stranger-host relationships (Gudykunst, 1983), frequency of contact (Bochner, 1982), and geographic distance (Furnham & Bochner, 1986). These dimensions neither discriminate sojourners from other groups nor suggest what different sojourner groups have in common. The first and most salient dimension is temporal—a sojourner spends a medium length of time (six months to five years) at a place, usually intending to return "home." Thus tourists spend too brief a period overseas to be thought of as sojourners, and migrants (and refugees) too long a period. The second dimension, more difficult to define, is specifically of purpose or motive. By and large, tourists travel for a variety of nonspecific motives (for example, relaxation, self-enlightenment) as do migrants, whose motives are equally vague and complex. Comparatively, sojourners' motives are more specific and goal-oriented.

Thus the independent variables in the sojourner experience are length of time and purpose. The dependent variables include the amount of difficulty or stress experienced, the quality of contact with the native or host population, and changes in self-concept and way of life. This chapter will be concerned with these dependent and independent variables.

MOTIVES OF SOJOURNERS

A number of different groups of people may be classified as sojourners: businesspeople, diplomats, foreign workers, students, and voluntary workers. Psychological research, however, has concentrated on some more than others. For instance, there is very little literature on diplomats, a limited (but increasing) amount on foreign workers and businesspeople, but a large amount on students and voluntary workers.

People usually have various motives and expectations when living in a foreign place. These motives and expectations help shape their reactions to their environment (Furnham & Bochner, 1986; Torbiorn, 1982).

As part of a major study, 69 Asian students who had returned from pursuing higher academic degrees overseas were interviewed in their homeland by Bochner (1973). They were asked why they had accepted their scholarships, and what they had hoped to get out of the experience of study abroad. Several measures of motivation (some direct and others indirect) were used. Of the 69 responses, 64 suggested that it was to get a degree or gain academic experience. Only two said their main reason was culture learning, and three (all from the Philippines) listed personal development (for example, to gain insight, to become better people, to find themselves). Similarly, in a large study of 2,536 foreign students in 10 different countries by Klineberg and Hull (1979), 71% of the respondents said that obtaining a degree or diploma was important. Again the acquisition of qualifications and experience ranked as the single most important reason for going to a foreign university.

Thus the overwhelming majority of foreign students are primarily interested in getting a degree or professional training rather than learning a second culture or achieving personal growth. What is utmost in their minds are concerns about the tangible payoffs a sojourn might provide in the shape of career advancement, prestige, and upward mobility. They withstood various hardships in their educational sojourn to achieve their purposes (Bochner, 1979; Bochner, Lin, & McLeod, 1979).

An examination of the motives of Peace Corp volunteers also revealed specific motivations for their sojourn. In a study, of approximately 300 trainees, Guthrie (1966) reports that about 80% evinced interests closely resembling those of the typical social worker. When interviewed they freely acknowledged that they had joined the Peace Corps because they wanted to do something significant and because they had not found a satisfying career at home. At the same time, many brought with them highly unrealistic notions as to what they could achieve, how quickly they could solve the problems of the region in which they served, or what tangible results could be expected from their work.

CULTURE SHOCK

Nearly all sojourners suffer from culture shock. The culture shock "hypothesis" or "concept" suggests that the experience of a new culture is a sudden, unpleasant feeling that may violate expectations of the new culture and cause one to evaluate one's own culture negatively. Nearly all users of the term have suggested that the experience is negative—though this may not necessarily be the case.

The anthropologist Oberg (1960) was first accredited with using the term. In a brief and largely anecdotal article he mentions at least six aspects of culture shock.

(1) *strain,* as a result of the effort required to make necessary psychological adaptation
(2) *a sense of loss* and *feelings of deprivation* in regard to friends, status, profession, and possessions
(3) *rejection* by and/or rejection of members of the new culture
(4) *confusion* in role, role expectations, values, feelings, and self-identity
(5) *surprise, anxiety*, even *disgust* and *indignation* after becoming aware of culture differences
(6) *feelings of impotence,* as a result of not being able to cope with the new environment

Some years later, Cleveland, Mangone, and Adams (1963) offered a similar analysis relying heavily on personal experiences, especially those at the two extremes—that is, those (American) migrants who act as if they "never left home" and those who immediately "go native."

Others have attempted to improve upon Oberg's (1960) multifaceted definition of culture shock. Guthrie (1975) has used the term "culture fatigue"; Smalley (1963), "language shock"; Byrnes (1966), "role shock"; and Ball-Rokeach (1973), "pervasive ambiguity." In doing so, different researchers have simply placed the emphasis on slightly different problems—language, physical irritability, role ambiguity—rather than actually helping to specify *how* or *why* or *when* different people do or do not experience different aspects of culture shock. No one has attempted to specify the *relationships* among the various facets of culture shock; to order their *importance*; to suggest in which *order* they are most likely to occur; whether certain *groups* are more vulnerable to one type of shock or another.

Bock (1970) has described culture shock as primarily an

emotional reaction that is consequent upon not being able to understand, control, and predict behavior, which appears to be a basic need. When people cannot do this, their usual accustomed, unthinking behavior changes to becoming unusual and unfamiliar as does that of others. This lack of familiarity extends to both the physical (design of buildings, parks) and the social environment (etiquette, clothing, and so on). Furthermore, the experience and use of time (mealtimes, time keeping) may all change (Hall, 1959), which may be profoundly disturbing. This theme is picked up by all of the writers in the field (Lundstedt, 1963; Hays, 1972)—many view culture shock as a stress reaction where salient psychological and physical rewards are generally uncertain and difficult to control or predict. Sojourners remain anxious, confused, and sometimes apathetic or angry until they have had time to develop a new set of assumptions that help them to understand and predict the behavior of others.

Others have attempted to describe culture shock in terms of individuals lacking points of reference, social norms, and rules to guide their actions and understand others' behavior. Hence the concept of *alienation* or *anomie* and ideas of powerlessness, meaninglessness, normlessness, self- and social estrangement, and social isolation (Seeman, 1959) are seen to apply. But even more salient are constructs, ideas associated with *anxiety* that pervade the culture-shock literature. A "free-floating" anxiety, lack of self-confidence, distrust of others, and mild psychosomatic complaints are common (May, 1970). Furthermore, people appear to lose their inventiveness and spontaneity and become obsessively concerned with orderliness (Nash, 1967). In-depth case studies, just as much as large surveys, on sojourners have again and again come up with findings such as this.

Central to the very concept of culture shock is change and adaptation. The fairly extensive literature on the U curve, the W curve, and the inverted U curve (Church, 1982; Torbiörn, 1982) have been proposed to describe adaptation over time. By and large, the empirical literature is highly equivocal, providing only very modest support for any one pattern. Part of the problem lies in the failure to differentiate between distinct subgroups of sojourners as well as adaptation to quite different phenomena such as food, language, climate, and so on.

Most attempts to investigate culture shock then have been descriptive. Little or no attempt has been made to explain *for whom* the shock will be more or less intense; what determines *which reaction* a person is likely to experience; *how long* they remain in a period of shock; what factors *inoculate against* shock, and the like. It is often suggested that *all* people will suffer culture shock, yet some do not experience any negative aspects of sojourning, indeed they *seek out* these experience for *enjoyment*. Sensation-seekers for instance might be expected not to suffer any adverse effects but to enjoy the highly arousing stimuli of the unfamiliar (Zuckerman, 1978).

Adler (1975) and David (1972) have offered an alternative view of culture shock, arguing that although it is most often associated with negative consequences it is often important for self-development and personal growth. Culture shock is seen as a transitional experience that can result in the adoption of new values, attitudes, and behavior patterns. The implication is that although it may be strange and possibly difficult, sojourning makes a person more adaptable, flexible, and insightful.

Although different writers have put emphasis on different aspects of culture shock (for example, alienation versus anxiety). Very few writers have stressed the positive or beneficial side of culture shock either for those individuals who revel in exciting and different environments or for those whose initial discomfort leads to personal growth.

MENTAL HEALTH OF STUDENTS

Many of the early studies were concerned with the relationship between mental health and academic performance of foreign students (Gunn, 1979; Kelvin, Lucas, & Ojha, 1965; Lucas, Kelvin, & Ojha, 1966; Rook, 1954). However, these studies did not separate foreign (overseas) from native (home) students, nor did they overcome the problems associated with suicide statistics (errors, differential registration procedures of death, religious sanctioning).

The literature on the difficulties of sojourning foreign students dates to immediately after the Second World War. Much of the earliest literature was nonempirical, descriptive, and impression-istic, although rich in detail and useful as a source of hypotheses (Carey, 1956; Tajfel & Dawson, 1965). Others have attempted systematic observations and interviews with a limited number of sojourning students; for instance, Schild (1962) studied 59 Jewish-American students on a one-year trip to Israel. A number of other studies in the 1950s and 1960s have looked specifically at the incidence of sojourning overseas students using university health facilities (Eldridge, 1960; Hopkins, Malleson, & Sarnoff, 1975; Rust, 1960).

Still (1961) looked at different types of reactions in overseas students from various countries and compared them to British students. On average, 14% of the British students showed evidence of psychological problems, although the percentage of foreign students with some psychological problems was always higher: Egypt, 22.5%; Nigeria, 28.1%; Turkey, 21.0%; Iraq, 28.1%; Iran, 29.7%; India, 17.6%; and Pakistan, 18.7%.

One of the most influential papers in this area was that of Ward (1967), who described "foreign student syndrome," which is characterized by vague, nonspecific physical complaints, a passive withdrawn interaction style, and a disheveled, unkempt appear-ance. He argued that depressed and culture-shocked overseas students tend to somatize their problem to avoid losing face, thus providing them with the justification for attending clinics for medical, as opposed to psychological, help. This tendency of foreign students would then be reflected in their university health services (Willmuth, Weaver, & Donlon, 1975). Indeed, Gunn (1979) found a higher incidence of digestive, dermatological, and sexual problems in overseas students.

Other studies have looked at the help-seeking behavior of psychologically disturbed students (Mechanic & Greenley, 1976; O'Neil, Lancee, & Freeman, 1984; Padesky & Hammen, 1981). In Britain there have been detailed studies of African students (Lambo, 1960; Noudehou, 1982). Anumonye (1970) divided student problems into inevitable (separation reactions) and avoidable (loneliness), while Singh (1963) described three prob-lems areas: emotional, academic, and adjustment. Bourne (1975) reviewed the history of Chinese students in the United States, and the particular problems they faced. Over a four-year period, he interviewed 24 Chinese students who presented themselves as patients and a control group of 24 nonpatients. From these interviews, Chinese students were observed to work harder and for longer hours than most other students. Also, Chinese males tended to be unassertive and shy and to have few friends, while Chinese females were less isolated but felt guilty about dating non-Asians.

The concept *culture distance* has been introduced to account for the amount of distress experienced by a student from one culture studying in another. Babiker, Cox, and Miller (1980) hypothesized that the degree of alienation, estrangement, and concomitant psychological distress was a function of the distance between the students' own culture and the host culture. They devised a culture distance index to provide objective assessment of disparity between the two cultures uncontaminated by the subject's perception of the differences or feelings about them. Items included climate, clothes, religion, food, and family structure. The instrument was then used on 121 foreign students at Edinburgh University to investigate the possible associations among culture distance and medical consultations, symptoms, and examination success. Correlational analysis showed that culture distance was significantly related to anxiety during the Easter term and the total number of medical consultations during the year, but not to academic success.

Babiker et al. interpreted the relationship between the CDI and medical consultations as an indication that (1) culturally distant students perceived the health services as an approachable safe haven; (2) they suffer more physical illness; or (3) the opportunity of free and expert medical checkups is being used. Clearly their study was unable to sort these variables.

In a similar study, Furnham and Bochner (1982) found that the degree of difficulty experienced by sojourners was directly related to the disparity (or culture distance) between the sojourners' culture and host society. The stress experienced by foreign students was viewed largely as a result of their lacking the requisite social skills with which to negotiate specific social situations. Many of the foreign students did not seek out host-culture friends from whom they might have been better able to learn the appropriate social skills necessary for a satisfying sojourn.

There have been reported some conflicting results regarding the mental health of foreign students. Davey (1957) found that British women students at Cambridge University had poorer mental health than the men students had. Yet Malleson (1954), who worked with British students at London University, found no gender differences. Furthermore, Kidd (1965), who worked at Edinburgh University, found British women to have better mental health than men. Anumonye (1970) found that male African students studying in Britain showed better adjustment and less emotional distress, but he found no differences between men and women with regard to academic stress.

Research findings on the differences in the mental health of native and overseas students based on medical consultation rates must be interpreted with caution. Foreign students may have no other source of help. In addition, their beliefs about illness may differ from those prevalent in the host country. For instance, disease seen as trivial by one society may not be seen as such by members of another culture. Foreign students may be more likely to seek medical assistance when they have minor infections than are natives. This might explain the large number of overseas students with supposedly hypochondriacal symptoms. Also, a higher average consulting rate of a group may arise from very frequent visits by only a small number of its members who are prone to visiting doctors. For a more accurate group comparison, the average number of visits per individual must be considered and, if the distribution is badly skewed, appropriate corrective statistics must be used.

Few studies have distinguished students in their first year (who are presumably more vulnerable to stress) from those in their second and third year (who have had more opportunities to adapt). Many studies have not collected information in a systematic way, which makes such comparisons difficult. In addition, some studies have concentrated on only one student nationality (for example, Indian), while others have haphazardly collected a wide range of foreign nationals.

Taking these research problems into consideration, Furnham and Trezise (1981) compared four groups of foreign students in Britain (Africans, Europeans, Middle Easterners, and Malaysians) with two British control groups (first year and second and third year). Using a reliable and valid self-report measure of mental health, they observed that overseas students, as a whole, showed evidence of significantly more psychological disturbance than either of the British groups, though there was no gender difference. Further, with the exception of the Malaysian students, the British students were significantly more satisfied with their social lives than were the other groups.

Klineberg and Hull (1979) surveyed 2,536 foreign students from 139 nations, studying in 11 countries, focusing on four major themes: the sources of satisfaction, the difficulties encountered, changes in attitude, and possible ways the sojourn experience might be improved. It was found that previous travel on the part of the respondents was associated with better coping skills, fewer difficulties, and more contact with local people during their sojourn. Those students who had made satisfactory social contact and established relationships with local people during their sojourn reported broader and more general satisfaction with their academic as well as nonacademic experiences. No support was found for the U-curve hypothesis of adjustment. Almost a third of the respondents reported that they had been the object of discrimination, and a quarter said that personal depression was a problem. About 15% of the respondents expressed a preference to remain in the sojourn country, evidence that the "brain drain" is still something of a problem despite the big improvement in the economies of the sending countries in recent times.

Overall, the two most important factors implicated in the coping process of students at a foreign university were found to be social contact with local people and prior foreign experience. Both of these findings are compatible with and support a culture-learning, social skills interpretation of the coping process. Furnham and Bochner (1982) have argued that foreign students face four areas of problems, two of which are exclusive to them (as opposed to native students). First, there are problems that confront anybody living in a foreign culture such as racial discrimination, language problems, accommodation difficulties, separation reactions, dietary restrictions, financial stress, misunderstandings, and loneliness. Second, there are the difficulties that face all late adolescents and young adults, whether they are studying at home or abroad, in becoming emotionally independent, self-supporting, productive, and responsible members of society. Third, there are academic stresses when students are expected to work very hard, often under poor conditions, and with complex material. Fourth, the national or ethnic role of overseas students is often prominent in their interactions with host members. In a sense, foreign students are being continually thrust into the role of ambassadors or representatives of their nations. Often, well-meaning individuals politely inquire about their home customs and national origins. Sometimes, however, prejudiced individuals may denigrate the policies or achievements of the student's country of origin. There may be a tendency for host members to speak slowly and clearly, on the assumption that the foreigner's English is poor. Motherly women on buses will want to know if the student is feeling homesick. These and other similar situations can be a burden to foreign students. In some instances, this can lead to misunderstandings and hostility between foreign students and host members (Huang, 1977).

These difficulties are shared by nearly all sojourners. However, business people experience less difficulty than students or other sojourners. They are usually posted in a foreign culture for a relatively short period of time, for a specific purpose. Conducting business abroad often increases the opportunities for their advancement on return. In contrast to students (and some migrants), business people are older and tend to be more mature. Also, businesses often provide accommodation enclaves, "old-hand" guides and a social support network that insulate the foreigner against the initial cultural difficulties and surprises. Because businesses are interested primarily in the work their employees do, the employees' time is carefully structured and scheduled. The social relationships both inside and outside the workplace are more likely to be on an equal footing for businesspeople than they are for students. Such equal-status peer-group interaction is a possible explanation for their better adjustment.

THEORIES OF SOJOURNER ADJUSTMENT

Despite the lack of any fully developed, formal theory that adequately explains sojourner adjustment, there are a number of theoretical approaches that have been fruitfully applied to this topic. Furnham and Bochner (1986) have identified eight such theoretical orientations.

Movement as Loss (Bereavement)

The geographic movement of the sojourner means the loss of specific relationships and significant objects (family, friends, occupational status, familiar foods, etc.). This loss is followed by individual grief or by more conventional types of mourning. Many particularly psychoanalytically oriented researchers have pointed to the similarities among typical grief reactions—intense anxiety, reduced resistance to stress, apathy and withdrawal, and anger. However, there are a number of problems with the analogy between grief and sojourner adjustment.

First, it is presumed that all sojourners experience negative, grieflike reactions. This is clearly not the case, as many sojourners thrive on the experience. Second, although the literature pertaining to the grief of the sojourner does not take into account individual and cultural differences, it makes no specific predictions as to what types of people suffer more or less grief, over what period, or what form the grief will take. Third, counseling for the grieving would seem highly inappropriate for sojourners who need information and support as much as therapy.

Fatalism (Locus of Control Beliefs)

This approach argues that many sojourners (particularly those from the Third World) have fatalistic, external locus of control beliefs before traveling, and that the initial experience of being a sojourner leads one to adopt fatalistic beliefs, along with passive and impaired coping strategies, and psychological distress. Sojourners tend to experience a loss of control and, therefore, lack the opportunity to manipulate the outcomes of their behavior.

The fatalism or locus of control explanation for the relationship between sojourning and adjustment is interesting but presents potential problems. The explanation does not account for the distress rates of different sojourning groups. Sojourners from a country in which the religious outlook is fatalistic or whose experiences render them more helpless should have more difficulty in adjusting than should migrants from a country where personal responsibility is valued. Also, most people who migrate have, by definition, an internal locus of control and are therefore relatively homogeneous without respect to their culture or origin. In order to migrate voluntarily (as a sojourner) one has to assume considerable personal responsibility and control over one's own affairs—financial, social, and familial. There must be other factors that account for the relationship between geographical movement and psychological well-being.

Selective Migration (Natural Selection)

This view is appealing in its simplicity and potential power. It suggests that those people who cope best with the exigencies of new environments become the prevailing type—the survival of the fittest. Hence the most carefully selected, or those who had the most hurdles to overcome in becoming a sojourner, will cope and adapt the best. This theory has a number of limitations, however. The theory stresses the relationship between selection processes and coping strategies. The evidence presented, however, is usually retrospective and the thesis itself more tautological than explanatory. Considering the selection obstacles of the sojourners, it is not clear which barriers or obstacles select for adaptation and which do not. The sheer number of obstacles alone does not imply that those people who necessarily overcome them will adapt well. For instance, education, physical fitness, language ability, and financial security may be important positive factors with regard to selection, while others, such as religion, may not. Rarely, if ever, do the optimally adaptive selectors exist in isolation from those factors that do not discriminate.

Positive selector obstacles may differ from country to country, from time to time, or from one sojourner group to another. Most receiving nations have specific general criteria of their own for the admission of sojourners. There are social, political, and economic reasons for these criteria that change over time. Hence it is extremely difficult to test the usefulness of this approach unless the precise nature of the adaptive selectors in both departure and arrival countries are specified and examined.

Appropriate Expectations

This approach suggests that the relationship between a sojourner's expectations (social, academic, economic) for sojourn and the fulfillment (or lack of fulfillment) is a crucial factor in determining adjustment. It has been shown that high (even unrealistic) expectations that cannot or do not get fulfilled are related to poor adjustment and that low expectations that are exceeded are related to good adjustment.

Again this approach is not without its problems. First, all sojourners have a wealth of expectations, some relating to social, economic, geographic, and political aspects of life in their new country. They are bound to be wrong about some, expecting too much or too little. What is unclear is *which* expectations about *what* aspect of life in the new country are most important to adjustment than others. Second, the process by which unfulfilled expectations lead to poor adjustment is far from clear. Third, having low expectations may be better for short-term adjustment but worse for overall social mobility (which would mean poor long-term adjustment).

Negative Life Events

This approach emphasizes that any *change* (major or minor, positive or negative) in one's daily routine is associated with adaptation stress and strain and associated psychological and physical illness. Sojourning involves drastic changes and the absolute amount of adjustment is directly related to the speed and type of adaptation. Problems of this approach lie in measurement of life events (quality versus quantity, various dimensions), identifying possible intervening variables, and the relatively small percentages of variance accounted for, among others. There is a problem in establishing cause and effect: Do psychologically distressed people cause the occurrence of many negative events, or do randomly occurring life events lead to depression? The cause relationship is likely to be bidirectional though the major causal direction may be from events to illness. Surprisingly, literature in the area of life events has not paid attention to the sojourner adjustment phenomena.

Social Support (Breakdown in Support Networks)

This explanation argues that social support is directly related to increased psychological well-being and to a lower probability of physical and mental illness. This approach draws on various traditions, including attachment theory, social network theory, and various ideas in psychotherapy. Because sojourning usually involves leaving one's family, friends, and acquaintances (work colleagues and neighbors), sources of social support are considerably reduced, hence a dramatic increase in physical and mental illness. Although few researchers claim that social support is the only, or the most important, determinant of sojourner adjustment, there is sufficient evidence to suggest that it is an important feature. This "theory," however, has to specify the quality as well as the quantity of social support in relations to aspects of adjustment. Also, the mechanism or process whereby social support prevents psychological problems needs to be spelled out.

A Clash of Values

The differences in values (social, moral, work, and so on) that exist among many cultures have been used to account for the misunderstandings, distress, and difficulties experienced by cross-cultural sojourners. Differences in values between the person's country of departure and country of arrival are assumed to be directly proportional to the amount of difficulty experienced by that person. Sociologists and psychologists have for many years seen links among deviance, delinquency, mental disorder, and a conflict in cultural values. There is a rich interdisciplinary literature on the definition and consequences of values. The idea is simply that differences in value systems cause related stress.

This approach also suggests that certain values (for example, stoicism, self-help) are more adaptive than others. It may, however, be that such values relate more to the reporting or not reporting of illness and unhappiness than they do to actual capacity to cope with stress. Value systems may be useful and necessary but not sufficient in predicting how much strain travelers feel.

Social Skills Deficit

It has been shown that socially inadequate or unskilled individuals have not mastered the social conventions of their society. They are unaware of or unable to abide by the rules of social behavior that regulate interpersonal conduct in their culture. From this perspective, socially unskilled persons are often like strangers in their own land and new arrivals in an alien culture or subculture are in a position similar to indigenous socially inadequate individuals. There is now considerable empirical evidence to indicate that the elements of social interaction listed earlier vary among cultures, and that many travelers do not easily learn the conventions of another culture. Ironically, individuals in this predicament (such as foreign students, businesspeople, diplomats, and missionaries) often tend to be highly skilled in the customs of their own society and find their sudden inadequacy in the new culture to be quite frustrating. The culture-learning, social skills model has clear implications for the comprehension and management of cross-cultural difficulties. Cross-cultural problems arise because sojourners have trouble negotiating everyday social encounters.

The social skills approach is favored by Furnham and Bochner (1986) not only for its explanatory power but also for its implications for culture learning. First, coping difficulties are attributed to a lack in appropriate skills rather than to some deficiency in the personality or cultural socialization of the sojourner. Second, the notion of "adjustment," with its ethnocentric overtones, is eliminated because sojourners are not expected to adjust themselves to a new culture. Rather, they learn selected aspects for instrumental reasons, which need not become part of their permanent repertoire. Culture learning makes a distinction between skills and values, between performance and compliance. Third, established courses exist for teaching second-culture skills, an extension of the developed and empirically assessed field of intracultural social skills training. Fourth, cultural social skills training is easier, more economic, and more effective than many other remedial approaches based on counseling and psychotherapy. Finally, the training can be used specifically to help people acquire bicultural competence.

CONCLUSION

This chapter has argued for the necessity of distinguishing among various groups of travelers such as tourists, sojourners, and migrants. In doing so, two dimensions, *motives* for travel and the *length* of time spent in the foreign country, have been presented. Although the latter is moderately straightforward and simple to measure, the former is highly complex. Indeed the many agencies who sponsor sojourners are quite unaware of the real aims and motives of those whom they support. Implicit in a great deal of literature on sojourners is that they will suffer from culture shock—a multifaceted negative reaction to changes in language, role, environment, and the like. Two major problems have been highlighted with regard to the concept of culture shock: (1) It is highly vague and imprecise, not specifying *how, why, who*, or *when* different people experience it, and (2) most researchers stress only the negative rather than the positive aspects of adaptation in a new culture. Also, the mental health in the adaptation of foreign students has been discussed, considering demographic, cultural, personality, social, and situational factors. Finally, eight plausible approaches to sojourners have been presented and evaluated. By and large this area of research has been atheoretical, with few major theories guiding research. Nevertheless, the eight perspectives have been borrowed from other areas of study by researchers in studying sojourner adjustment.

Research findings in this relatively new area are often ambiguous and inconsistent. In future studies, individual differences need to be taken more into account. First, researchers need to consider psychological differences in personality (for example, self-concept and beliefs) of sojourners before and after any sojourning experiences. Second, there are demographic differences (for example, age, sex, national group, religion, and schooling) that condition a sojourner's worldview and expectations. Third, actual experiential differences in the new country need to be examined, including the native population's reactions. All of these variables have been examined in the past. The problem has been that, in concentrating on one set of variables, others have been ignored (or worse still, confounded). For a more systematic and comprehensive understanding of the sojourn experience, these and other relevant variables must be investigated simultaneously in a given research.

REFERENCES

Adler, P. (1975). The transitional experience: An alternative view of culture shock. *Journal of Humanistic Psychology, 15*, 13-23.

Alatas, S. (1972). The captive mind in development studies. *International Social Science Journal, 24*, 9-25.

Alatas, S. (1975). The captive mind and creative development. *International Social Science Journal, 27*, 691-700.

Anumonye, A. (1970). *African students in alien cultures*. London: Black Academy Press.

Babiker, I., Cox, J., & Miller, P. (1980). The measurement of culture distance and its relationship to medical consultations, symptomatology and examination performance of overseas students at Edinburgh University. *Social Psychiatry, 15*, 109-116.

Ball-Rokeach, S. (1973). From pervasive ambiguity to a definition of the situation. *Sociometry, 36*, 43-51.

Bochner, S., & Wicks, P. (Eds.). (1972). *Overseas students in Australia*. Sydney: New South Wales University Press.

Bochner, S. (1973). *The mediating man: Cultural interchange and transnational education*. Honolulu: Culture Learning Institute.

Bochner, S. (1979). Cultural diversity: Implications for modernization and international education. In K. Kumar (Ed.), *Bonds without bondage*. Honolulu: University of Hawaii Press.

Bochner, S. (Ed.). (1982). *Cultures in contact: Studies in cross-cultural interaction*. Oxford: Pergamon.

Bochner, S., Lin, A., & McLeod, B. (1979). Cross-cultural contact and the development of an international perspective. *Journal of Social Psychology, 107*, 29-41.

Bock, P. (Ed.). (1970). *Culture shock: A reader in modern anthropology*. New York: Knopf.

Bourne, P. (1975). The Chinese student-acculturation and mental illness. *Psychiatry, 38*, 269-277.

Boxer, A. (1969). *Experts in Asia: An inquiry into Australian technical assistance*. Canberra: ANU.

Byrnes, F. (1966). Role shock: An occupational hazard of American technical assistants abroad. *Annals of the American Academy of Political and Social Science, 368*, 95-108.

Carey, A. (1956). *Colonial students*. London: Secker & Warburg.

Cattell, R., Breul, H., & Hartman, H. (1951). An attempt at a more refined definition of the cultural dimensions of syntality in modern nations. *American Sociological Review, 17*, 54-68.

Cattell, R., Graham, R., & Woliver, R. (1979). A reassessment of the factorial cultural dimension of modern nations. *Journal of Social Psychology, 108*, 241-258.

Church, A. (1982). Sojourner adjustment. *Psychological Bulletin, 91*, 540-572.

Cleveland, H., Mangone, G., & Adams, J. (1963). *The overseas Americans*. New York: McGraw-Hill.

Curle, A. (1970). *Educational strategy in developing societies*. London: Tavistock.

Davey, B. (1957). The disappointed undergraduate. *British Medical Journal, 2*, 547-550.

David, K. (1972). Intercultural adjustment and applications of reinforcement theory to problems of "culture shock." *Trends, 4*, 1-64.

Eldridge, J. (1960). Overseas students at Leicester University: Some problems of adjustment and communication. *Race, 2*, 50-59.

Furnham, A., & Bochner, S. (1982). Social difficulty in a foreign culture: An empirical analysis of culture shock. In S. Bochner (Ed.), *Cultures in contact: Studies in cross-cultural interaction*. Oxford: Pergamon.

Furnham, A., & Bochner, S. (1986). *Culture shock: Psychological reactions to unfamiliar environments*. London: Methuen.

Furnham, A., & Trezise, L. (1981). The mental health of foreign students. *Social Science and Medicine, 17*, 365-370.

Gudykunst, W. (1983). Toward a typology of stranger-host relationship. *International Journal of Intercultural Relations, 7*, 401-413.

Gunn, A. (1979). National health problems in student care. *Journal of the American College Health Association, 27*, 322-323.

Guthrie, G. (1966). Cultural preparation for the Philippines. In R. Textor (Ed.), *Cultural frontiers of the Peace Corps*. Cambridge: MIT Press.

Guthrie, G. (1975). A behavioral analysis of culture learning. In R. Brislin, S. Bochner, & W. Lonner (Eds.), *Cross-culture perspectives on learning*. New York: Wiley.

Hall, E. (1959). *The silent language*. Garden City, NY: Doubleday.

Hays, R. (1972). Behavioral issues in multinational operations. In R. Hayes (Ed.), *International business*. Englewood Cliffs, NJ: Prentice-Hall.

Hofstede, G. (1982). *Culture's consequences: International differences in work-related values*. Newbury Park, CA: Sage.

Hopkins, J., Malleson, N., & Sarnoff, I. (1975). Some non-intellectual correlates of success and failure among university students. *British Journal of Sociology, 9*, 25-36.

Huang, R. (1977). Campus mental health: The foreigner at your desk. *Journal of the American College Health Association, 25*, 217-219.

Kelvin, R., Lucas, C., & Ojha, A. (1965). The relation between personality, mental health and academic performance in university students. *British Journal of Social and Clinical Psychology, 4*, 244-252.

Kidd, C. (1965). *Epidemiological factors in mental illness: Psychiatric morbidity among students*. Unpublished thesis, University of Edinburgh.

Klineberg, O., & Hull, W. (1979). *At a foreign university: An international study of adaptation and coping*. New York: Praeger.

Lambo, T. (1960). A report on the study of social and health problems of Nigerian students in Britain and Ireland. In *Nigeria Government Primer* (pp. 13-21). Western Nigeria.

Lucas, C., Kelvin, R., & Ojha, A. (1966). Mental health and student wastage. *British Journal of Psychiatry, 112*, 277-284.

Lundstedt, S. (1963). An introduction to some evolving problems in cross-cultural research. *Journal of Social Issues, 19*, 1-9

Malleson, N. (1954). The distressed student. *Lancet, 1*, 824.

Malpass, R., & Salancik, G. (1977). Linear and branching formats in culture assimilator training. *International Journal of Interculture Relations, 1*, 76-87.

May, R. (1970). The nature of anxiety and its relation to fear. In A. Elbing (Ed.), *Behavioral decisions in organizations*. New York: Scott, Foresman.

Mechanic, D., & Greenley, J. (1976). The prevalence of psychological distress and help-seeking in a college student population. *Social Psychiatry, 11*, 1-11.

Mortimer, R. (1973). Aiding the "under developed" countries. *Australia's Neighbors, 4*, 1-5.

Nash, D. (1967). The fate of Americans in a Spanish setting: A study of adaptation. *Human Organization, 26*, 3-14.

Noudehou, A. (1982). Deracines avant d'etre partis. *Journal de Geneve, 8*, 213-215.

Oberg, K. (1960). Culture shock: Adjustment to new culture environments. *Practical Anthropology, 7*, 197-182.

O'Neill, M., Lancee, W., & Freeman, S. (1984). Help-seeking behavior of depressed students. *Social Science and Medicine, 18*, 511-514.

Padesky, C., & Hammen, C. (1981). Sex differences in depressive symptom expression and help-seeking among college students. *Sex Roles, 7*, 309-317.

Rook, A. (1954). Student suicides. *British Medical Journal, 1*, 599-603.

Rust, R. (1960). Epidemiology of mental health in college. *Journal of Psychology, 49*, 235-248.

Schild, E. (1962). The foreign student, as a stranger, learning the norms of host-culture. *Journal of Social Issues, 18*, 41-54.

Seeman, M. (1959). On the meaning of alienation. *American Sociological Review, 24*, 783-791.

Singh, A. (1963). Culture shock, language shock, and the shock of self-discovery. *Practical Anthropology, 10*, 49-56.

Still, R. (1961). Mental health in overseas students. *Proceedings of the British Health Association*. Working paper.

Tajfel, H., & Dawson, J. (Eds.). (1965). *Disappointed guests*. Oxford: Oxford University Press.

Torbiörn, I. (1982). *Living abroad: Personal adjustment and personnel policy in the overseas setting*. New York: Wiley.

Wade, N. (1975). Third World: Science and technology contribute feebly to development. *Science, 189*, 770-776.

Ward, L. (1967). Some observations of the underlying dynamics of conflict in foreign students. *Journal of the American College Health Association, 10*, 430-440.

Willmuth, L., Weaver, D., & Donlan, S. (1975). Utilization of medical services by transferred employees. *Archives of General Psychiatry, 2*, 182-189.

Zuckerman, M. (1978). Sensation seeking and psychopathy. In R. Hare & D. Schalling (Eds.), *Psychopathic behavior*. New York: Wiley.

3

Psychological Acculturation of Immigrants

JOHN W. BERRY • UICHOL KIM • PAWEL BOSKI •
Queen's University at Kingston, Ontario

Individuals who experience acculturation (by migration, displacement, or colonization) must deal with their new circumstances in some way. This process of psychological acculturation is conceptualized, and a model of alternative modes of adaptation is presented. Within this model, five types of acculturating groups (immigrants, refugees, native peoples, ethnic groups, and sojourners) are considered to manifest varying modes of acculturation, with differing attitudes and differing experience of stress. Variation in adaptation also occurs because of differences in host or dominant culture characteristics and because of the cultural and psychological interactions occurring between the two groups in contact. Research in Canada is reviewed to illustrate the general model and to provide some substantive results from this one plural society.

The concept of *adaptation* has a long and complex history in the social and behavioral sciences (Cohen, 1968) as well as in the biological sciences (Dubos, 1965). Without attempting to cover the numerous debates, it is nonetheless useful to identify some of the various meanings that have attended the concept. We will then specify the resent use of the concept.

First, we should note that it can refer both to a *process* and to a *state* (resulting from the process). The former refers to *changes* in a system, so that the parts of the system fit or function together better than before the changes occurred; the latter refers to the *outcome*, in which the parts now function better together.

Second, it is important to note that different disciplines can focus on different parts of the system: Biologists can examine how organisms are adapted to their habitat; anthropologists can seek to discover how features of culture may fit in with the ecological context; and psychologists can study how individuals come to grips with the social, cultural, or ecological setting in which they find themselves (Honigmann, 1976).

Third, there are different *strategies of adaptation* (as a process) that lead to different *varieties of adaptation* (as a state). In the case of the individual, three such strategies have been identified (Berry, 1976). These have been termed *adjustment, reaction,* and *withdrawal,* and may be defined in the following way. In the case of adjustment, behavioral changes are in a direction that reduces the conflict (that is, increases the congruence or fit) between the environment and the behavior by bringing the behavior into harmony with the environment. In general, this strategy is the one most often intended by the term *adaptation* and may indeed be the most common form. In the case of reaction, behavioral changes are in a direction that retaliates against the environment; these may lead to environmental changes that, in effect, increase the congruence or fit between the two, but not by way of cultural or behavioral adjustment. In the case of withdrawal, behavior is in a direction that reduces the pressures from the environment. In a sense, it is a removal from the adaptive arena. These three strategies of adaptation are similar to the distinctions in the psychological literature (Lewin, 1936; Horney, quoted in Munroe, 1955) made among *moving with or toward, moving against,* and *moving away from* a stimulus.

It is important to note that the third strategy (withdrawal) is often not a real possibility, either from physical-environmental pressures for those living at subsistence level, or from accultura-tion pressures for those being influenced by larger and more powerful cultural systems. For the second strategy (reaction) many traditional peoples cannot successfully engage in retaliatory responses. This is either a result of the absence of an advanced technology to change the physical environment, or of the absence of political power to divert acculturative pressures. Thus individual change to adapt to the context (the adjustment strategy of adaptation) is often the only realistic alternative. This is true for peoples confronting both natural environments (as in the case of ecological adaptation) and dominant cultures (as in the case of acculturation).

We can now define *psychological acculturation* as the process by which individuals change their psychological characteristics, change the surrounding context, or change the amount of contact in order to achieve a better fit (outcome) with other features of the system in which they carry out their life. These other features can be physical, cultural, or social in nature and constitute the adaptive context in which the person lives (Berry, Wintrob, Sindell, & Mawhinney, 1982). Note that this definition incorporates both the process and state features of the concept and can take place by way of the adjustment, reaction, or withdrawal strategies of adaptation.

ACCULTURATION

Here, the new context in which psychological adaptation is taking place is that which exists during the process of acculturation. *Acculturation* has been defined as culture change that results from continuous, firsthand contact between two distinct cultural groups (Redfield, Linton, & Herskovits, 1936). While originally proposed as a group-level phenomenon, it is now also widely recognized as an individual-level phenomenon, and is termed *psychological acculturation* (Graves, 1967). At this second level, acculturation refers to changes in an individual (both overt behavior and covert traits) whose cultural group is experiencing acculturation collectively.

What kinds of changes may occur as a result of acculturation? First, *physical* changes may occur: A new place to live, a new type of housing, increasing population density, more pollution, and so forth, are all common with acculturation. Second, *biological* changes may occur: New nutritional status, new diseases (often devastating in force), and interbreeding yielding mixed (metis, mestizo) populations are all common. Third, *cultural* changes, which are at the heart of the definition, necessarily occur: Original political, economic, technical, linguistic, religious, and social institutions become altered, or new ones take their place. Fourth, new sets of *social* relationships, including ingroup-outgroup and dominance patterns, may become established. Finally, as noted above, *psychological* changes (including changes in mental health status) almost always occur as individuals attempt to adapt to their new milieu. While it is important to measure all five categories of change (see Berry, Trimble, & Olmeda, 1986), it is the latter three that are discussed in this chapter.

Psychological adaptation to acculturation is likely to vary as a function of many contextual features of the contact situation.

One of the contextual features is the way the larger society exercises its dominance. In those societies that insist on changes being made by members of the acculturating group, the adjustment strategy will be prevalent; however, those that are more tolerant of diversity may permit the other two strategies. Moreover, even within the adjustment mode, individuals and groups may select the domains (for example, language, food, dress, religion) in which they will change and those in which they will not change.

Just as there are strategies of adaptation, so too are there varying ways by which individuals can acculturate (Berry, 1980). Corresponding to the view that *adjustment* is not the only strategy of adaptation, we take the view that *assimilation* is not the only mode of acculturation. This position becomes clear when we examine the framework proposed by Berry (1984a). The model is based upon the observation that in culturally plural societies, individuals and groups must confront two important issues. One pertains to the maintenance and development of one's ethnic distinctiveness in society, deciding whether one's own cultural identity and customs are of value and should be retained. The other issue involves the desirability of interethnic contact, deciding whether relations with the larger society are of value and should be sought. These are essentially questions of values, even ideologies, and may be responded to on a continuous scale from positive to negative. For conceptual purposes, however, they can be treated as dichotomous (yes or no) decisions, thus generating a fourfold model that serves as the basis for our discussion (see Figure 3.1). Each cell in this fourfold classification is considered to be an option (both a strategy and an outcome) available to individuals and to groups in plural societies. These four options are *assimilation, integration, separation,* and *marginalization.*

When the first question is answered no and the second is answered yes, the assimilation option is defined, namely, relinquishing one's cultural identity and moving into the larger society. It can take place by way of absorption of a nondominant group into an established dominant group, or it can be by way of the merging of many groups to form a new society, as in the melting pot concept. In a detailed analysis of this form of acculturation, Gordon (1964) distinguishes a number of subvarie-

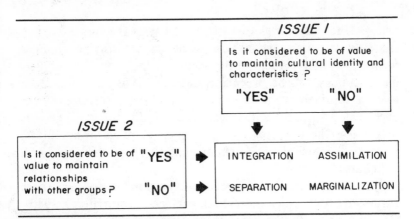

Figure 3.1   Four Modes of Acculturation

ties or processes; most important among these are *cultural* or *behavioral assimilation*, in which collective and individual behaviors become more similar, and *structural assimilation*, in which the nondominant groups participate in the social and economic systems of the larger society.

The integration option implies some maintenance of the cultural integrity of the group, as well as the movement by the group to become an integral part of a larger societal framework. Therefore, the option taken is to retain cultural identity and move to join with the dominant society. In this case there is a large number of distinguishable ethnic groups, all cooperating within a larger social system. Such an arrangement may occur where there is some degree of structural assimilation but little cultural and behavioral assimilation (to use Gordon's terms).

When there are no substantial relations with the larger society, accompanied by a maintenance of ethnic identity and traditions, another option is defined. Depending upon which group (the dominant or nondominant) controls the situation, this option may take the form of either segregation or separation. When the pattern is imposed by the dominant group, classic "segregation to keep people in their place" appears. On the other hand, the maintenance of a traditional way of life outside full participation in the larger society may lead to the desire for an independent existence, as in the case of separatist movements. Here, segregation and separation differ mainly with respect to which group or groups have the power to determine the outcome.

Finally, there is an option that is difficult to define precisely, possibly because it is accompanied by a good deal of collective and individual confusion and anxiety. It is characterized by striking out against the larger society and by feelings of alienation, loss of identity, and what has been termed *acculturative stress* (Berry & Annis, 1974). This option is *marginalization*, in which groups lose cultural and psychological contact with both their traditional culture and the larger society. When imposed by the larger society, it is tantamount to ethnocide. When stabilized in a nondominant group, it constitutes the classical situation of marginality (Stonequist, 1937).

Two points should be made with respect to the model in Figure 3.1. First, these options pertain to both individuals and groups in plural societies. One individual may follow a course toward assimilation, whereas another may not; any one ethnic group through its formal organizations may opt for separation, whereas another may seek integration. It should be obvious, however, that choices among the options are not entirely independent. If, for example, one's group pursues assimilation collectively, one is left without a membership group, rendering the other options meaningless.

Second, the various options may be pursued by politically dominant or nondominant groups. For example, if assimilation is sought by a particular ethnic group, it is an example of the "melting pot," whereas if it is enforced as national policy, we may characterize it as a "pressure cooker." Similarly, as we have noted, separation occurs when a group wishes to set up shop on its own, whereas the classic forms of segregation exist when such apartness is forced on it by the dominant groups.

To summarize these points, the model in Figure 3.1 can be viewed at three distinct levels. First, at the level of the dominant or larger society, *national policies* can be identified as those encouraging assimilation, integration, separation/segregation, or marginalization. In Canada, the official policy is clearly toward integration (termed *multiculturalism* by the federal government; see Berry, 1984b), while other societies' policies can be identified as leaning toward other alternatives. Second, at the level of ethnic or minority groups, these communities can articulate their wishes and goals, and communicate them to their members and to the larger society. Generally, in Canada, most ethnic groups are pursuing an integrationist goal, although there are expressions of assimilationist and separatist views from time to time by some groups. Third, at the level of individuals, attitudes toward or preferences for these four alternatives can be assessed using standard attitude measurement techniques. These *acculturation attitudes* will be presented in the next section.

This framework sets the stage for the examination of the kinds of psychological adaptation made by individuals during the course of acculturation. It should be evident that there are some correspondences intended between strategies of adaptation and modes of acculturation: Assimilation clearly involves adjustment, and separation clearly involves withdrawal. However, marginalization is not really a form of adaptation, but suspends individuals and groups among options. Finally, integration involves both some degree of adjustment and some degree of reaction in order to change the dominant group.

SELECTED CANADIAN STUDIES

In the balance of this chapter a selection of recent and current work on such adaptation is drawn mainly from the Canadian literature. This is not intended to be a comprehensive review, but only to illustrate the concepts outlined up to this point, to provide some empirical evidence for them, and to stimulate further work on these topics. Before examining these studies, however, it will be useful to consider, first, the types of acculturating groups that are available for study, and, second, a framework for sampling across them.

Many of the phenomena of psychological adaptation to be reviewed in this chapter vary according to the nature of the acculturating group being examined. Figure 3.2 illustrates five kinds of groups: immigrants, refugees, native peoples, ethnic groups, and sojourners. Across these categories, there are variations in the degree of voluntariness, movement, and permanence of contact, all factors that might affect the psychological adaptation of members of the group. Those involved voluntarily in the

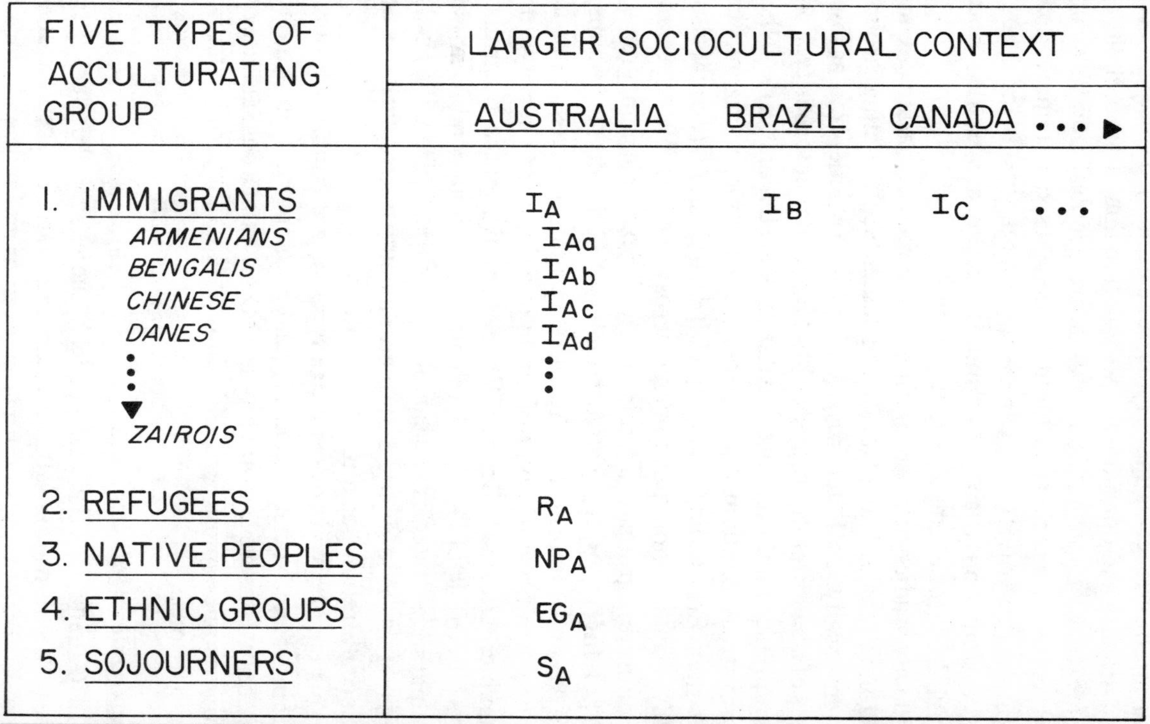

Figure 3.2 Five Types of Acculturating Groups

FIVE TYPES OF ACCULTURATING GROUP	LARGER SOCIOCULTURAL CONTEXT			
	AUSTRALIA	BRAZIL	CANADA ... ▲	
1. IMMIGRANTS *ARMENIANS* *BENGALIS* *CHINESE* *DANES* ••• ► *ZAIROIS*	I_A I_{Aa} I_{Ab} I_{Ac} I_{Ad} •••	I_B	I_C	•••
2. REFUGEES	R_A			
3. NATIVE PEOPLES	NP_A			
4. ETHNIC GROUPS	EG_A			
5. SOJOURNERS	S_A			

69

acculturation process (immigrants, for example) may experience less difficulty and opt more for assimilation than those with little choice (for example, refugees and native peoples); and those in contact only temporarily, without permanent social supports (for example, sojourners), may experience more problems and desire less assimilation than those more permanently settled and established (for example, ethnic groups).

Ideally studies of acculturation should be comparative. Our long-term goal is to study a particular acculturating group systematically, both across larger or host societies and across types of acculturating groups within a particular host society. For example (see Figure 3.3), we could study societies that vary on the pluralist/assimilationist dimensions (for example, immigrants in Australia, Brazil, and Canada, I[A], I[B], I[C] . . .). We could also study acculturation phenomena across the varying types of acculturating groups in a single society (for example, immigrants, I[A]; refugees, R[A]; native peoples, NP[A]; ethnic groups, EG[A]; and sojourners, S[A], in Australia), or across cultural groups within a single type of group in a single host society (for example, Armenian, Bengali, Chinese immigrants in Australia: I[Aa], I[Ab], I[Ic] . . .). And, of course, we could combine these comparative strategies and sample systematically from the resulting matrix (as in Figure 3.3) to give a comparative overview of the acculturation phenomenon of interest.

This chapter will cover all five types of acculturating groups within a single society (Canada), and is comparative in this one way only. However, within types, there are numerous samples of native peoples, sojourners, and ethnic groups that permit internal comparisons.

Acculturation Attitudes

In Canada, a series of empirical studies were conducted to assess acculturation attitudes among various acculturating groups. These studies involved the development and validation of acculturation-attitude scales, the search for some psychological and behavioral correlates of acculturation attitudes, and for variations among the samples. This section will summarize this series of empirical studies conducted in Canada and reported in Berry, Kim, Power, Young, and Bujaki (in press).

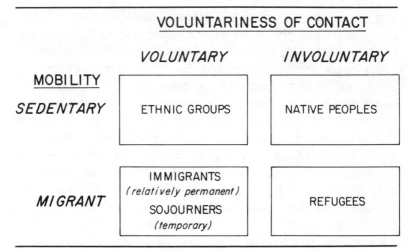

Figure 3.3 Framework for the Comparative Study of Acculturation

A total of 900 individuals have been studied. Of these, 534 are native peoples, representing four distinct cultures (3 samples of Cree, 3 samples of Ojibway, 2 samples of Carrier, and 2 samples of Tshimshian). The other samples are residents of Ontario: French-Canadians living in Kingston (N = 49); Portuguese immigrants living in Kingston (31 families, N = 117); Korean immigrants living in Toronto (N = 150); and Hungarian refugees living in Ottawa (30 first-generation and 20 second-generation, N = 50).

For each study, scales were developed based on the researchers' knowledge and understanding of important topics and dimensions that are relevant to a particular group. An initial pool of statements was generated to reflect the ideas inherent in the four modes of acculturation presented in Figure 3.1. These items were then given to judges who were asked to sort these items into four categories, representing the four acculturation attitudes. Items were selected when agreement was found among most of the judges. Half of the items were worded positively, and the other half negatively. Items were then back-translated (Brislin, 1980).

Reliability estimates (Cronbach's alpha) were generally satisfactory usually in the 0.70 to 0.85 range. To check the validity of the acculturation attitude scales, several behavioral measures (for example, club membership, newspaper readership) and psychological measures (for example, ethnic identity, language preference) were used. For newspaper readership (as an example), we predicted that, compared to other forms of newspaper readership, respondents reading only Canadian newspapers will have a higher assimilation score; respondents reading only ethnic newspapers will have a higher separation score; respondents reading both ethnic and Canadian newspapers will have a higher integration score; and respondents not reading any newspaper will have a higher marginalization score. Similar predictions were made for validation checks with other criteria. In all studies we have some validation support for assimilation, integration, and separation. Formal schooling (used as an index of exposure to Euro-Canadian life) revealed a consistent positive correlation with assimilation, a negative correlation with separation, and a moderate positive correlation with integration. For marginalization, we found concurrent validation within the Korean-Canadian sample (correlation of 0.54 with the marginality scale of Mann, 1958). In addition to predictions based on measured behavioral and psychological variables, we predicted that the scales representing the diagonal opposites in the model (Figure 3.1) would be correlated negatively (assimilation-separation and integration-marginalization dyads). These predictions were generally verified in most of the samples.

If we compare the overall means for the four acculturation attitudes for all of the samples, we can assess which mode is preferred. In *all* samples, integration had the highest sample mean. Moreover, the mean scores for integration were always on the agree side of the scale, buttressing the evidence that it is the favored mode of acculturation.

Correlational analyses were conducted to assess the relationships between acculturation attitudes and other measured variables. For example, in the studies of native peoples, an index of Westernization (measures such as formal education, wage employment, and ownership of Euro-Canadian manufactured goods) was found to be correlated positively with assimilation, correlated moderately positively with integration, and correlated negatively with separation. In the French-Canadian study, ethnic identity, club membership, high education, socioeconomic status, and travel experience were correlated negatively with assimilation and marginalization, and positively with integration and separation.

Correlational analyses were conducted to assess the relationships between acculturation attitudes and other measured variables. For example, in the studies of native peoples, index of Westernization (measures such as formal education, wage employment, and ownership of Euro-Canadian manufactured goods) was found to be correlated positively with assimilation, correlated moderately positively with integration, and correlated negatively with separation. In the French-Canadian study, ethnic identity, club membership, high education, socioeconomic status, and travel experience were correlated negatively with assimilation and marginalization, and positively with integration and separation.

To summarize, the acculturation attitudes scales show consistent and stable reliability and validity. Second, the conceptual model has been supported by interscale correlations and a series of simple and multiple correlational analyses. The pattern of results provides a coherent set of results supporting the overall scientific merit of the model. Third, these studies showed that the integration mode is preferred over all the other modes. Cutting across cultural variations, voluntariness of contact, and mobility, all groups favored integration. Clearly, assimilation is not taking place in Canada as some researchers have assumed in other societies (see Glazer & Moynihan, 1963; Gordon, 1964). Taft (1986a) has noted that after 10 years of research in acculturation, the assumption of linear progressive assimilation was abandoned in Australia and researchers there adopted a multifaceted model similar to one proposed by Berry (1980). Preference for the Integration mode over all the other modes is now a common result from other studies in the United States (for example, with Korean-Americans, Hurh & Kim, 1984; Y. Kim, 1978; with Mexican-Americans, Mendoza & Martinez, 1981). Other researchers have come to develop similar models of acculturation, and the integration mode of acculturation shares similar characteristics to "cultural pluralism" (Newman, 1973), "adhesive adaptation" (Hurh & Kim, 1984), "reconciliation" (Born, 1970), "cultural incorporation" (Mendoza & Martinez, 1981), "controlled acculturation (Eaton, 1952), "accomodative pluralism"

(Kurokawa, 1979) and "acculturation without assimilation" (Rosenthal, 1970). These researchers all agree that assimilation is only one possible mode of acculturation. Further research is needed in order to clarify, theoretically and empirically, the integration mode of acculturation.

Finally, the present model of acculturation has both scientific and practical merits. Acculturation attitudes can be used to assess individual preferences directly with respect to various policy options in plural societies. This information can then be used to assist in government policy and program development.

Acculturative Stress

The concept of *stress* has had wide use in the recent psychological and medical literature (for example, Dohrenwend & Dohrenwend, 1974; Lazarus & Folkman, 1984; Selye, 1979). For our purposes *stress* is defined to be a state of the organism, brought about by the experience of *stressors*, and which requires some reduction (for normal functioning to occur), through a process of *coping* until some satisfactory *adaptation* to the new situation is achieved. The concept of *acculturative stress* refers to a particular kind of stress, that in which the stressors are identified as having their source in the process of acculturation. There is often a particular set of stress behaviors that occur during acculturation, such as lowered mental health status (specifically: confusion, anxiety, depression), feelings of marginality, and alienation. heightened psychosomatic symptom level, and identity confusion. Acculturative stress is thus a reduction in the health status of individuals and may include physical, psychological, and social aspects; to qualify as *acculturative stress*, these changes should be related in a systematic way to known features of the acculturation process as experienced by the individual.

Recently, Berry and Kim (1986) conducted a review of the literature identifying the psychological, social, and cultural factors that moderate the relationship between acculturation and stress. These moderating factors have been divided broadly into five categories: (1) the nature of the larger society, (2) the type of acculturating group, (3) the mode of acculturation being experienced, (4) a number of demographic, psychological, and social characteristics of acculturating individuals, and (5) interactions among these four sets of factors.

Here we summarize a series of empirical studies, conducted in Canada, explicitly examining the above factors. Numerous acculturating groups have been researched in Canada in order to investigate acculturative stress systematically. An integrated discussion of the general findings are reported in Berry, Kim, Minde, and Mok (1985). In these studies the nature of the larger society is held constant (that is, all of the studies were conducted in Canada).

A total of 1,197 individuals were studied. Of these, 534 were native people, representing four distinct cultures. These four cultures are the same as those reported in the previous section. The other samples are residents of Ontario. They are Korean immigrants living in Toronto (N = 150); Vietnamese refugees living in Kingston (N = 72); three samples of student sojourners, including Malaysian students living in Kingston and other urban areas of Ontario (N = 72); Chinese students from Singapore and Hong Kong, all studying at Queen's University (N = 71); a cross section of foreign students attending Queen's University from the United States, the United Kingdom, India, Hong Kong, South America, and Africa (N = 97); four ethnic groups, including a sample from Westport, a rural Anglo-Celtic community in southern Ontario (N = 48), a sample from Sioux Lookout, a frontier resource town in northern Ontario, of mixed but largely Northern and Eastern European origin (N = 40), and two samples of Canadian Queen's University students (N = 49 and N = 64), who are of mixed, but largely Anglo-Celtic origin.

Among the various measures employed, a common instrument has been used in all the studies for comparative purposes; this instrument is a stress scale developed by Cawte (1972). Cawte selected 20 items from the Cornell Medical Index (CMI) of Brodman, Erdman, Lorge, Gershenson, and Wolff (1952) on the basis of clinical and statistical judgment using data from Aboriginal populations in Australia. The first 10 items are from the somatic section of the CMI, but they are considered to be primarily *psycho*somatic. The second 10 items cover the psychological areas of anxiety, depression, and irritability.

Within the series of studies conducted by Berry et al. (1985), the scale proved to be a reliable and valid measure of acculturative stress. The internal consistency of the scale tends to be rather high: Cronbach's alpha is usually in the 0.7 to 0.8 range. For validity, we have found several measures of support. For example, we have found significant correlations in the stress scale with a self-report measure of respondents' physical health status in the study with mixed sojourners. Of particular interest is that prior to our actual investigations, we made theoretically based predictions guided by our knowledge of the literature. We expected that the two groups that were not in voluntary contact (native peoples and refugees) to exhibit higher levels of stress compared to the three voluntary groups (immigrants, ethnic groups, and sojourners). As we shall see below, the results of our studies confirmed our predictions providing "known group" validation.

An overall mean for the stress scale was calculated for five types of acculturating groups. As we have predicted, the two involuntary groups had the highest overall means (5.5 for native peoples and 5.6 for refugees). The two voluntary groups had the two lowest means (3.1 for immigrants and 2.7 for ethnic groups). Sojourners, although a voluntary group, fell between the involuntary and other voluntary groups with a mean score of 4.1. The higher stress level of sojourners compared with other voluntary groups may be a result of their impermanence of contact, their relative youth, and their student status.

In addition to voluntariness of contact, there are several other factors that could explain the variation among the five types of groups. First, these samples vary not only by voluntariness of contact, but also by their mobility (see Figure 3.2). This factor, however, seems to have relatively little impact: The two sedentary and established groups (native peoples and ethnic groups) exhibit the highest and lowest sample means, respectively, while the two mobile and recent migrants (refugees and immigrants) similarly vary widely at the group level. Second, within the 10 native samples, we have a measure of cultural distance from Euro-Canadian society. We predicted and found that those samples most culturally different experienced relatively greater acculturative stress. Cultural distance, however, cannot explain all the variations found among the groups. Three groups (Koreans, Chinese, and Vietnamese), all of whom come from one cultural area (East Asia), differ considerably from the largely European-derived character of Canadian society, but they vary widely in the experience of stress.

In addition to overall group differences, we have identified a number of individual, social, and demographic characteristics that were related to stress. First, *education* appears as a consistent predictor of low stress in all the native samples—among the Korean immigrants, among Vietnamese refugees, and among Malay and mixed student sojourners. Moreover, in the studies of natives, a variety of tests of cognitive ability have been used and these measures correlate negatively with stress, even when education is controlled.

A second major class of variables related to stress are the *acculturation attitudes*. For all native samples, those favoring the integration mode experience less stress, while those preferring the separation mode tend to experience greater stress. Within the Korean sample, those respondents who score high in separation and marginalization modes score high on stress.

Third, variables that tap *prior cultural experiences* have also been found to be related to the experience of stress. For Malaysian students, the extent of prior travel, knowing more languages, and having lived in an urban (usually culturally plural) as opposed to a rural (usually unicultural) setting, were all predictive of lower stress.

Fourth, variables that assess *contact experiences* were related to stress. Among the native samples, an Acculturation Index was constructed to reflect a community's general contact with the participation in the larger society. Greater participation both at the community level and at the individual level was associated with lower stress levels. Similar results were found for Korean immigrants and Malay, Chinese, and mixed student sojourners at the individual level. Chance (1965) proposed that in addition to actual contact, the congruity between desired and actual contact can be an important factor. He found that among the Alaskan Inuit, those people who had less contact than they desired exhibited higher levels of stress than those with greater congruity. In our study, for both Chinese and mixed sojourner samples, similar results were obtained: The total contact incongruity score correlated positively with stress.

Social support variables were found to mediate the experience of stress. Among Korean immigrants, sponsored immigrants (as opposed to independent immigrants), Christians (rather than non-Christians), and those with close Korean friends scored lower on stress. People in the former categories have access to social supports that can serve to buffer stressful situations. Similarly, among Malay, Chinese, and mixed sojourners, having close friends and spending time with various other people were associated with lower stress.

Reviewing the general literature and the present series of empirical studies, we conclude that the relationship between acculturation and stress is probabilistic rather than deterministic: The experience of acculturative stress is likely, but not inevitable, as it can be mediated by the numerous factors noted in these studies.

We should note that acculturative stress falls under the general concept of mental health. Berry and Kim (1986) noted that mental health involves the effective functioning of individuals in their daily lives and in their ability to deal with new situations. Inherent in the definition are the absence of distress and dysfunction and the positive qualities of well-being. The discussion on acculturative stress so far has focused on the negative aspects of mental health. However, the positive aspects of health have been emphasized with recent interest in the concept of "quality of life." Researchers are acknowledging the importance of understanding such factors as emotional stability, meaningful interpersonal relationships, and satisfaction in various aspects of one's life rather than focussing on the absence of disease and illness as indicators of mental health (Scott & Stumpf, 1984; Taft, 1986a, 1986b). In Australia, these authors have found that life satisfaction is an important indicator of successful adaptation. In our series of studies, we have measures of satisfaction as indicators of positive aspects of mental health in two studies (the Chinese and mixed sojourner samples). These two studies mirror the results obtained for acculturative stress. Respondents who reported higher life satisfaction had fewer mental health problems (as measured by the Stress scale and CMI), greater contact the participation in the larger society, greater knowledge of English, positive motivation (that is, they have chosen to come to Canada), felt at home in Canada, and had fewer problems dealing with homesickness, language, prejudice, loneliness, and general adaptation. Moreover, in the mixed sojourner sample, those respondents with less difference in the diet and climate between their country of origin and Canada, higher scores of Hofstede's cultural distance measures, and contact incongruity, reported higher satisfaction levels. For academic satisfaction, respondents with higher TOEFL scores, low number of courses dropped, higher academic averages, and fewer courses failed had higher satisfaction levels.

Finally, our presentation may have implied that stress is always a negative experience, something to be avoided or reduced. However, this may not be true. A case can be made that acculturative stress is an adaptive psychological state, insofar as it alerts an acculturating population to new situations that require action on their part. Without such stress, disappearance of the cultural group (for lack of response) might be the long-term outcome. Alternatively, too much stress may inhibit effective responses to acculturation, leading to disintegration and eventual disappearance. Thus, as in the case of the Yerkes-Dobson Law that has established a curvilinear relationship between arousal and performance, there may be an optimal level of acculturative stress that alerts a population to impending changes and dangers and that motivates and facilitates effective response; in contrast, either too little or too much stress may prevent such long-term adaptation to the new circumstances of their lives.

Ethnic Identity

Until very recently, ethnicity has been an area dominated by sociologists and other social scientists operating with census-type data (Anderson & Frideres, 1981; De Vos & Romanucci-Ross, 1975; Glazer & Moynihan, 1975; Goldstein & Bienvenue, 1980; Isajiw, 1980). Psychological theorizing and methods of investigation have entered this field only recently (Aboud, 1981; Berry, Kalin, & Taylor, 1977).

In the psychological tradition many researchers have asked a practical empirical question: "What type of ethnic labels do individuals use (defined by some objective or external criteria of ethnicity), and what are the determinants and correlates of such self-labeling decisions?" Typical of this approach are the survey studies of O'Bryan, Reitz, and Kuplowska (1976) and Berry et al. (1977). The research paradigm established in those works provides for three basic self-labeling categories: "Canadian/Canadien;"

ethnic Canadian" (hyphenated ethnicity); and an "ethnic" identification (usually one's ancestral country of origin).

The O'Bryan et al. (1976) work was concerned primarily with the issue of the maintenance of nonofficial languages in Canada, and ethnic labeling was only one of many variables. Predictably, attitudinal favorability toward heritage-language maintenance was correlated strongly with ethnic labeling: Respondents who felt "ethnic" expressed the strongest support for nonofficial language maintenance. These authors were able to present their data in a path-analytical model with ethnic labeling being determined by generational status and command of their heritage language, and having consequences in language use (behavior) and positive attitudes toward its maintenance.

Berry et al. (1977) dealt mainly with English and French Canadian attitudes to government's policies of multiculturalism. In a follow-up analysis of their data (Kalin & Berry, 1979) some ethnic labeling questions were investigated more thoroughly. First of all, the distribution of identification labels (Canadian/hyphenated/ethnic) depended on a number of objective sociodemographic criteria. Using a compound measure of objective ethnicity, these authors found 84% of Anglo-Celts calling themselves "Canadian" as compared with 66% of other ethnics (comparable with O'Bryan et al., 1976), and 17% of French Canadians deciding on a "Canadien" self-label.

Kalin and Berry (1979) also sought to discover what factors make one decide on a Canadian, hyphenated, or ethnic label. For the French, determinants of "Canadien" were living and visiting outside Quebec and exogamy; "Canadien Francais" were those living in Quebec, older, and more religious; "Quebecois" were younger, less religious, and wealthier than "Canadien Francais." For Anglo-Celts, who, as noted above, felt predominantly "Canadian," only generational status was a strong predictor of that identity. Results for other ethnics paralleled exactly the findings reported by O'Bryan et al. (1976): The self-label "Canadian" was chosen by those with longer family residence in Canada (generational status) who did not desire heritage-language maintenance, were younger, less religious, lived outside Quebec, and were exogamous.

Within the framework of social cognition, it has been proposed

(Boski, 1985) that ethnic self-identity should be defined in terms of one's distance to ethnic *prototypes* of the two groups conceived (for example, Canadian and Portuguese, Canadian and Polish, and so on). To use Tajfel's (1981) terms, prototypes are represented in *criterial attributes* as the best exemplars of a category (Cantor & Mischel, 1979). *Correlated attributes*, on the other hand, represent schematic content of such prototypes and of an individual's self-concept as well. They enable measuring the degree of self-prototype similarity (distance).

It was hypothesized that ethnic schemata should reflect acculturative adaptation, and be a function of length of residence in the receiving country. In particular, first generation Polish immigrants with a long period in Canada should have higher Canadian ethnic schemata and lower Polish ethnic schemata than those recently arrived. Theoretically, this relationship should be moderated by acculturation attitudes. Second, because of their presumably more extensive acculturative adaptation in terms of objective social criteria, immigrants with a longer time in Canada should express a higher degree of life satisfaction in the country of settlement.

To test these hypotheses, a study was conducted (Boski, 1985) with 32 Polish immigrants (male and female) who differed in their length of stay in Canada. *Old* were the World War II veterans (or their wives) who arrived in Canada between 1947-1952. Their present age range was 60-69. The remaining were *new* immigrants, recruited from the recent "Solidarity" wave. Their dates of arrival in Canada were 1980-84, and their age range was 32-40. Hence generation and length of time in Canada were the criteria separating (but also confounding) those groups.

To measure ethnic schemata there were 75 items of culture-related behavioral descriptions; care was taken to select a pool of correlated attributes, yet with presumably different frequencies in the two cultures. The research instrument was designed as a Q-sort technique, which forces a normal distribution of responses. The extreme ends of the distribution were named "Most like me (him)" and "Least like me (him)," and, as such, were considered equally diagnostic or schematic; items from the middle section of distribution were poorly descriptive or aschematic.

To link this work to the previous section, life satisfaction in Canada was measured with three scales: degree of self-fulfillment, quality of family life, and evaluation of socioeconomic status. Correlations between self and Polish prototype's sortings was $r = +.32$, $p < .01$; while between self and Canadian prototype, $r = -.20$. The difference between these two mean coefficients measured with the t-test for paired measures is highly significant ($p < .001$). It indicates that Polish immigrants tend to retain their primary ethnic schemata rather than acquire a Canadian one. Our hypothesis, which predicted differences in ethnic schemata between old and new immigrants, was not confirmed: Living 3 of 30 years did not matter for the degree of positive correlation between self and Polish prototype, nor of negative correlation between self and Canadian prototype. However, interaction of gender and generation was found, showing new immigrant women more pro-Polish, and old immigrant women more pro-Canadian.

Correlations among schematic representations of Polish and Canadian prototypes were also negative ($r = -.26$, $p < .05$); here, however, generation affects the width of this distance: It is larger for New immigrants ($r = -.38$, $p < .01$) than for Old immigrants ($r = -.10$), $F(1,28) = 5.78$, $p < .05$. It shows that contrasts among Polish and Canadian cultures (symbolized by their psychological prototypes) have mellowed with the length of stay in the receiving country.

Since the three life-satisfaction subscales were highly intercorrelated (mean $r = +.79$), scores were aggregated into one index of life satisfaction. In line with the hypothesis, old immigrants indeed reported higher life satisfaction levels than the new immigrants ($p < .05$). Neither Canadian nor Polish ethnic schemata showed any significant correlation with life satisfaction, but the two prototypes' schematic similarity did ($r = +.39$, $p < .05$). The latter moderates the effect of generation on life satisfaction.

As has been already documented, *integration* is the mode that best protects immigrants from acculturative stress. Blending or mellowing of cultural differences among cultural prototypes could be interpreted as indicative of the integrative acculturative outcome accomplished by old immigrants. This solution has positive consequences on life satisfaction, which is a healthy counterpart of destructive acculturative stress.

Language

One of the most dramatic changes that can occur as a result of acculturation is the rapid decline in heritage-language knowledge and use. O'Bryan et al. (1976) conducted a pioneering study examining heritage-language knowledge, use, and support among 10 major ethnic groups (Chinese, Dutch, German, Greek, Hungarian, Italian, Polish, Portuguese, Scandinavian, and Ukranian) residing in five major cities across Canada (Montreal, Toronto, Winnipeg, Edmonton, and Vancouver). A total of 2,433 respondents were interviewed.

Knowledge of heritage language was assessed by a self-report measure of an individual's ability to understand, speak, read, and write. The most dramatic finding was that heritage-language knowledge virtually disappears after two generations. Among the first generation, 71% reported fluent knowledge, 27% reported some knowledge, and only 2% reported no knowledge. For the second generation, only 11% reported fluent knowledge, 64% reported some knowledge and 24% reported no knowledge. For the third generation only 0.6% reported fluent knowledge, 38% reported some knowledge, and 61% reported no knowledge. heritage-language knowledge was greatest among Greeks, Hungarians, Italians, Portuguese, and Chinese (in descending order). Heritage-language knowledge drops off and is lowest among Scandinavians, Polish, Ukranian, German, and Dutch, respectively. These ethnic-group variations, however, are minor compared to the generation effect.

Although there is a dramatic drop in language knowledge and use across generations, there is strong support for heritage-language retention. Overall, 30% of the respondents strongly supported language retention, 41% were somewhat supportive, 20% were indifferent, and only 9% opposed it and found it undesirable. The support for heritage-language retention was greatest among the first generation. A majority of the third generation supported the retention of heritage language with 18% strongly supporting it, 41% somewhat supporting it, 27% indifferent, and 14% against.

Relating support for heritage-language retention with identity, those who identified themselves by using an ethnic label (for example, Italian) had the highest support for heritage-language retention, followed by those using a hyphenated identity (for example, Italian-Canadian). However, the majority of respondents who identified themselves simply as a Canadian also supported heritage-language retention. O'Bryan et al. (1976, p. 172) concluded that "in the minds of many ethnic group members, to become a true Canadian is not to become Anglocized or Francocized. Their definition of a Canadian does not stipulate abandonment of one's cultural tradition and complete conformity to the North American norm." These findings agree with the strong and consistent support for the integration mode of acculturation by all the groups reported earlier in this chapter.

Second language acquisition research in Canada focuses mainly on the effects of learning one of the two "official languages" (English and French). Researchers have found that individuals must have both language aptitude and motivation to learn a second language (for a review, see Gardner, 1977; Gardner & Lambert 1972). They have articulated two important motivations for learning a second language: instrumental and integrative. Instrumental motives involve practical consideration: a means to the desired goal such as a better job or position. Integrative motivation involves a desire to learn more about the language group, to interact with them and to become part of the group. While both motivations were important in predicting the success of second language competence, integrative motivation produced better long-term effects.

The outcome of these studies examining the effects of learning a second language generally showed positive results. English Canadians who have been enrolled in French immersion classrooms benefited from positive cognitive and social consequences (for example, increased cognitive flexibility and tolerance for other groups), without suffering from the feared retardation in native language, and academic, personal, and social developments (for a review, see Genesee 1983, 1984; Lambert, 1978).

However, Lambert and Taylor (1984) point out that these studies have focused on English-Canadians who are economically and socially established in Canada. Lambert (1978) argued that these individuals are economically and socially secure and can afford to increase their linguistic and cognitive skills without facing a threat to their native language development; he labeled this process as "additive bilingualism." Lambert and Taylor (1984, p. 208) also point out that for French-Canadians and other acculturating groups "subtractive" bilingualism can occur. Subtractive bilingualism refers to learning a new language that can hinder, suppress, and even eradicate the previously learned language. When ethnic children enter school they are faced with a situation where a "high-prestige, socially powerful group's language, such as English, is introduced as the exclusive language of instruction." The rapid decline in heritage-language knowledge with academic, personal, and social disruptions have been documented where a single dominant language has been used as a sole medium of communication (for a review, see Cummins, 1984). Taylor, Meynard, and Rheault (1977) found that there is a negative motivation for learning a second language that can threaten one's ethnic identity. Because learning the language of the dominant group can result in the loss of one's first language, people may be fearful of learning a second language. It can create fear for one's ethnic identity, intergenerational conflict (Frasure-Smith, Lambert, & Taylor, 1975), and feelings of anomie (Lambert, Gardner, Barik, & Turnstall, 1963).

CONCLUSIONS

In this chapter, we have attempted to illustrate the concept of *psychological adaptation* during acculturation, using a series of studies carried out in one plural society (Canada). Of course, while valid for this one society, generalization to others should be made with caution; parallel studies are required in other societies in order to develop cross-culturally valid statements about the nature and course of psychological adaptation to acculturation.

A central point of view expressed in this chapter is that there are both group and individual differences in adaptation to acculturation *and* there are some commonalities across groups and individuals. Put in terms of current issues in cross-cultural methodology, there may well prove to be *universal processes* of psychological adaptation, but with local (specific group and individual) expressions of these commonalities.

Another key point is that the conceptualization and measurement of adaptation phenomena can be done at both the group and individual levels of analysis. Moreover, there are identifiable and consistent interrelations between these two levels that establish the merit of continuing to blend the sociocultural and psychological research traditions in the investigation of acculturation.

REFERENCES

Aboud, F. E. (1981). Ethnic self-identity. In R. C. Gardner & R. Kalin (Eds.), *A Canadian Social Psychology of Ethnic Relations*. Toronto: Methuen.

Anderson, A. B., & Frideres, J. S. (1981). *Ethnicity in Canada*. Toronto: Butterworths.

Berry, J. W. (1976). *Human ecology and cognitive style: Comparative studies in cultural and psychological adaptation*. New York: Sage/Halsted.

Berry, J. W. (1980). Acculturation as varieties of adaptation. In A. Padilla (Ed.), *Acculturation: Theory, model and some new findings*. Washington, DC: AAAS.

Berry, J. W. (1984a). Cultural relations in plural societies: Alternatives to segregation and their sociopsychological implications. In N. Miller & M. Brewer (Eds.), *Group in contact*. New York: Academic Press.

Berry, J. W. (1984b). Multicultural policy in Canada: A social psychological analysis. *Canadian Journal of Behavioural Science, 16*, 353-370.

Berry, J. W., & Annis, R. C. (1974). Acculturative stress: The role of ecology, culture and differentiation. *Journal of Cross-Cultural Psychology, 5*, 382-406.

Berry, J. W., Kalin, R., & Taylor, D. M. (1977). *Multiculturalism and ethnic attitudes in Canada*. Ottawa: Government of Canada.

Berry, J. W., & Kim, U. (1986). Acculturation and mental health. In P. Dasen, J. W. Berry, & N. Sartorius (Eds.), *Health and cross-cultural psychology: Towards application*. London: Sage.

Berry, J. W., Kim, U., Minde, T., & Mok, D. (1985). *Acculturative stress in Canada*. Paper presented at the Annual Conference of the Canadian Psychological Association, Halifax.

Berry, J. W., Kim, U., Power, S., Young, M., & Bujaki, M. (in press). Acculturation attitudes in plural societies. *International Review of Applied Psychology*.

Berry, J. W., Trimble, J., & Olmeda, E. (1986). Assessment of acculturation. In W. J. Lonner & J. W. Berry (Eds.), *Field methods in cross-cultural research*. London: Sage.

Berry, J. W., Wintrob, R., Sindell, P., & Mawhinney, T. (1982). Psychological adaptation to culture change among the James Bay Cree. *Naturaliste Canadien, 109*, 965-975.

Born, D. O. (1970). Psychological adaptation and development under acculturative stress. *Social Science and Medicine, 3*, 529-547.

Boski, P. (1985). *On becoming a Canadian or remaining a Pole: Stability and change in ethnic self-schemata among Polish immigrants in Canada*. Paper presented at the Canadian Ethnic Studies Association Conference, Montreal.

Brislin, R. W. (1980). Translation and content analysis of oral and written material. In H. C. Triandis & J. W. Berry (Eds.), *Handbook of cross-cultural psychology* (Vol. 2). Boston: Allyn and Bacon.

Brodman, K., Erdmann, A. J., Lorge, E., Gershenson, C. P., & Wolff, H. G. (1952). The Cornell Medical Index Health Questionnaire. *Journal of Clinical Psychology, 8*, 119-124.

Cantor, N., & Mischel, W. (1979). Prototypes in person perception. In L. Berkowitz (Ed.), *Advances in experimental social psychology* (Vol. 12) New York: Academic Press.

Cawte, J. (1972). *Cruel, poor and brutal nations.* Honolulu: University of Hawaii.

Chance, N. A. (1965). Acculturation, self-identification and personality adjustment. *American Anthropologist, 67*, 372-393.

Cohen, Y. (1968). *Man in adaptation.* Chicago: Aldine.

Cummins, (1984). *Bilingualism and special education: Issues in assessment and pedagogy.* Clevedon, England: Multilingual Matters.

de Vries, J. (1977). Language in contact: A review of Canadian research. In W. H. Coons, D. M. Taylor, & M. A. Tremblay (Eds.), *The individual, language and society in Canada.* Ottawa: Canada Council.

DeVos, G., & Romanucci-Ross, L. (1975). *Ethnic identity: Cultural continuities and change.* Palo Alto, CA: Mayfield.

Dohrenwend, B. S., & Dohrenwend, B. P. (Eds.). (1974). *Stressful life events: Their nature and effects.* Toronto: Wiley.

Dubos, R. (1965). *Man adapting.* New Haven, CT: Yale University Press.

Eaton, J. (1952). Controlled acculturation: A survival technique of the Hutterites. *American Sociological Review, 17*, 331-340.

Frasure-Smith, N., Lambert, W. E., & Taylor, D. M. (1975). Choosing the language of instruction for one's children—A Quebec study. *Journal of Cross-Cultural Psychology, 6*, 131-155.

Gardner, R. C. (1977). Social factors in second language acquisition and biliguality. In W. H. Coons, D. M. Taylor, & M. A. Tremblay (Eds.). *The individual, language and society in Canada.* Ottawa: Canada Council.

Gardner, R. C., & Lambert, W. E. (1972). *Attitudes and motivation in second language learning.* Rowley: Newbury House.

Genesee, F. (1983). Bilingual education of majority language children: The immersion experiments in review. *Applied Linguistics, 4*, 1-46.

Genesee, F. (1984). Beyond bilingualism: Social psychological studies of French immersion programs in Canada. *Canadian Journal of Behavioural Science, 16*, 338-352.

Glazer, N., & Moynihan, D. P. (1963). *Beyond the melting pot.* Cambridge: Harvard University Press.

Glazer, N., & Moynihan, D. P. (Eds.). (1975). *Ethnicity: Theory and experience.* Cambridge: Harvard University Press.

Goldstein, J. E., & Bienvenue, R. M. (1980). *Ethnicity and ethnic relations in Canada.* Toronto: Butterworths.

Gordon, M. (1964). *Assimilation in American life.* New York: Oxford University Press.

Graves, T. (1967). Psychological acculturation in a tri-ethnic community. *Southwestern Journal of Anthropology, 23*, 337-350.

Hamilton, D. (Ed.). (1980). *Cognitive process in stereotyping and intergroup behavior.* Hillsdale: Lawrence Erlbaum.

Honigmann, J. J. (1976). Personal adaptation as a topic for cultural and social anthropological research. Paper presented at the symposium on *The Concept of Adaptation in Studies of American Native Culture Change,* American Anthropological Association, Washington, DC.

Hurh, W. M. (1977). *Comparative study of Korean immigrants in the United States: A typological approach.* San Francisco: R & E Research Associates.

Hurh, W. M., & Kim, K. C. (1984). Adhesive sociocultural adaptation of Korean immigrants in the U.S.: An alternative strategy of minority adaptation. *International Migration Review, 18,* 188-216.

Isajiw, W. W. (1980). Definition of ethnicity. In J. W. Goldstein & R. M. Bienvenue (Eds.), *Ethnicity and ethnic relations in Canada.* Toronto: Butterworths.

Kalin, R., & Berry, J. W. (1979). *Determinants and attitudinal correlates of ethnic identity in Canada.* Paper presented to Canadian Psychological Association, Quebec.

Kim, U. (1986, May). Living in two cultures: Psychological acculturation of Korean university students living in Toronto. *Contact: Korean-Canadian University of Toronto Newsletter,* pp. 3-14.

Kim, U., & Berry, J. W. (1986). *The dynamic relationship between language and culture: An acculturation study of Korean immigrants in Toronto, Canada.* Paper presented at the 21st International Congress of Applied Psychology, Jerusalem.

Kim, Y. Y. (1978). A communication approach to the acculturation process: A study of Korean immigrants in Chicago. *International Journal of Intercultural Relations, 2,* 197-223.

Klineberg, O. (1980). Stressful experience of foreign students at various stages of sojourn: Counselling and policy implications. In G. V. Coelho & P. I. Ahmed (Eds.), *Uprooting and development.* New York: Plenum.

Kurokawa, M. (Ed.). (1970). *Minority responses: Comparative views of reactions to subordination.* New York: Random House.

Lambert, W. E. (1978). Some cognitive and sociocultural consequences of being bilingual. In J. E. Alatis (Ed.) *International dimensions of bilingual education.* Washington: Georgetown University Press.

Lambert, W. E., Gardner, R. C., Barik, H. C., & Turnstall, K. (1963). Attitudinal and cognitive aspects of intensive study of a second language. *Journal of Abnormal and Social Psychology, 66,* 358-368.

Lambert, W. E., & Taylor, D. M. (1984). Language in the education of ethnic minority children in Canada. In R. J. Samuda, J. W. Berry, & M. Lafferriere (Eds.), *Multiculturalism in Canada: Social and educational perspectives.* Toronto: Allyn & Bacon.

Lazarus, R. S., & Folkman, S. (1984). *Stress, appraisal and coping.* New York: Springer-Verlag.

Lewin, K. (1936). *Principles of topological psychology.* New Haven: McGraw-Hill.

Lyman, S. M. (1972). *The Black American in sociological thought.* New York: G. P. Putnam.

Mann, J. (1958). Group relations and the marginal man. *Human Relations, II,* 77-92.

Mendoza, R. H., & Martinez, J. L. (1981). The measurement of acculturation. In A. Baron, J. (Ed.), *Explorations in Chicano psychology.* New York: Praeger.

Munroe, R. (1955). *Schools of psychoanalytic thought.* New York: Holt, Rinehart & Winston.

Murphy, H.B.M. (1975). Low rate of mental hospitalization shown by immigrants to Canada. In C. Zwingmann & G. Pfister-Ammendes (Eds.), *Uprooting and after.* New York: Springer-Verlag.

Newman, W. M. (1973). *American pluralism: A study of minority groups and social theory.* New York: Harper & Row.

O'Bryan, K. G., Reitz, J. G., & Kuplowska, O. M. (1976). *Non-official languages: A study in Canadian multiculturalism.* Ottawa: Government of Canada.

Park, R. E. (1950). *Race and culture*. Glencoe, IL: Free Press.

Redfield, R., Linton, R., & Herskovits, M. J. (1936). Memorandum on the study of acculturation. *American Anthropologist, 38*, 149-152.

Richmond, A. H. (1974). *Aspects of absorption and adaptation of immigrants*. Ottawa: Department of Manpower and Immigration.

Rosenthal, E. (1970). Acculturation without assimilation. *American Journal of Sociology, 66*, 275-288.

Scott, W. A., & Stumpf, J. (1984). Personal satisfaction and role performance: Subjective and social aspects of adaptation. *Journal of Personality and Social Psychology, 47*, 812.

Selye, H. (1979). *The stress of life* (rev. ed.). New York: Van Nostrand Reinhold.

Spielberger, C. D., Gorsuch, R. L., & Lushene, R. E. (1970). *The STAI Manual for the State-Trait Anxiety Inventory (Self-Evaluation Questionnaire)*. California: Consulting Psychologists.

Stonequist, E. V. (1937). *The marginal man*. NY: Scribners.

Taft, R. (1965). *From stranger to citizen*. London: Tavistock.

Taft, R. (1986a). The adaptation of recent Soviet immigrants in Australia. In I. Reyes-Lagunes & Y. H. Poortinga (Eds.), *From a different perspective: Studies of behavior across cultures*. Lisse: Swets and Zeitlinger.

Taft, R. (1986b). The psychological study of the adjustment and adaptation of immigrants to Australia. In N. T. Feather (Ed.), *Survey of Australian psychology: Trend for research*. Sydney: Allen and Unwin.

Tajfel, H. (1981). Social stereotypes and social groups. In J. C. Turner & H. Giles (Eds.), *Intergroup behavior*. Oxford: Basil Blackwell.

Taylor, D. M. Meynard, R., & Rheault, E. (1977). Threat to ethnic identity and second-language learning. In H. Giles (Ed.), *Language, ethnicity and intergroup relations*. London: Academic Press.

4

Communication in Assimilation, Deviance, and Alienation States

MICHAEL McGUIRE ● STEVEN McDERMOTT ●
University of Georgia

Assimilation and alienation are conceptualized as states between which human beings may alternate through a crucial period of relative deviance. These states are conceptualized as temporary outcomes or functions of both host and immigrant communication behaviors. A theoretical, communication-based, process model is presented to account for the movement of immigrants from one state to another.

In 1970, Kim Giffin published a perceptive, farsighted discussion of the role of communication denial in producing and reinforcing the psychological state of alienation (Giffin, 1970). Giffin showed that, in *intra*cultural, interpersonal relationships the denial of communication leads to alienation, a state opposite to assimilation. *Inter*cultural communication researchers have been focusing attention lately, as the theme of this volume shows, on achieving the opposite end state of alienation, which is assimilation or acculturation.

Our purpose in this chapter is to offer a theoretical, communication-based process model to account for the motion of human beings toward one or the other of these end states. We will argue that specific communication behaviors and patterns are related to the processes of assimilation or to the opposing state of alienation. Our model will focus attention, not on the end states of assimilation or alienation alone, but on the crucial intermediate state of "deviance." Many of the behaviors Giffin identified as producing alienation characterize this stage.

The uniqueness of our theoretical perspective is presenting assimilation and alienation not as permanent outcomes but rather as temporary states. Everyone—no matter how well integrated into a culture—deviates from some norm(s), and experiences feelings of greater or lesser alienation and assimilation at different times. Research on acculturation or assimilation, however, continues to investigate outcomes and end states of acculturation. For instance, Wiseman and Abe (1984) and Gudykunst and Hammer (1984) argue about the cultural specificity of perceived intercultural effectiveness as though effects occur in intercultural communication and acculturation that are permanent. "Dealing with frustration," for example, is not a constant or permanent skill or outcome of intercultural or intracultural communication as we perceive them. Wong-Rieger (1984), in a study that, at first glance, seemed not to have made this error of assuming permanence but offered a theory-based model of acculturation, commits a similar mistake. Wong-Rieger, however, asserts that one learns norms, acquires behavior skills, and modifies the self-concept, but makes no provision for the possibility (which we see as an inevitability) that learning and skills are not permanently acquired, nor are they permanently, equally useful, and that the self-concept is a variable. In short, data reported offering descriptions of acculturation as an outcome and not as a variable cannot be consistent either with each other or with elegant theory. The pattern in acculturation research is beginning to resemble the earliest research on deviance, to which we turn for help.

Early discussions of deviance focused largely on its psychological effects and sociological causes (Merton, 1957). Moreover, deviance has been seen as a negative trait of individuals or a problem in normless societies and not frequently (even by Merton, who acknowledged it) as a necessary, temporary state of an individual's relations with others. More recently, there has been a paradigm shift from a focus on the deviant toward the action of and reaction to the deviant (Archer, 1985). Our approach is in line with this conception, but differs in that we emphasize the exact nature of interpersonal communication in the process, whereas others are more macro in approach (see Archer, 1985). We are also in conceptual agreement with Y. Kim (1979, p. 441), who presented a fundamental axiom stating that the communication/acculturation process is a function of the relationships between the individual immigrant and the social-cultural environment.

We intend to show that as the quantity and quality of deviance increases, specific, transactional communication patterns between deviates and the dominant culture or group result, which may lead toward assimilation or alienation. The model we offer should have explanatory utility for *intra*cultural and *inter*cultural communicators, but our concern here is its application to the acculturation of "immigrants" by a "host culture." Toward that end we have divided over discussion into three main sections— treating assimilation, deviance, and alienation—and conclude with suggestions for further research.

ASSIMILATION STATE

We are interested in a model of a process that may link intercultural communication with intracultural communication and social psychology. We believe that the processes of alienation and assimilation are extremely similar for immigrants and natives of a culture—that, as Sarbaugh (1979, p. 15) suggested, "As one begins to identify the variables that operate in the communication being studied, . . . it becomes apparent that they are the same for both intercultural and intracultural settings." Research in psychology may help shed light on the interactive processes by which people become alienated in their own or a foreign culture. Moreover, we will argue that the transactional process of assimilation is best conceived of as an effect of communication (J. Kim, 1980; Y. Kim, 1977). In doing so we are following the leads of the theories of interpersonal and intercultural communication researchers that have emerged recently and seem, to us, especially fruitful (Gudykunst & Kim, 1984; Miller & Steinberg, 1975).

Our intention, then, is to conceptualize *alienation, assimilation*, and *deviance*, not as traits (or worse, personality types) of an individual, but as different, temporary outcomes of human communication transactions. That is, in an ongoing process of interaction—anyone may one day feel assimilated, the next day alienated. Our goal is to describe the communication behaviors that produce these outcomes. In this section, we will focus on the behaviors associated with the two assimilation processes. That task is made more difficult because our model sees these temporary outcomes of communication as leading toward behaviors that cause other communication behaviors, and that may accelerate or reverse an individual's behaviors, producing particular communications and outcomes. That is, the relationship between the individual and the communication he or she receives is a dialectical one: We both produce and are produced by the communication behaviors others exhibit toward us (Berger & Luckmann, 1967).

It would seem that the behaviors associated with assimilation would be the easiest to isolate and describe intuitively. We all know how it feels to be included, to be "part of things." But it turns out that, perhaps because we "know" these things so well and take them for granted, these behaviors are the least researched and thought about of the group with which we are concerned here.

We believe that *individuals (or groups) have achieved the assimilation state when their perceptions are of receiving positive reinforcement from others' communications.* Very differently, we believe that *the group accomplishes an assimilation state when an individual conforms to expected norms.* To explore both, we need to distinguish further between the "factist" and "definitionist," or objective and subjective-perceptual issues (Ritzer, 1975). Individual assimilation is almost purely perceptual, although there doubtless exists factual artifacts by which we could measure the "accuracy" of the individual's perceptions. The group's assimilation achievements, we believe, are best measured by factual variables, that is, specific communication behaviors elicited by the immigrant (or deviate) from the host culture, and an absence of deviant behavior. That claim will be supported only by our entire analysis, however, and cannot be established here.

Our process model of assimilation shows what we believe is the relationship among assimilation, deviance, and alienation (ADA, see Figure 4.1).

Assimilation and alienation are end states, outcomes of a process of communication. As deviance by immigrants increases, the quantities and kinds of communication they receive are affected. What we call "neglectful communication" is the response of the host culture to deviance. The forms of this response include qualitative and quantitative features: First, neglectful communi-

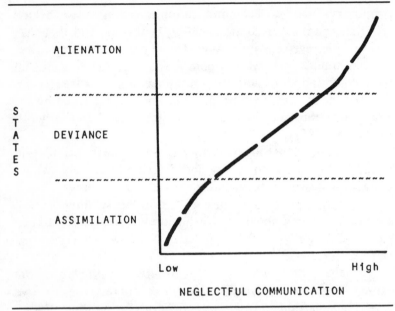

Figure 4.1 Assimilation, Deviance, and Alienation (ADA) Model

cation is negative messages (of any quantity) that seek to dissuade a deviate by showing negative consequences to deviance; second, neglectful communication is an absence of messages. The absence of messages has been shown to be a last stage of this process, which we assume does not occur until the host culture abandons efforts or hopes of assimilating the deviant immigrant (Giffin, 1970; Berger & Luckmann, 1967).

Assimilation behaviors by the host culture, then, are those that characterize low neglectful communication; assimilation behaviors by the immigrant characterize low deviance. Some host-culture assimilative (low neglect) communication behaviors are:

1. Verbal praise for immigrants' behaviors.
2. Availability for immigrants' interactions.
3. Absence (or very low level) of ethnocentric derogation.
4. Verbal encouragement to adopt and follow host norms.
5. Dine together in public.
6. Ask about immigrants' well-being and happiness.
7. Offer to share or provide transportation.
8. Creation and use of affectionate nickname for immigrant.

Some immigrant assimilative communication behaviors are:

1. Verbal praise of host culture's lifestyle (including material goods, services, government, media).
2. Seeks interactions with host culture members.
3. Humorous or serious criticism of native ethnicity norms.
4. Adoption of host norms, for example, dress and grooming.
5. Disclosure of happiness to live in host culture.
6. Consume the media that host-culture members recommend.
7. Increase fluency in host culture's language and gesture.

These behaviors, we suggest, are the same as those we would find in attempts to reassimilate to a culture natives who have become (slightly) deviant, or in attempts by deviates to reassimilate to their culture (see under Deviance State, below). Such behaviors have been conceptualized as "therapeutic," because they seek to restore to "normalcy" those who have begun to deviate (Berger & Luckmann, 1967). In an intercultural interaction, we might appropriately label such behaviors "conversionist," because they are aimed at securing not a return, but an initial conversion to norms.

Foreign immigrants can be assimilated and deviates can be reassimilated. In the case of foreigners, which interests us most here, communication patterns with the host culture and the ethnic group have been shown to be of significance in the achievement of assimilation (see, for example, Y. Kim, 1977; J. Kim, 1980). What we are now interested in exploring are the specific communication behaviors of a host culture toward deviates and the behaviors of deviates in response. The behaviors in this critical stage of interaction can lead, we will argue, either toward assimilation or alienation. It remains now to specify the behaviors and directions in which they are likely to lead.

DEVIANCE STATE

The deviance state follows the assimilation state, where, it will be argued, low self-esteem and neglectful communication are evident. Here, a person experiences tension with the new culture where the socialized norms from the native culture come into conflict with the norms of the new culture. Whether one takes the factists' position with a focus on identifying the behavior of the deviant, or the social-definitionist position that examines the process by which people come to be defined as deviant (see, Ritzer, 1975), tension results when the culture ". . . disallow(s) participants control over their activities" (Twinning, 1980. p. 422).

A lack of control is a function of *observed behaviors* from members of the host culture and from the immigrant, or, to a greater or lesser extent, a *perceived* lack of control over the immigrant's new environment. The latter state defines one who has low self-esteem (Rosenberg, 1965) and does not define true alienation—although it may be classified as partial alienation (Twinning, 1980). This state, where self-esteem is low, is both a result and a determinant of an inability to learn, adapt or understand new norms.

Given these conceptions, two research lines are available for intercultural analyses. The first should be an attempt to recognize the observable behaviors that come from the host culture in communicating to immigrants in the deviance state. Here, research will benefit by examining the types of communication messages that are determinants and correlates of deviance and low self-esteem. Researchers can identify those communication messages that move immigrants from an assimilation state to the second state, those that maintain the deviance position, and those that move the immigrant from deviance to state three, full alienation.

The second research line made apparent by the new conception allows for the examination of the communication responses of immigrants as a result of being in the second state. Identification of responses to the host culture's communication messages, as outlined above, should be fruitful, but those particular messages that the immigrant may give in bringing about responses in the host culture can also be identified. Significant variables from both of these lines are outlined below.

Communication from the Host Culture

Communication patterns in the deviance state are defined as neglectful. These types of communication include patterns of partial denial (Giffin, 1970) and low levels of personal communication, as well as some level of overt negativity. It is assumed that some communication is evident (unlike the alienation state, where it is often totally absent or consistently negative) and is much like what Giffin described as a condition of partial alienation:

> When a person is partially alienated he is . . . convinced that he will be denied the opportunity for communication with another person (or persons) on certain topics, at certain times, or under certain conditions. (p. 348)

It is also assumed that negative communication conforms to the same pattern as denial: It is a result of inconsistencies.

Lack of communication from members of a culture is related to the inability to learn or understand norms (McClosky & Schaar, 1965). This, in turn, leads to a reduced ability to interact successfully (deviance) in the new culture because of the failure to learn the beliefs and values of the culture. Yum (1982) found that communicative integration of Korean immigrants in Hawaii appears to be related to norm acquisition as informational gain. And as both volume and intimacy of interpersonal communication from the new culture are related to acculturation among Korean (Y. Kim, 1979), Mexican (Y. Kim, 1979), and Indo-Chinese (Y. Kim, 1980) immigrants, reduced communication levels may be considered neglectful.

The parallel findings in self-concept theory and research support this neglectful communication conception. Although most self-concept theorists (for example, Coopersmith, 1967) are concerned with child development, some of the best documented findings may apply to acculturation in ways similar to primary socialization. For self-concept theorists, inconsistent messages (for children it's the unscheduled use of discipline) are related to lower self-concepts; and although completely ignoring children occurs rather infrequently, when it does happen, it lowers self-concept (Ashmore & Del Boca, 1976).

Giffin's (1970) seminal work on communication and alienation (within culture) focused on communication denial. Denial was identified as: (1) ignoring communication from another, (2) contradictions between verbal and nonverbal communication, (3) refusal to interact, (4) differing interpretations of communication events, and (5) lack of personal validation. In the present model, we conceptualize the refusal to interact and lack of personal validation as evidence for total alienation. On the other hand, communication that partially ignores, contradictions between verbal and nonverbal behavior, and differing interpretations of communication events represent the neglectful communication stage as discussed above. Contradictions between verbal and nonverbal communications or differing interpretations of interactions constitute inconsistencies that have negative effects.

Low levels of *personal* communication would also be part of the neglectful stage. Gudykunst and Y. Kim (1984) argue—on the basis of Miller and Steinberg's (1975) conception of interpersonal communication as that which requires psychological levels of prediction—that most intercultural interactions occur on a cultural or sociocultural level. At these levels, personal uncertainty is high. Berger and Calabrese (1975) theorize that in interaction among strangers, a process of uncertainty reduction leads to increased intimacy, information seeking, reciprocity, and affiliative expressiveness. Decreased intimacy, information seeking, reciprocity, and affiliative expressiveness should therefore be associated with neglectful communication and deviance. Although few intercultural studies have explored these relationships, Gudykunst and Nishida (1984) found uncertainty to be related to nonverbal affiliative expressiveness among Japanese and to information seeking and self-disclosure when uncertainty was high and where cultural dissimilarity was present among potential interactants.

In summary, it can be expected that neglectful communication from the host culture would include:

1. A relative lack of communication.
2. Low levels of intimacy.
3. Low levels of information seeking.
4. Nonreciprocity or negative feedback.
5. Low levels of affiliative expressiveness.
6. Inconsistent messages.

Communication from the Neglected Deviate

Giffin (1970) states that denial of communication can be responded to by (1) repetition of the initial communication, (2) asking about the denial, (3) escalating demands for recognition, and (4) accepting that he or she cannot communicate with the other person under the existing conditions. Extrapolating from his analysis of within-culture situations to intercultural communication, we can identify those communication attempts that will move the immigrant toward the assimilation state, maintain the deviance state, or accelerate the immigrant toward total alienation.

Repetition of the initial communication—for our analysis, repeated attempts to communicate—might bring about responses from the host culture that lead either to assimilation or to greater deviation. In the first case, observations of the host culture could lead to the conclusion that the host culture is responding positively. In fact, members of the host culture would be responding positively if the communication were positive *and* at the appropriate level (that is, psychological and personal when desired; sociocultural when necessary). This positive communication should begin to influence the deviate toward assimilation. On the other hand, observations may be misleading: Communication that appears positive may be superficial, noninterpersonal, or even merely phatic. When this is the case, communication should reinforce the deviate or move the immigrant toward alienation.

Initiation of communication about the denial is probably unlikely, as Giffin (1970) argues, especially if an immigrant is uncertain what the norms of the host culture are. However, conflict researchers argue that metacommunication would be an appropriate strategy for at least managing conflict (for example, Hocker & Wilmot, 1985). So, we believe that inquiry about denial would help move that deviate toward the assimilation state.

Escalated demands for recognition or even aggression (Giffin, 1970) may be one response to communication denial, but it is questionable whether this would be likely if the immigrant does not have the support of a cultural subgroup. Those who identify or are well integrated into a culturally similar subgroup may be more likely to engage in escalated demands. For instance, Bulhan

(1978) found that Somali students in the U.S. who measured as socially close to members of their own and similar cultures were likely to indicate hostility toward Euro-American ideology. Furthermore, failure at demands for recognition and aggressive responses should lead to withdrawal (Storr, 1968) and alienation from the host culture.

If the immigrants come to believe that they cannot communicate with members of the host culture, it is assumed that alienation will be the final outcome as a result of not wanting to acquire the host culture's norms. This highly unfortunate circumstance is related to speech anxiety, which Giffin and Groginsky (1970) distinguish from alienation, that is, total withdrawal from, rather than just avoidance of, interaction. It is our position that avoidance will lead to total withdrawal in intercultural communication because the host culture will label avoidance as deviance, which is responded to by denying accurate information about cultural norms.

Thus far we have tried to suggest some likely responses to deviant behavior by a host culture that might lead toward assimilation or alienation. We also have tried to explain how the immigrant or deviate perceives and reacts to communications from the host culture. We have discussed familiar aspects of assimilation above, and turn now to a discussion of alienation as an end state of a communication transaction.

ALIENATION STATE

The very term *alienation* carries the implicit affirmation that persons suffering it are not "of" the host culture, whether they once were or not. They feel themselves to be and are perceived as being aliens. The phenomenon of alienation, which may be found in individuals or in groups, has been studied under different definitions and from different perspectives. In literature, Dostoevsky's underground man represents the quintessential alienated being; philosophers such as Nietzsche and Sartre have presented the alienated being as a too sensitive one reaching a crisis regarding the norms and values of society; Marx expressed concern about the individual alienated from the material reality of culture; Merton (1957) raised the phenomenon for consideration as an artifact of complex society.

We will pass up the temptation to explore the existential approach to alienation in the literary expressions familiar to most readers. We reject the "psychological" approach to deviance for studying intercultural communication for important reasons. However useful such a psychoanalytical theory may be for intracultural deviants, it misses the central mark of a communication centered approach. Freud's work was seminal to the drive-centered psychological approach, characterized by Moore (1969, p. 300) as one that explains deviance as resulting from "autonomous drives by the individual which occasionally break through the restraints of civilization." We prefer the sociological approach that emphasizes the transaction between an individual (or group) and the host culture. (For one final reason, we assume a similarity of drives in human beings from all cultures, and so reject drive theory as useful to our inquiry regarding immigrants.)

The sociological paradigm views deviance and alienation as natural consequences of a complex society. It therefore argues that deviance from a particular norm may be attributable, not to an individual in conflict with that norm, but rather (in many cases) to an individual exhibiting behavior that conforms to a different social norm (Merton, 1957). Thus, alienation may result not only in individuals who are in conflict with specific norms of a culture, but also in individuals who perceive the presence of different norms from which to choose.

Prominent sociological theorists of alienation, most notably Dean (1961) and Seeman (1959), have conceptualized alienation as consisting of different components; both theorists included the two components we believe are important to a communication based intercultural model: normlessness and social isolation. Dean, following Durkheim and others, interprets normlessness as the feeling that goals are unattainable or nonexistent, and social isolation as a feeling of exclusion from the group or of lacking access to group norms. These feelings, however, need not involve hostility, aggression, or conflict. Alienation, then, may result from an individual feeling unable or unwilling to cope with ambiguous or contradictory norms. Contradictory norms may come from different cultures: host and native or ethnic.

Host culture communications may bring about or reinforce alienation for an immigrant. Moreover, some host culture behaviors are responses to the perception of alienation, signalled by extreme deviance. Some behaviors likely to maintain or strengthen alienation include:

1. Total refusal to interact interpersonally.
2. Use of abusive or obscene language or gestures.
3. Obviously reluctant, forced, phatic interaction.
4. Use of ethnic slurs.
5. Coercive, intimidating or violent acts.
6. Public ridicule.
7. Deception about host culture behavior norms.

The alienated immigrant is likely to respond with:

1. Withdrawal into isolation (refusal to interact).
2. Withdrawal into native culture or alienated subculture.
3. Hostility or violence toward host culture.
4. Public acknowledgement of "inferiority."
5. Inattention to host culture media.
6. Refusal to use host culture's language.

These behaviors, we argue, would describe not only the transactions between a host culture and an immigrant, but also the behaviors a culture would exhibit toward a former member who deviated too extremely to be reassimilated. Deviates can be isolated and alienated totally; immigrants can be isolated and alienated totally. So far we have specified behaviors and transactions of the assimilation state, the alienation state, and the very important deviance state. Most of the human condition, we argue, is the deviance state. Few people are totally assimilated or totally alienated; even in conformity there are variations, and sometimes in deviation one finds approbation or affection.

We conclude by offering and explaining our process model of assimilation, deviance and alienation.

THE ADA MODEL AND
SOME CONCLUSIONS

Our contention has been that the possibility for social alienation depends upon the delicate balance of neglectful communication with deviance. When neglectful communication and
deviance are counterbalanced, the system is at its deviance state
(see Figure 4.1). When neglectful communication is infrequent
and deviance is low, the system is moving toward the assimilation
state. When neglectful communication is frequent and deviance is
high, the system is moving toward the alienation state. Given that
we conceptualize a mutually causal, therefore reversible, link
between deviance and neglectful communication, a change in
deviance will lead to a change in neglectful communication.
Persons in the alienation state are highly deviant and for that
reason perceive (even if not accurately) highly neglectful communication. Persons in the assimilation state are low deviant (and,
by definition, must know it) and perceive communication as not
neglectful.

In sum, the ADA Model here advanced assumes that changes
in either amount or kind of deviance or amount or kind of
neglectful communication will push an individual toward or into
either the alienation state or the assimilation state. Increases in
deviance cause increases in neglectful communication, propelling
the individual toward alienation; reciprocally, increases in neglectful communication will lead to further deviance and the alienation
state (except for those forms of constructive, negative feedback
that seek to assimilate, so do not actually meet our definition of
neglectful communication). Alienation or assimilation, therefore,
of a group or individual is an outcome of the relationship between
deviant behavior and neglectful communication.

One difficulty with connecting our theoretical model to
previous empirical research on acculturation is that the body of
available studies neglects, almost completely, examining behaviors of the host culture, which we have argued are very important.
In one of few studies even mentioning host behaviors as a decisive
variable, Wong-Rieger (1984) argued that abusive treatment
from host-culture members produces anger and lowered self-

esteem. Other studies, as we mentioned in introducing this chapter, do not explore the content of communications in the process of acculturation, even if they use frequency or quantity of communications as a variable (for example, J. Kim, 1980). Pursuing effects instead of processes and causes, researchers ask about perceptions of communication outcomes, not about what communications actually occur (for example, Wiseman & Abe, 1986).

Our purpose in offering the ADA model and explaining its states as we have, is to emphasize the functional role of communication in acculturation. That role, as we see it, is to move the individual toward either the socially functional assimilation state or the socially dysfunctional and personally miserable alienation state. A few researchers have commented, and we echo their still-true observations, that research on acculturation has not adequately featured the central role of communication. We hope to have suggested some possible starting points for exploration of communication in acculturation.

REFERENCES

Archer, D. (1985). Social deviance. In G. Lindzey & E. Aronson (Eds.), *The handbook of social psychology: Vol. II* (pp. 743-804). New York: Random House.

Ashmore, R. D., & Del Bocca, F. (1976). Psychological approaches to understanding intergroup conflicts. In P. Katz (Ed.), *Toward the elimination of racism*. Elmsford, NY: Pergamon.

Berger, C., & Calabrese, R. (1975). Some explorations in initial interaction and beyond. *Human Communication Research, 1*, 99-112.

Berger, P., & Luckmann, T. (1967). *The social construction of reality*. New York: Doubleday and Anchor Books.

Bulhan, H. A. (1978). Reactive identification, alienation, and locus of control among Somali students. *Journal of Social Psychology, 104*, 69-80.

Coopersmith, S. (1967). *The antecedents of self-esteem*. San Francisco: W. H. Freeman.

Dean, O. G. (1961). Alienation: Its meaning and measurement. *American Sociological Review, 27*, 753-758.

Giffin, K. (1970). Social alienation by communication denial. *Quarterly Journal of Speech, 56*, 347-357.

Giffin, K., & Groginski, B. (1970). *A study of the relationship between communication denial and social alienation*. Unpublished manuscript, University of Kansas, Communication Research Center.

Gudykunst, W. B., & Hammer, M. R. (1984). Dimensions of intercultural effectiveness: Culture specific or culture general? *International Journal of Intercultural Relations, 8*, 1-10.

Gudykunst, W. B., & Kim, Y. Y. (1984). *Communicating with strangers: An approach to intercultural communication.* New York: Random House.

Gudykunst, W. B., & Nishida, T. (1984). Individual and cultural influences on uncertainty reduction. *Communication Monographs, 51*, 23-36.

Hocker, J. L., & Wilmot, W. W. (1985). *Interpersonal conflict.* Dubuque, IA: Wm. C. Brown.

Kim, J. (1980). Explaining acculturation in a communication framework. *Communication Monographs, 47*, 155-179.

Kim, Y. Y. (1977). Communication patterns of foreign immigrants in the process of acculturation. *Human Communication Research, 4, 66-77.*

Kim, Y. Y. (1979). Toward an interactive theory of communication-acculturation. In D. Nimmo (Ed.), *Communication Yearbook 3* (pp. 435-453). New Brunswick, NJ: Transaction Books.

Kim, Y. Y. (1980). *Indo-Chinese refugees in the state of Illinois: Vol. 4. Psychological, social, and cultural adjustment of Indo-Chinese refugees.* Vol. 4. Chicago: Travelers' Aid Society.

McClosky, H., & Schaar, J. H. (1965). Psychological dimensions of anomie. *American Sociological Review, 30*, 14-40.

Merton, R. K. (1957). *Social theory and social structure.* Glencoe, IL: Free Press.

Miller, G. R., & Steinberg, M. (1975). *Between people.* Chicago: Science Research Associates.

Moore, W. E. (1969). Social structure and behavior. In G. Lindzey & E. Aronson (Eds.), *The handbook of social psychology* (pp. 283-322). Reading MA: Addison-Wesley.

Ritzer, G. (1975). *Sociology: A multiple paradigm science.* Boston: Allyn and Bacon.

Rosenberg, M. (1965). *Society and the adolescent self-image.* Princeton, NJ: Princeton University Press.

Sarbaugh, L. (1979). *Intercultural communication.* Rochelle Park, NJ: Hayden.

Seeman, M. (1959). On the meaning of alienation. *American Sociological Review, 24*, 783-791.

Storr, A. (1968). *Human aggression.* New York: Atheneum.

Twinning, J. E. (1980). Alienation as a social process. *The Sociological Quarterly, 21*, 417-428.

Wiseman, R. L., & Abe, H. (1984). Finding and explaining differences: A reply to Gudykunst and Hammer. *International Journal of Intercultural Relations, 8*, 11-16.

Wiseman, R. L., & Abe, H. (1986). Cognitive complexity and intercultural effectiveness: Perceptions in American-Japanese dyads. In M. McLaughlin (Ed.), *Communication Yearbook 9.* (pp. 611-622). Newbury Park, CA: Sage.

Wong-Rieger, D. (1984). Testing a model of emotional and coping responses to problems in adaptation: Foreign students at a Canadian University. *International Journal of Intercultural Relations, 8*, 153-183.

Yum, J. O. (1982). Communication diversity and information acquisition among Korean immigrants in Hawaii. *Human Communication Research, 8*, 154-169.

5

Strangers and Hosts
An Uncertainty Reduction Based Theory of Intercultural Adaptation

WILLIAM B. GUDYKUNST • *Arizona State University*
MITCHELL R. HAMMER • *University of Wisconsin-Milwaukee*

The purpose of this chapter is to present an initial extension of uncertainty-reduction theory to intercultural adaptation. It is assumed that the reduction of uncertainty and anxiety are necessary and sufficient conditions for intercultural adaptation. Axioms are generated that relate these two processes to their "basic" causes. Theorems are deducted from the axioms and support for the derived statements is assessed. Finally, we discuss implications of the theory for research and training.

Uncertainty reduction theory is one of the major theories used to explain human communication. In the context of this theory, uncertainty refers to the ability to predict accurately how others will behave and the ability to explain the behavior of others (Berger & Calabrese, 1975). Uncertainty reduction, therefore, involves the creation of proactive predictions and retroactive explanations about the behavior of others. The major assumption of the theory is that individuals try to reduce uncertainty about others when they provide rewards, behave in a deviant fashion, or are likely be encountered in future interactions (Berger, 1979). Berger and Calabrese's (1975) initial formulation of the theory posited 7 axioms and 21 theorems specifying the interrelations among uncertainty, amount of communication, nonverbal affiliative expressiveness, information seeking, intimacy level of communication content, reciprocity, similarity, and liking.

Cross-cultural studies suggest that the theory can account for differences in initial interactions (Gudykunst & Nishida, 1984), as well as explain communication in developed relationships across cultures (Gudykunst, Yang, & Nishida, 1985). Recent research

AUTHORS' NOTE: *The manuscript benefited from the comments and suggestions of Charles Berger, Young Yun Kim, and Ronald Perry.*

(Gudykunst & Hammer, in press) also reveals that the theory can reveal ethnic differences in initial interactions, account for differences in intra- and interethnic communication (Gudykunst, 1986), and explain communication between people from different cultures (Gudykunst, 1985a, b; Gudykunst, Chua, & Gray, 1987). Since previous research has demonstrated its application to intercultural phenomena, it should be possible to generalize uncertainty reduction theory to situations where individuals are entering new cultural environments. The purpose of this chapter, therefore, is to extend uncertainty-reduction theory by offering a preliminary explanation of intercultural adaptation based on the theory.

FOUNDATIONS OF THE THEORY

Uncertainty and Anxiety

Ruben (1983, p. 137) argues that "adaptation is a consequence of an ongoing process in which a system strives to adjust and readjust itself to challenges, changes, and irritants in the environment. The (adaptation) cycle is triggered when discrepancies between the demands of an environment and the capabilities of a system emerge, creating disequilibrium, or *stress*." Intercultural adaptation, therefore, involves working out a fit between the person and the new cultural environment.

To understand communication among sojourners, immigrants, tourists, and other travelers and members of the host culture and the travelers' adaptation to living in the culture, it is necessary to recognize that these people are "strangers" in the host culture. Georg Simmel (1950) introduced the concept in his classic essay "Der Fremde" ("The Stranger," published in German in 1908) arguing that strangers are physically present and participating in a situation (that is, the host culture), but at the same time, are outside the situation because they are from a different place (that is, a different culture).

Schuetz (1944, p. 499) views a stranger as "an adult individual . . . who tries to be permanently accepted or at least partially tolerated by the group which he [or she] approaches." Because strangers lack "intersubjective understanding," or an understanding of the social world inhabited by the members of the host culture, their interactions in the host culture are experienced as a series of crises. Taking this position suggests that first assumption of the theory:

Assumption 1: Sojourners, immigrants, tourists, and other travelers are strangers when they enter a host culture for the first time.

Herman and Schield (1961, p. 165) point out that "the immediate psychological result of being in a new situation is lack of security. Ignorance of the potentialities inherent in the situation, of the means to reach a goal, and of the probable outcomes of an intended action, causes insecurity." Attempts to adapt to the ambiguity of new situations involve a cyclical pattern of behaviors to reduce tension and seek information (Ball-Rokeach, 1973). Information seeking is directed toward individuals increasing their ability to predict or explain the behavior of themselves and others in the environment, that is, reducing cognitive uncertainty. Tension reduction, on the other hand, is directed toward reducing the anxiety that individuals experience in "foreign" cultural environments. Stephan and Stephan (1985, p. 159) point out that "anxiety stems from the anticipation of negative consequences. People appear to fear four types of negative consequences: psychological or behavior consequences for the self, and negative evaluations by members of the outgroup and the ingroup." These observations suggest:

Assumption 2: The initial experiences of strangers in the host culture are manifested as a series of crises; that is, strangers are not cognitively sure of how to behave (they have uncertainty) and they experience the feeling of a lack of security (anxiety).

Before proceeding, the relationship between uncertainty and anxiety needs to be addressed. For purpose of the initial extension of uncertainty reduction theory to intercultural adaptation, it is assumed that uncertainty and anxiety are independent aspects of the adaptation process. While social cognitive processes (uncertainty reduction) and affective processes (reducing anxiety) are related, the influence of social cognitive processes on intercultural communication is mediated through behavioral intentions and the influence of affective processes is not (Gudykunst, 1987). It is possible for strangers to reduce uncertainty and still have high levels of anxiety and vice versa (see concluding section for a more complete discussion of this issue). A third assumption, therefore, is needed:

> *Assumption 3*: Uncertainty and anxiety are independent dimensions of intercultural adaptation.

In developing a theory of intercultural adaptation, it is possible to assume that there are many "causes" of adaptation or, alternatively, that there are only a few. Lieberson (1985, p. 186) argues that "the dependent variable in a typical setting is actually responding to a small number of causes," He refers to the variables that are actually generating the outcome in the dependent variable as the "basic" causes. The variables that "appear to be responsible," in contrast, are the "superficial" or "surface" causes. It will be assumed that there are two "basic" causes of intercultural adaptation for purposes of the initial statement of the theory: the reduction of uncertainty and the reduction of anxiety. Uncertainty reduction and controlling/reducing anxiety are each viewed as a necessary, but not sufficient, cause for intercultural adaptation. The combination of the two (reducing anxiety and uncertainty), however, is assumed to provide both necessary and sufficient conditions for intercultural adaptation.

> *Assumption 4*: Uncertainty reduction and controlling/reducing anxiety, in combination, are necessary and sufficient conditions for intercultural adaptation.

Culture and Communication

Strangers are socialized members of one culture (native culture), but are confronting a new, "foreign" culture (host culture). To explain their adaptation, it is necessary to understand what culture is. Keesing (1974, p. 89) borrows the distinction between "competence" and "performance" from linguistics to explain culture:

> It is his [or her] *theory of what his [or her] fellows know, believe,
> and mean*, his [or her] theory of the code being followed, the game
> being played . . . It is this theory to which a native actor *refers* in
> interpreting the unfamiliar or the ambiguous, in interacting with
> strangers (or supernaturals) . . . But note that the actor's "theory"
> of his [or her] culture, like his [or her] theory of his [or her]
> language, may be in large measure unconscious. Actors follow
> rules of which they are not consciously aware.

This conceptualization suggests that culture forms an "implicit"
theory that individuals use to guide their behavior and interpret
the behavior of others. Much behavior in which individuals
engage in their own culture is habitual; that is, following habits.
Habits "are situation-behavior sequences that are or have become
automatic, so that they occur without self-instruction. The
individual is not usually 'conscious' of these sequences" (Triandis,
1980, p. 204). Individuals become conscious of their habitual
behavior, however, when they enter new situations (including
entering a new culture). Because of the heightened awareness,
Gudykunst and Kim (1984) contend that individuals are more
conscious of their behavior when they are communicating with
people from other cultures than when they are communicating
with someone from their own culture. This suggests a fifth
assumption of the perspective being presented:

> *Assumption 5*: The behavior of strangers in the host culture takes
> place at relatively high levels of awareness.

Communication among host nationals and strangers is based,
at least in part, upon group membership. Sherif (1966, p. 12)
argues that "whenever individuals belonging to one group
interact, collectively or individually, with another group or its
members *in terms of their group identification*, we have an
instance of intergroup behavior." Tajfel and Turner (1979) extend
Sherif's position by describing behavior as varying along a
continuum from purely interpersonal (all behavior is based on the
individual) to intergroup (all behavior is based on the categories
to which individuals belong). Gudykunst and Lim (1986), however, argue that a single dimension oversimplifies the situation

and both interpersonal and intergroup factors are salient in the same encounter; therefore, two dimensions are needed: low-to-high intergroup salience and low-to-high interpersonal salience. This implies:

Assumption 6: Both intergroup and interpersonal factors influence the interactions of strangers with host nationals.

When intergroup factors are salient, research suggests that strangers do not give the "proper" weight to situational factors in predicting or explaining the behavior of host culture members; in other words, they tend to underestimate its influence. Jaspars and Hewstone (1982) argue that the tendency is to attribute the positive behavior of in-group members (other strangers) to dispositional factors and the positive behavior of out-group (members of host culture) members to situational factors. Negative behavior by in-group members, in contrast, is attributed to situational factors, while negative behavior of out-group members is attributed to dispositional factors. The attributions of strangers during the process of intercultural adaptation are influenced highly by cultural differences and, therefore, the dispositional factor used to explain the behavior of host nationals is often culture. A seventh assumption, therefore, emerges:

Assumption 7: Strangers overestimate the influence of culture in explaining host nationals' behaviors, especially with respect to negative behaviors.

Definitions

The preceding overview introduced the three primary constructs that form the core of the theory: the adaptation of strangers to new cultural environments, uncertainty reduction, and anxiety. For purposes of the present analysis, the following definitions are stipulated:

Definition 1: Intercultural adaptation refers to the fit between individuals and their environment. Individuals who have adapted to "foreign" environments have worked out a "good" fit between themselves and their environment.

Definition 2: Uncertainty reduction refers to the ability of individuals to predict and explain their own behavior and that of others during interactions.

Definition 3: Anxiety refers to the fear of negative consequences in a "foreign" cultural environment.

AXIOMS

The assumptions suggest that uncertainty reduction and controlling/reducing anxiety mediate the influence of other variables linked traditionally to intercultural adaptation. As indicated above, these two processes are viewed as the "basic" causes of intercultural adaptation. The variables linked to adaptation in previous research (for example, contact, status), in contrast, are viewed as "superficial" or "surface" causes. These "superficial" causes of adaptation, however, are treated as "basic" causes of reducing uncertainty or anxiety in the theory. The effects of reducing uncertainty and anxiety on intercultural adaptation are stated as assumptions because they have not been tested in previous research; that is, the assumptions are untested, not untestable.

To formulate the theory, axioms were generated that state the relationships between reducing uncertainty or anxiety and their "basic" causes (which are referred to as "primary variables"). Blalock (1969, p. 18) states that axioms are "those propositions that involve variables that are taken to be directly linked causally; axioms, therefore, should be statements that imply direct causal links among variables" (italics omitted). A review of the literature revealed 16 primary variables. To preview, eight of the variables were found to be related to both reducing uncertainty and anxiety: knowledge of host culture, shared networks, intergroup attitudes, favorable contact, stereotypes, cultural identity, cultural similarity, and second language competence; four were related only to reducing uncertainty, that is, intimacy, attraction, display of nonverbal affiliative expressiveness, and the use of appropriate uncertainty reduction strategies; and four were associated only with reducing anxiety, that is, the motivation of strangers to live permanently in the host culture, attitudes of host nationals, intergroup host culture policy toward strangers, and psychological differentiation of strangers. Once the axioms were formulated, theorems were deduced from the axioms to complete the theory (Blalock, 1969). The relationships isolated from the literature are presented schematically in Figure 5.1.

Knowledge of Host Culture

Miller and Steinberg (1975) argue that individuals use three types of data when making predictions about the behavior of others: cultural, sociological, and psychological. People in any culture behave generally in a regular fashion because of their norms, rules, and values, and this regularity allows for making predictions on the basis of "cultural" data. Miller and Sunnafrank (1982, pp. 226-227) elaborate:

> Knowledge about another person's culture—its language, dominant values, beliefs, and prevailing ideology—often permits predictions of the person's probable response to certain messages. . . . Upon first encountering a . . . [member of the host culture], cultural information provides the only grounds for communicative predictions. This fact explains the uneasiness and perceived lack of control most people experience when thrust into an alien culture: they not only lack information about the individuals with whom they must communicate, they are bereft of information concerning shared cultural norms and values.

"Sociological" predictions are based on memberships in or aspirations to particular social groups. Miller and Sunnafrank (1982) argue that sociological data are the principal kind used to predict the behavior of people from the same culture. At the "psychological" level predictions are based on the specific people with whom strangers are communicating. At this level strangers are concerned with how individuals are different from or similar to other members of the host culture and of the groups to which they belong.

The preceding analysis suggests that intercultural attributional confidence (the inverse of uncertainty) is affected by cultural knowledge. Cultural knowledge involves an understanding of the norms and communication rules of the other culture so that the behavior of people from that culture can be interpreted accurately.

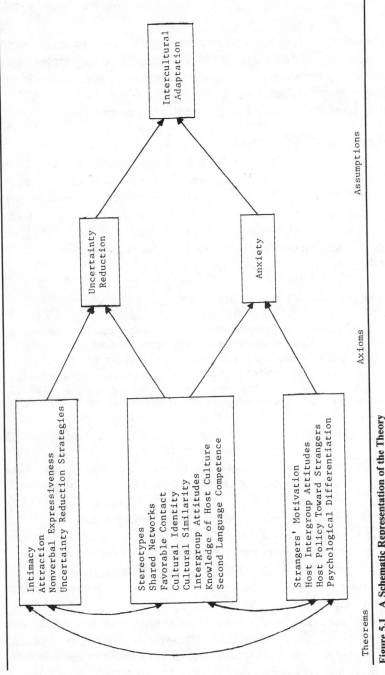

Figure 5.1 A Schematic Representation of the Theory

Intercultural Adaptation

Uncertainty Reduction

Anxiety

Intimacy
Attraction
Nonverbal Expressiveness
Uncertainty Reduction Strategies

Stereotypes
Shared Networks
Favorable Contact
Cultural Identity
Cultural Similarity
Intergroup Attitudes
Knowledge of Host Culture
Second Language Competence

Strangers' Motivation
Host Intergroup Attitudes
Host Policy Toward Strangers
Psychological Differentiation

Assumptions

Axioms

Theorems

For individuals from one culture to predict accurately the behavior of people from another culture, they must have knowledge about the other culture (Gudykunst & Kim, 1984). Stephan and Stephan (1984) also suggest that lack of knowledge of the other group is one of the major causes of intergroup anxiety. This suggests:

> *Axiom 1*: An increase in strangers' knowledge of the host culture will produce an increase in the accuracy of strangers' predictions and explanations of the behavior of host nationals.
>
> *Axiom 2*: An increase in strangers' knowledge of the host culture will produce a decrease in the anxiety strangers experience upon entering the host culture.

Knowledge of the host culture per se does not appear to have been examined in previous research on sojourner adjustment. Indirect evidence for the positive influence of knowledge of the host culture, however, can be inferred from research on the positive effects of cultural assimilator training on sojourner adjustment (Fieldler, Mitchell, & Triandis, 1971), as well as from Padilla's (1980) research on cultural awareness. Studies of cultural learning (Bochner, 1972; Guthrie, 1975) indicate that cultural learning often is trial-and-error and that inaccurate knowledge can have negative consequences for adjustment (Bochner, 1972; Hull, 1978). Knowledge of the host culture is, in part, a function of prior experience in the host culture that does not reinforce negative stereotypes (DuBois, 1956).

Intergroup Attitudes

The reduction of uncertainty and anxiety are influenced by intergroup attitudes such as prejudice (Pettigrew, 1978) and social representations (Hewstone, Jaspars, & Laljee, 1982). There is conflicting evidence, however, with respect to ethnocentrism. O'Driscoll and Feather's (1983) study indicated that ethnocentrism influences the social distance among members of different ethnic groups. Taylor and Jaggi (1974) also found that ethnocentrism influences attributions Hindus make about Muslims, but research by Hewstone and Ward (1985) suggests that this may not be a universal tendency. Their research revealed that the influence of ethnocentrism may be mediated by the stereotypes of the out-group or social identity vis-à-vis the in-group.

Intergroup attitudes influence not only attributions, they influence anxiety. Stephan and Stephan (1985), for example, posited a negative relationship between ethnocentrism and level of anxiety. Their research revealed a weak negative relationship for interaction among ethnic groups in the United States. In the interaction of strangers with members of the host culture, this relationship should be stronger because of the increase in the cultural dissimilarity. In addition to the attitudes of strangers toward the host culture, the attitudes of host nationals toward strangers influence the degree of anxiety strangers experience (Dyal & Dyal, 1981; Gudykunst, 1983b). Three axioms emerge from the preceding:

Axiom 3: An increase in negative intergroup attitudes (that is, prejudice and ethnocentrism) will produce a decrease in the accuracy of strangers' predictions and explanations regarding the behavior of host nationals.

Axiom 4: An increase in negative intergroup attitudes by strangers toward host nationals will produce an increase in the anxiety strangers experience upon entering the host culture.

Axiom 5: An increase in the negative intergroup attitudes by host nationals toward strangers will produce an increase in the anxiety strangers experience upon entering the host culture.

Studies of Peace Corp volunteers (Mischel, 1965) and international students (Basu & Ames, 1970) appear to support the relationships posited in Axioms 3 and 4. This research revealed a weak negative relationship between authoritarianism and adjustment. Negative intergroup attitudes are, at least in part, a function of the attitudes of parents, friends, and peers (Stephan & Stephan, 1984) and the norms guiding behavior in the situation (see research summarized in Stephan, 1985), as well as individual factors such as level of education (Wagner & Schonbach, 1984).

Stereotypes

Information used in making predictions about members of the host culture is generated by inferences based on observations. Once strangers obtain information about host nationals, an impression of individuals or "typical" members of the culture is made through inferences about expected relationships. Research suggests that the need to make inferences is greater when dealing with people who are unfamiliar than when dealing with those who are familiar (Koltuv, 1962). When strangers deal with members of the host culture there is limited information available and many gaps must be filled and, therefore, extreme inferences often are necessary.

Observing host nationals, either personally or through mass media, is one way of gaining information. The mass media provide most of the information for those who have not had contact with the host culture (Hartmann & Husband, 1972). Individuals who have had little contact also tend to perceive the media's content to be "real" (Murray & Kippax, 1979). The media, therefore, provide strangers who have had little experience in the host culture with stereotypes that are perceived to be accurate. Rothbart, Dawes, and Park (1984, p. 130) point out that stereotypes emerge more from secondary sources (that is, the media) than they do from primary sources (that is, contact):

> Our mental representations of groups include both stereotypic and individual components. . . . We view the stereotypic component as embodying generic, culturally shared features, generated in large part by "secondary" sources such as media, schools, and parents, whereas the individual component incorporates concrete episodic experiences generated by "primary" interaction with specific individuals or specific groups of individuals.

Stereotypes influence several aspects of strangers' communication with host nationals. Drawing on Hewstone and Giles's (1986) analysis of stereotypes, at least four generalizations appear to be warranted: (1) stereotyping is the result of cognitive biases stemming from illusory correlations between group membership and psychological attributes; (2) stereotypes influence the way information is processed, in other words, more favorable information is remembered about in-groups and more unfavorable information is remembered about out-groups; (3) stereotypes create expectancies (hypotheses) about others and individuals try to confirm these expectancies; and (4) stereotypes constrain others' patterns of communication and engender stereotype-

confirming communication—they create self-fulfilling prophe-
cies. Inaccurate stereotypes, however, lead to inaccurate predictions regarding host national behaviors. Stephan and Stephan's
(1985) research also indicated that negative stereotypes are
related to anxiety experienced during intergroup contact. Extending these conclusions to the adaptation of strangers to new
cultural environments leads to two additional axioms:

> *Axiom 6:* An increase in the accuracy of strangers' stereotypes of
> host nationals will produce an increase in the accuracy of their
> predictions and explanations of the behavior of host nationals.
>
> *Axiom 7:* An increase in the negative stereotypes of host nationals
> will produce an increase in the anxiety strangers experience upon
> entering the host culture.

Since most research has focused on intergroup attitudes, there
is limited research on the impact of stereotypes, per se, on the
adjustment of strangers in the host culture. It does appear,
however, that inaccurate stereotypes inhibit adjustment to the
host culture (DuBois, 1956). Yum and Wang's (1983) research
further suggests that accuracy of stereotypes is mainly a function
of interpersonal contact with members of the stereotypes, but
they also are influenced by educational level and occupational
status. Detweiler's (1975) work further reveals that strangers who
use narrow categories to interpret the behavior of members of the
host culture tend to form inaccurate expectancies (that is,
stereotypes).

Uncertainty Reduction Strategies

Berger (1979) isolated three major strategies individuals use to
reduce uncertainty about others: passive, active, and interactive.
Strangers can use all three strategies prior to departing their
native culture and after arrival in the host culture to gain
information about host nationals. The passive strategies strangers
use to reduce uncertainty about the behavior of host nationals
include, but are not limited to, reading books, watching television
or movies, and observing host nationals interacting with each
other. A large portion of the passive strategies involve the use of
secondary sources about host nationals and, therefore, play a role

in the creation of stereotypes that are perceived to be accurate, assuming little or no contact has occurred with host nationals. Active strategies (that is, asking other strangers about host nationals), in contrast, can play a role in changing attitudes and/or increasing the accuracy of stereotypes. Hamilton and Bishop (1976), for example, found that Whites in an integrated housing area changed their racial attitudes as a function of indirect methods of collecting information about Blacks; that is, discussion with other Whites.

When contact takes place with strangers, information can be obtained using interactive strategies such as interrogation, self-disclosure, and deception detection (Berger, 1979). Accurate information, however, can be obtained only if the contact occurs under favorable conditions (that is, conditions that do not increase prejudice and/or ethnocentrism). According to Amir (1969, p. 338), these conditions include:

> (a) when there is equal status contact between members of the various ethnic groups, (b) when the contact is between members of a majority group and *higher* status members of a minority group, (c) when an "authority" and/or the social climate are in favor of and promote the intergroup contact, (d) when the contact is of an intimate rather than casual nature, (e) when the ethnic intergroup contact is pleasant or rewarding, (f) when the members of *both* groups in the particular contact situation interact in functionally important activities or develop common goals or superordinate goals that are higher ranking in importance than the individual goals of the groups.

Available research suggests that actual intergroup contact is not likely to meet these "favorable" conditions (Rose, 1981). Stephan and Stephan's (1985) research, however, suggests that when previous contact has occurred under favorable conditions, there is less anxiety experienced in new contact situations. This suggests:

> *Axiom 8:* An increase in the "favorable" contact strangers have with members of the host culture will produce an increase in the accuracy of their predictions and explanations of the behavior of host nationals.

Axiom 9: An increase in the "favorable" contact strangers have with host nationals will produce a decrease in the anxiety they experience upon entering the host culture.

Axioms 8 and 9 are related closely to a large portion of previous research on sojourner adjustment and immigrant acculturation. Many researchers conclude that "positive" interaction with host nationals is a necessary condition for sojourner adjustment (Selltiz, Christ, Havel, & Cook, 1963; Gudykunst, Wiseman, & Hammer, 1977; Klineberg & Hull, 1979). Similarly, studies of immigrant acculturation suggest that acculturation is a function of the immigrants' communication with members of the host culture (Kim, 1977a, 1977b). Lack of interaction with host nationals also is associated with high levels of anxiety (Gullahorn & Gullahorn, 1966). Whether or not favorable contact occurs is a function of the host culture's attitude toward strangers (Gudykunst, 1983b), the stranger group's (that is, the stranger enclave's) attitude toward host nationals (Herman & Schield, 1961), the attitudes of strangers' friends (Stephan & Stephan, 1984), the public or private nature of the contact (Stephan, 1985), and the strangers' motivation (Cook, 1969; Torbiörn, 1982), to name only a few of the major influences.

The use of uncertainty reduction strategies (Berger, 1979) has been linked to the reduction of uncertainty in intercultural and intercultural relationships (Gudykunst & Nishida, 1984; Gudykunst, Yang, & Nishida, 1985). The inappropriate application of these strategies in intercultural relationships, however, could increase uncertainty, rather than reduce it. The "appropriateness" of the strategies must be judged vis-à-vis the host culture in the case of the intercultural adaptation of strangers. The use of inappropriate strategies can create "surprising events" (violations of expectations) that can either increase or decrease uncertainty (Sodetani & Gudykunst, 1986). The use of uncertainty reduction strategies appropriate in the host culture, in contrast, should reduce uncertainty. Axiom 10, therefore, is based on the use of "appropriate" strategies:

Axiom 10: An increase in the use of appropriate uncertainty reduction strategies by strangers will produce an increase in the accuracy of their predictions and explanations of the behavior of host nationals.

The type of uncertainty reduction strategies strangers use appear to be affected by the degree to which they monitor their own behavior (Snyder, 1974; for an intercultural application see Gudykunst, 1985a). Wilder and Allen's (1978) research further indicates that individuals tend to seek information regarding dissimilarities for members of out-groups. Similarly, McPherson's (1983) study revealed that individuals with a low tolerance for ambiguity tend to seek out information that is supportive of their own beliefs, rather than information that is objective.

Cultural Similarity

Gudykunst's (1983a) research indicates that people ask more questions when others are culturally dissimilar and self-disclose more when others are culturally similar. Simard's (1981) research further suggests that people are more confident in predicting the behavior of culturally similar individuals than they are in predicting the behavior of culturally dissimilar individuals. Chance and Goldstein (1981) also found that individuals are more willing to draw inferences about subjective attributes of culturally similar others than they are for culturally dissimilar others.

With respect to anxiety, Stephan and Stephan's (1985) research revealed that the greater the perceived cultural dissimilarities, the more anxiety individuals experienced during intergroup contact. Research further suggests that small cultural differences in assimilationist societies produce stress in strangers, while large cultural differences in pluralist societies produce less stress in strangers (Murphy, 1973; Berry, 1975). Three axioms, therefore, emerge:

Axiom 11: An increase in the similarity between the host and native culture will produce an increase in the accuracy of strangers' predictions and explanations of the behavior of host nationals.

Axiom 12: An increase in the similarity between the host and native culture will produce a decrease in the anxiety strangers experience upon entering the host culture.

Axiom 13: An increase in pluralist tendencies in the host culture will produce a decrease in the anxiety strangers experience upon entering the host culture.

Culture similarity is assumed to be related to sojourner adjustment and immigrant acculturation (Morris, 1960; David, 1971), but the relationship is supported only to a limited extent by empirical research (Morris, 1960; Taft, 1966; Hull, 1978). Cultural similarity, however, appears to be inversely related to the difficulty strangers experience in new cultures; the more similar the host and native culture, the less difficulty experienced (Furnham & Bochner, 1982).

Cultural dissimilarity appears to have a different impact depending on the type of relationship. Most interpersonal relationships (that is, acquaintances, role relationships) are guided by cultural norms. Friendships, in contrast, are less influenced by normative expectations. Altman and Taylor (1973) contend that cultural stereotypes do not influence communication in friendships. If cultural stereotypes are broken down in friendships and not in earlier stages, the level of cultural similarity should have a differential impact on uncertainty-reduction processes in different relationships. This position is supported by extensive research (Gudykunst, 1985a, b; Gudykunst, Chua, & Gray, 1987).

Berger and Calabrese's (1975) theory further posits that attraction and the display of nonverbal affilitative expressiveness reduce uncertainty. Parks and Adelman's (1983) research also revealed that shared networks are related to uncertainty reduction. Gudykunst's (1985a) study indicated that attraction and shared networks are related to attributional confidence, even when the communicators are culturally dissimilar. Similarly, Gudykunst, Chua, and Gray (1987) found that all three variables are correlated with uncertainty reduction under conditions of cultural dissimilarity. Finally, research suggests that shared networks in the host culture reduces the anxiety strangers experience in the culture (Katz, 1974; Dyal & Dyal, 1981). This suggests five axioms:

Axiom 14: Under conditions of cultural similarity or dissimilarity, an increase in the intimacy of the relationship that strangers form with members of the host culture will produce an increase in the accuracy of their predictions and explanations of the behavior of host nationals.

Axiom 15: Under conditions of cultural similarity or dissimilarity, an increase in the attraction of strangers to members of the host culture will produce an increase in the accuracy of their predictions and explanations of the behavior of host nationals.

Axiom 16: Under conditions of cultural similarity or dissimilarity, an increase in the display of nonverbal affiliative expressiveness by strangers will produce an increase in the accuracy of their predictions and explanations of the behavior of host nationals.

Axiom 17: Under conditions of cultural similarity or dissimilarity, an increase in the networks that strangers share with members of the host culture will produce an increase in the accuracy of their predictions and explanations of the behavior of host nationals.

Axiom 18: Under conditions of cultural similarity or dissimilarity, an increase in shared networks will produce a decrease in the anxiety strangers experience upon entering the host culture.

There does not appear to be research that has examined the relationship between nonverbal behavior or attraction and intercultural adaptation. Research on adjustment, however, suggests that developing intimate relationships (that is, friendships) with host nationals facilitates the adjustment of strangers (Selltiz et al., 1963). Similarly, there are extensive studies that demonstrate that not sharing communication networks (living in stranger-enclaves of fellow nationals) is associated negatively with adjustment in the host culture (Herman & Schield, 1961; Gullahorn & Gullahorn, 1966).

The attraction strangers have for host nationals is a function, at least in part, to the proximity of the cultures; strangers are attracted more to members of cultures close to them than they are to those farther away (Brewer & Campbell, 1976). The intimacy of the relationships established appears to be related to the strangers' motivation (Cook, 1969), while the degree to which they share networks with host nationals is related to the strength of this ethnic enclave in the host culture (Herman & Schield,

1961). Finally, psychological differentiation may affect the relationship between cultural dissimilarity and anxiety. Witkin and Berry (1975), for example, found that field independents experience less stress upon entering a new culture than do field dependents, regardless of the degree of cultural dissimilarity. This finding suggests:

> *Axiom 19:* An increase in the psychological differentiation of strangers will produce a decrease in the anxiety experience upon entering the host culture.

Cultural Identity

Giles and Byrne (1982) argue that when identification with the in-group is weak, interethnic comparisons yield little awareness of alternatives to inferiority, in-group vitality is perceived as low, in-group boundaries are perceived to be open and soft, there is strong identification with other social categories that provide adequate group identities, and second language competence increases. These five factors are indicators of the strength of group identifications by individuals and their perceptions of the relations between their own and other groups. Giles and Byrne's (1982) analysis suggests that the likelihood of a stranger learning the host language increases when strangers do not identify with their native culture. Recent work by Gudykunst, Sodetani, and Sonoda (1987) extends Giles and Byrne's analysis to uncertainty reduction. Their study demonstrated that ethnolinguistic identity in general, and ethnolinguistic vitality and interethnic comparisons in particular, is related positively to interethnic attributional confidence. It also appears that ethnic identity influences the anxiety that strangers experience in new cultures; the stronger the identification with the native culture, the more anxiety (Padilla, 1980; Dyal & Dyal, 1981). By substituting cultural identity for ethnolinguistic identity, two additional axioms can be posited:

> *Axiom 20:* An increase in the strength of strangers' cultural identity will produce an increase in the accuracy of their predictions and explanations of the behavior of host nationals.

Axiom 21: An increase in the strength of strangers' cultural identity will produce an increase in the anxiety they experience upon entering the host culture.

Closely related to cultural identity is the motivation of strangers toward the host culture. That is, does the stranger desire to visit (a tourist), live in the host culture (a business person assigned to work in the culture for a few years), or reside permanently in the host culture (an immigrant). Recent work (Dyal & Dyal, 1981; Gudykunst, 1983b) suggests that these different motivations have differential influences on strangers' anxiety; the more permanent the relocation, the greater the anxiety. This, therefore, suggests:

Axiom 22: An increase in the permanency of the strangers' stay in the host culture will produce an increase in the anxiety they experience upon entering the host culture.

There is no direct research on strength of cultural identity and adjustment, but there is indirect evidence. Studies of sojourner adjustment (Morris, 1960) indicate that perceived loss of status in the host culture is related negatively to adjustment, especially for strangers from "lower status" cultures (Church, 1982). Padilla's (1980) study also demonstrated that ethnic loyalty is related negatively to acculturation. Other research (Bochner & Perks, 1971) reveals that strangers perceive that host nationals look at them in cultural terms. Barnett and McPhail's (1980) study further suggests that the more television programming viewed from another culture, the weaker the cultural identity.

Second Language Competence

Research indicates that second language competence increases an individual's ability to cope with uncertainty (Naiman, Frohlich, Stern, & Todesco, 1978). Gudykunst's (1985b) model of uncertainty reduction during intercultural encounters further posits a direct impact of second language competence on attributional confidence. Two axioms emerge from these studies:

Axiom 23: An increase in the second language competence of strangers will produce an increase in the accuracy of their predictions and explanations of the behavior of host nationals.

Axiom 24: An increase in the second language competence of strangers will produce a decrease in the anxiety experienced upon entering the host culture.

Axioms 23 and 24 are related to selected work on sojourner adjustment and immigrant acculturation. Some research (Morris, 1960; Gullahorn & Gullahorn, 1966), for example, displays a weak relationship between second language competence and sojourner adjustment. Similarly, analyses of immigrant acculturation (Kim, 1977a; Berry, 1980) indicate that second language competence is related indirectly to acculturation.

Second language competence is influenced by several factors. Previous research, for example, demonstrates that experience in the host culture facilitates second language competence (Burstall, 1975). The ability of strangers to use the host language also is a function of the degree to which they desire to integrate into the host culture and their motivation to study the language (Gardner, 1985).

THEOREMS

It is possible to combine the 24 axioms and derive statements of relationships among the primary variables (that is, those that influence reducing uncertainty and/or anxiety directly). A large number of statements can be derived by combining the primary variables from the axioms. At least 28 have been the subject of previous research. These are presented below and research supporting the derived relationships cited where applicable.

Theorem 1: Knowledge of the host culture is associated negatively with negative intergroup attitudes.

Theorem 2: Knowledge of the host culture is associated positively with accurate stereotypes.

Theorem 3: Knowledge of the host culture is associated positively with favorable contact.

Theorem 4: Knowledge of the host culture is associated positively with strangers developing intimate relationships with host nationals.

Theorem 5: Favorable contact is associated positively with strangers developing intimate relationships with host nationals.

Theorem 6: Favorable contact is associated positively with pluralist tendencies in the host culture.

Theorem 7: Favorable contact is associated inversely with negative intergroup attitudes held by host nationals.

Theorem 8: Knowledge of the host culture is associated positively with degree of cultural similarity.

Theorem 9: Negative intergroup attitudes are associated inversely with favorable contact.

Support for the first nine theorems emerges from research on the contact hypothesis. Downs and Stea (1977) argue that information, not necessarily understanding, emerges from contact. When contact occurs under favorable conditions, however, understanding should develop. This is supported by Stephan and Stephan's (1984) study of Anglo attitudes toward Chicanos. Their research revealed that contact with Chicanos under favorable conditions influenced positively Anglos' knowledge of Chicano culture and knowledge, which in turn, influenced attitudes positively. Their research also reveals a positive relationship between favorable contact and positive attitudes toward Chicanos, the central tenet of the contact hypothesis. Since part of favorable contact as defined by Amir (1969) is intimate rather than casual contact and positive attitudes by the majority group, there is indirect support for the relationship derived between knowledge and intimate relationships as well as that between contact and host attitudes. Also, pluralist societies support intergroup contact more than do assimilationist societies, therefore, there is support for Theorem 6. DuBois (1956) also found that experience in the host culture that reinforced negative stereotypes is not associated with understanding the host culture, providing indirect support for the relationship between knowledge and accurate stereotypes.

Theorem 10: Negative intergroup attitudes are associated positively with strangers' identification with native culture.

Theorem 11: Strangers' identification with native culture is associated negatively with shared networks with host nationals.

These two theorems are directly or indirectly supported by the work of Tajfel and associates and by Giles and associates. Tajfel's research, for example, reveals that categorization of others into outgroups leads to negative intergroup attitudes (Tajfel & Turner, 1979). Giles and Byrne's (1982) work on ethnolinguistic identity and second language competence further suggests that soft language boundaries among ethnic groups (that is, overlapping networks) are associated with weaker identification with a specific ethnic group.

Theorem 12: The degree of similarity between the host and native culture is associated positively with strangers' shared network with host nationals.

Theorem 13: The degree of similarity between the host and native cultures is associated positively with strangers' use of appropriate uncertainty reduction strategies.

Support for Theorems 12 and 13 can be found in two different lines of research. Blau and Schwartz (1984) found that the greater the degree of cultural similarity, the more networks overlap. Research by Gudykunst (1983b) and Simard (1981) further indicates that individuals know how to get to know others when they come from the same culture, but are not sure how to do this when people come from different cultures.

Theorem 14: The use of appropriate uncertainty reduction strategies by strangers is associated positively with their second language competence.

Theorem 15: Cultural similarity is associated positively with the second language competence of the strangers.

Theorem 16: Shared networks are associated positively with second language competence.

Theorem 17: Intimacy is associated positively with the second language competence of the strangers.

Theorem 18: The attraction of strangers to host nationals is associated positively with the second language competence of the strangers.

Theorem 19: Strangers' identification with the host culture is associated positively with second language competence.

Theorem 20: Negative intergroup attitudes are associated inversely with the second language competence of the strangers.

Theorem 21: Favorable contact is associated positively with the second language competence of the strangers.

Theorem 22: Accurate stereotypes are associated positively with second language competence.

Previous research demonstrates that experience in the host culture facilitates learning the language of that culture (Burnstall, 1975). There also is data to indicate that the more similar the native and host cultures, the easier it is for strangers to learn the host language (Whyte & Holmberg, 1956; Gudykunst, 1985b). Favorable contact with members of the host culture and second language competence have been found to be reciprocally related by researchers studying adjustment (Selltiz et al., 1963; Gullahorn & Gullahorn, 1966). Competence in a second language is also influenced by shared communication networks. Larson and Smalley's (1972) work, for example, reveals that participation in a language community affects fluency in the language. This finding is supported by research on learning a second language in informal environments (Klein & Dittmar, 1979). In addition to being attracted to and sharing networks, forming intimate relationships with host nationals is related to second language competence (Gudykunst, 1985b). Gudykunst's (1985b) research also exhibits a relationship between second language competence and the uncertainty-reduction strategies used. Yum and Wang's (1983) study further supports the posited relationship between accurate stereotypes and second language competence. Finally, the relationship derived between cultural identity and second language competence is consistent with Giles and Byrne's (1982) analysis, while the relationship between negative intergroup attitudes and second language competence is compatible with most models of second language competence (see Gardner, 1985, for a recent review).

Theorem 23: Attraction and intimacy are associated positively.

Theorem 24: Attraction and display of nonverbal affiliative expressiveness are associated positively.

Theorem 25: Attraction and shared networks are associated positively.

Theorem 26: Intimacy and display of nonverbal affiliative expressiveness are associated positively.

Theorem 27: Intimacy and shared networks are associated positively.

Theorem 28: Shared networks and display of nonverbal affiliative expressiveness are associated positively.

The previous six theorems are all consistent with statements that could be derived directly from Berger and Calabrese's (1975) original version of uncertainty reduction theory or Parks and Adelman's (1983) elaboration. All six theorems are supported under conditions of cultural dissimilarity (Gudykunst & Nishida, 1984; Gudykunst, 1985a; Gudykunst, Chua, & Gray, 1987).

Many additional statements can be derived from the logical combination of the axioms. Some of these statements, however, are not supported by previous research. The relationship between cultural similarity and intimacy, for example, is not supported by Gudykunst's (1985b) study. Other statements generated from combinations of the axioms appear to involve the "fallacy of the excluded middle"; that is, one of the other primary variables appears to intervene between the two variables in the derived statement. To illustrate, it appears reasonable to argue that favorable contact intervenes to mediate the relationship between shared networks and favorable intergroup attitudes. Relationships such as this are not included; rather, only those statements that appear to be plausible are derived. The 22 statements proffered below are theorems that do not appear to be tested in previous research and, therefore, are hypotheses for future research.

Theorem 29: Knowledge of the host culture is associated positively with strangers' use of appropriate uncertainty reduction strategies.

Theorem 30: Knowledge of the host culture is associated positively with strangers sharing networks with host nationals.

Theorem 31: Knowledge of the host culture is associated negatively with strangers' identification with native culture.

Theorem 32: Knowledge of the host culture is associated positively with strangers' second language competence.

Theorem 33: Negative intergroup attitudes are associated inversely with strangers' use of appropriate uncertainty reduction strategies.

Theorem 34: Negative intergroup attitudes are associated inversely with accurate stereotypes.

Theorem 35: Accurate stereotypes are associated positively with favorable contact.

Theorem 36: Accurate stereotypes are associated positively with strangers' use of appropriate uncertainty reduction strategies.

Theorem 37: Accurate stereotypes are associated negatively with strangers' identification with native culture.

Theorem 38: Favorable contact is associated positively with strangers' use of appropriate uncertainty reduction strategies.

Theorem 39: Favorable contact is associated positively with the attraction of strangers to host nationals.

Theorem 40: Favorable contact is associated positively with strangers sharing networks with host nationals.

Theorem 41: Favorable contact is associated negatively with strangers' identification with native culture.

Theorem 42: The use of appropriate uncertainty reduction strategies by strangers is associated positively with attraction to host nationals.

Theorem 43: The use of appropriate uncertainty reduction strategies by strangers is associated positively with strangers developing intimate relationships with host nationals.

Theorem 44: The use of appropriate uncertainty reduction strategies by strangers is associated positively with strangers sharing networks with host nationals.

Theorem 45: The use of appropriate uncertainty reduction strategies by strangers is associated negatively with strangers' identification with native culture.

Theorem 46: The attraction of strangers to host nationals is associated negatively with strangers' identification with native culture.

Theorem 47: Strangers' motivation to live in the host culture is associated positively with their identification with host culture.

Theorem 48: Strangers' motivation to live in the host culture is associated positively with their second language competence.

Theorem 49: Strangers' motivation to live in the host culture is associated positively with their knowledge of the host culture.

Theorem 50: Strangers' motivation to live in the host culture is associated inversely with negative intergroup attitudes of host nationals.

CONCLUSION

The major assumption underlying the theory is that intercultural adaptation is a function of uncertainty reduction and reducing/controlling anxiety. The reduction of uncertainty and anxiety is a function of stereotypes, favorable contact, shared networks, intergroup attitudes, cultural identity, cultural similarity, second language competence, and knowledge of the host culture. Reducing uncertainty also is influenced by the appropriate use of uncertainty reduction strategies, the display of nonverbal affiliative expressiveness, attraction, and, intimacy. Reducing anxiety, in contrast, is affected by strangers' motivation, strangers' psychological differentiation, host nationals' attitudes toward strangers, and the host cultures' policy toward strangers. (For a schematic representation of the theory, refer to Figure 5.1 presented earlier).

Other axioms might be warranted. It could be argued, for example, that psychological differentiation not only influences anxiety (Axiom 19), but also attributional confidence. This position can be supported *indirectly* from research on communication acculturation, which reveals a relationship between cognitive complexity and information acquisition (Kim, 1977a). Research by Selltiz and his associates, (1963) also suggests that intimacy and attraction influence anxiety, in addition to affecting attributional confidence (Axioms 14 & 15). Similarly, Mehrabian's (1971) work would be used to develop an argument that non-verbal affiliative expressiveness influences anxiety, as well as attributional confidence as posited in Axiom 16. Support for these relationships, however, is not as direct as that used to generate the axioms and they, therefore, were omitted in the present version of the theory.

If uncertainty and anxiety are conceived of as the two axes of a graph, different patterns of intercultural adaptation can be described (see Figure 5.2). Four general patterns emerge: (I) high uncertainty, high anxiety; (II) high uncertainty, low anxiety; (III) low uncertainty, high anxiety; and (IV) low uncertainty, low anxiety. The first pattern (Quadrant I: high, high) involves a lack of adaptation, while the fourth (Quadrant III: low, low) represents total adaptation. The remaining two patterns reflect different strategies for adaptation. The second pattern (Quadrant II: high uncertainty; low anxiety), for example, describes the typical pattern of adaptation used by strangers who live and engage in all, or most, of their interaction within stranger enclaves. These strangers are unsure of how to behave in the host culture or do not wish to associate with host nationals and, therefore, stay with their "own kind" in the enclave. Since behavioral patterns within the enclave are similar to those at home, anxiety is low. This pattern requires relatively complete stranger communities in the host culture (that is, institutional completeness, Breton, 1964; cohesive stranger groups, Herman & Schield, 1961; or strong contracultures, Gudykunst & Hallsall, 1980). Finally, the third pattern (Quadrant III: low uncertainty, high anxiety) depicts those strangers who "understand" the host culture, but do not like it. That is, they interact effectively with host nationals, but this interaction requires that they behave in ways inconsistent with their values; they, therefore, experience anxiety to some degree. It would appear reasonable to argue that strangers whose adaptation fits this pattern may be high self-monitors (Snyder, 1974); people who adjust their behavior to situational demands. Low self-monitors, in contrast, would appear to be more likely to choose the second pattern of adaptation.

Understanding that these variations exist allows for multiple forms of intercultural adaptation by strangers, rather than one continuous outcome (low to high adaptation) as used in most analyses. The inclusion of self-monitoring as a factor influencing which pattern of adjustment emerges, further links the theory proffered with recent statements of uncertainty reduction theory (Berger & Bradac, 1982), as well as a major line of research in social psychology (see Synder & Ickes, 1985).

To conclude, the theory outlines in this chapter is an initial

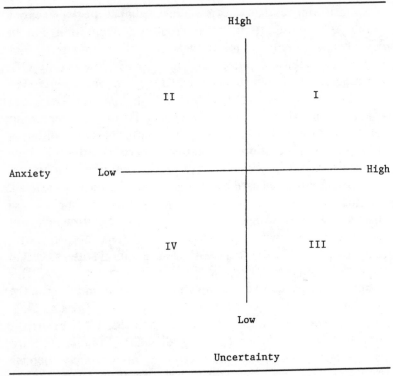

Figure 5.2 Patterns of Adaptation

attempt to explain intercultural adaptation using uncertainty-reduction theory. The argument that reducing uncertainty and anxiety are necessary and sufficient conditions for intercultural adaptation is plausible and, indirectly, consistent with previous research (Ball-Rokeach, 1973; Padilla, Wagatsuma, & Lindholm, 1985). This, however, is an assumption in the present version of the theory. As pointed out, the assumption is not untestable, only untested. The first step in testing the theory proffered, therefore, is to examine empirically this assumption. The assumption that uncertainty and anxiety are independent aspects of intercultural adaptation also should be examined in future research. The different patterns of adaptation described above obviously would not be warranted if anxiety and uncertainty are correlated linearly. Further, the theorems derived from the axioms must be tested in order to ascertain the interrelations among the major variables. Ideally, in fact, the complete theory (assumptions, axioms, and theorems) should be tested and modified as necessary. Once it has been tested, the theory can be used as a template for the design and implementation of intercultural training programs to facilitate the adaptation of strangers to new cultural environments. As Kurt Lewin said, "there is nothing so practical as a good theory."

REFERENCES

Altman, I., & Taylor, D. (1973). *Social penetration: The development of interpersonal relationships.* New York: Holt, Rinehart & Winston.

Amir, Y. (1969). The contact hypothesis in ethnic relations. *Psychological Bulletin, 71* 319-342.

Ball-Rokeach, S. J. (1973). From pervasive ambiguity to a definition of the situation. *Sociometry, 36,* 378-389.

Barnett, G. A., & McPhail, T. (1980). An examination of the relationship of United States television and Canadian identity. *International Journal of Intercultural Relations, 4,* 219-232.

Basu, A. K., & Ames, R. G. (1970). Cross-cultural contact and attitude formation. *Sociology and Social Research, 55,* 5-16.

Berger, C. R. (1979). Beyond initial interactions. In H. Giles & R. St. Clair (Eds.), *Language and social psychology.* Oxford: Basil Blackwell.

Berger, C. R., & Bradac, J. J. (1982). *Language and social knowledge: Uncertainty in interpersonal relations.* London: Edward Arnold.

Berger, C. R., & Calabrese, R. (1975). Some explorations in initial interactions and beyond: Toward a developmental theory of interpersonal communication. *Human Communication Research, 1,* 99-112.

Berry, J. W. (1975). Ecology, cultural adaptation, and psychological differentiation. In R. Brislin, S. Bochner, & W. Lonner (Eds.), *Cross-cultural perspectives on learning.* Newbury Park, CA: Sage.

Berry, J. W. (1980). Acculturation as varieties of adaptation. In A. Padilla (Ed.), *Acculturation: Theory, models, and new findings.* Boulder, CO: Westview Press.

Blalock, H. H. (1969). *Theory construction: From verbal to mathematical formulations.* Englewood Cliffs, NJ: Prentice Hall.

Blau, P., & Schwarts, J. (1984). *Cross-cutting social circles.* New York: Academic Press.

Bochner, S. (1972). Problems in culture learning. In S. Bochner & P. Wicks (Eds.), *Overseas students in Australia* Randwick, Australia: New South Wales University Press.

Bochner, S., & Perks, R. W. (1971). National role evocation as a function of cross-national interaction. *Journal of Cross-Cultural Psychology, 2,* 157-164.

Brenton, R. (1964). Institutional completeness of ethnic communities and the personnel relations of immigrants. *American Journal of Sociology, 70,* 193-205.

Brewer, M., & Campbell, D. (1976). *Ethnocentrism and intergroup attitudes.* New York: Wiley.

Burstall, C. (1975). French in the primary schools: The British experiment. In H. Stern, C. Burstall, & B. Harley (Eds.), *French from age eight or eleven?*. Toronto: Ontario Studies in Education.

Chance, J. E., & Goldstein, A. (1981). Depth of processing in response to own-and other-race faces. *Personality and Social Psychology Bulletin, 7,* 475-480.

Church, A. (1982). Sojourner adjustment. *Psychological Bulletin, 91,* 540-572.

Cook, S. W. (1969). Motives in a conceptual analysis of attitude-related behavior. In W. Arnold & D. Levine (Eds.), *Nebraska symposium on motivation* (Vol. 17). Lincoln: University of Nebraska Press.

David, K. H. (1971). Culture shock and the development of self awareness. *Journal of Contemporary Psychotherapy, 4,* 44-48.

Detweiler, R. (1975). On inferring the intentions of a person from another culture. *Journal of Personality, 43,* 591-611.

Downs, R., & Stea, D. (1977). *Maps in minds.* New York: Harper and Row.

DuBois, C. A. (1956). *Foreign students and higher education in the United States.* Washington, DC: American Council on Education.

Dyal, J. A., & Dyal, R. Y. (1981). Acculturation, stress, and coping. *International Journal of Intercultural Relations, 5,* 301-328.

Fiedler, F. E., Mitchell, T., & Triandis, H. C. (1971). The culture assimilator: An approach to cross-cultural training. *Journal of Applied Psychology, 55,* 95-102.

Furnham, A., & Bochner, S. (1982). Social difficulty in a foreign culture. In S. Bochner (Ed.), *Cultures in contact.* Elmsford, NY: Pergamon.

Gardner, R. C. (1985). *Social psychology and second language learning.* London: Edward Arnold.

Giles, H., & Byrne, J. L. (1982). An intergroup approach to second language acquisition. *Journal of Multilingual and Multicultural Development, 3,* 17-40.

Gudykunst, W. B. (1983a). Similarities and differences in perceptions of initial intracultural and intercultural encounters. *The Southern Speech Communication Journal, 49,* 40-65.

Gudykunst, W. B. (1983b). Toward a typology of stranger-host relationships. *International Journal of Intercultural Relations, 7,* 401-415.

Gudykunst, W. B. (1985a). The influence of cultural similarity, type of relationship, and self-monitoring on uncertainty-reduction processes. *Communication Monographs, 52,* 203-217.

Gudykunst, W. B. (1985b). A model of uncertainty reduction in intercultural encounters. *Journal of Language and Social Psychology, 4,* 79-98.

Gudykunst, W. B. (1986). Intraethnic and interethnic uncertainty-reduction processes. In Y. Kim (Ed.), *Current research in interethnic communication.* Newbury Park, CA: Sage.

Gudykunst, W. B. (1987). Cross-Cultural comparisons. In C. Berger & S. Chaffee (Eds.), *Handbook of communication science.* Newbury Park, CA: Sage.

Gudykunst, W. B., Chua, E., & Gray, A. (1987). Cultural dissimilarities and uncertainty reduction process. In M. McLaughlin (Ed.), *Communication yearbook 10.* Newbury Park, CA: Sage.

Gudykunst, W. B., & Hallsall, S. J. (1980). The application of a theory of contracture to intercultural communication. In D. Nimmo (Ed.), *Communication yearbook 4.* New Brunswick, NJ: Transaction.

Gudykunst, W. B., & Hammer, M. R. (in press). The effect of ethnicity, gender and dyadic composition on uncertainty reduction in initial interactions. *Journal of Black Studies.*

Gudykunst, W. B., & Kim, Y. Y. (1984). *Communicating with strangers: An approach to intercultural communication.* New York: Random House.

Gudykunst, W. B., & Lim, T. S. (1986). A perspective for the study of intergroup communication. In W. Gudykunst (Ed.), *Intergroup communication.* London: Edward Arnold.

Gudykunst, W. B., & Nishida, T. (1984). Individual and cultural influences on uncertainty reduction. *Communication Monographs, 51,* 23-36.

Gudykunst, W. B., Sodetani, L., & Sonoda, K. (1987). Uncertainty reduction in Japanese-American-Caucasian relationships in Hawaii. *Western Journal of Speech Communication, 51,* 256-278.

Gudykunst, W. B., Wiseman, R., & Hammer, M. (1977). Determinants of sojourners' attitudinal satisfaction. In B. Ruben (Ed.), *Communication yearbook 1.* New Brunswick, NJ: Transaction.

Gudykunst, W. B., Yang, S. M., & Nishida, T. (1985). A cross-cultural test of uncertainty reduction theory: Comparisons of acquaintance, friend, and dating relationships in Japan, Korea, and the United States. *Human Communication Research, 11,* 407-455.

Gullahorn, J. E., & Gullahorn, J. T. (1966). American students abroad. *The Annals of the American Academy of Political and Social Science, 368,* 43-59.

Guthrie, G. M. (1975). A behavioral analysis of culture learning. In R. Brislin, S. Bochner, & W. Lonner (Eds.), *Cross-cultural perspectives on learning.* New York: Wiley.

Hamilton, D. L., & Bishop, G. D. (1976). Attitudinal and behavioral effects of initial integration of White suburban neighborhoods. *Journal of Social Issues, 32,* 47-67.

Hartmann, P., & Husband, C. (1972). The mass media and racial conflict. In D. McPhail (Ed.), *Sociology of mass communication.* Hammondsworth, England: Penguin.

Herman, S., & Schield, E. (1961). The stranger group in a cross-cultural situation. *Sociometry, 24,* 165-176.

Hewstone, M., & Giles, H. (1986). Social groups and social stereotypes in intergroup communication. In W. Gudykunst (Ed.), *Intergroup communication.* London: Edward Arnold.

Hewstone, M., Jaspers, J., & Laljee, M. (1982). Social representations, social attribution, and social identity. *European Journal of Social Psychology, 12,* 241-269.

Hewstone, M., & Ward, C. (1985). Ethnocentrism and causal attribution in Southeast Asia. *Journal of Personality and Social Psychology, 48,* 614-623.

Hull, W. F. (1978). *Foreign students in the United States of America: Coping behavior within the educational environment.* New York: Praeger.

Jaspers, J., & Hewstone, M. (1982). Cross-cultural interaction, social attribution, and inter-group relations. In S. Bochner (Ed.), *Cultures in contact.* Elmsford, NY: Pergamon.

Katz, P. (1974). *Acculturation and social networks of American immigrants in Israel.* Unpublished doctoral dissertation. State University of New York, Buffalo, NY.

Keesing, R. (1974). Theories of culture. *Annual Review of Anthropology, 3,* 73-97.

Kim, Y. Y. (1977a). Communication patterns of foreign immigrants in the process of acculturation. *Human Communication Research, 41,* 66-76.

Kim, Y. Y. (1977b). Inter-ethnic and intra-ethnic communication. In N. Jain (Ed.), *International and Intercultural Communication Annual* (Vol. IV). Annandale, VA: Speech Communication Association.

Klein, W., & Dittmar, N. (1979). *Developing grammars: The acquisition of German syntax by foreign workers.* New York: Springer-Verlag.

Klineberg, O., & Hull, W. F. (1979). *At a foreign university: An international study of adaptation and coping.* New York: Praeger.

Koltuv, B. (1962). Some characteristics of intrajudge trait intercorrelations. *Psychological Monographs, 76*(33), Whole No. 552.

Larson, D. N., & Smalley, W. A. (1972). *Becoming bilingual: A Guide to language learning.* South Pasadena, CA: William Carey Library.

Lieverson, S. (1985). *Making it count: The improvement of social research and theory.* Berkeley: University of California Press.

McPherson, K. (1983). Opinion-related information seeking. *Personality and Social Psychology Bulletin, 9,* 116-124.

Mehrabian, A. (1971). *Silent messages.* Belmont, CA: Wadsworth.

Miller, G. R., & Steinberg, M. (1975). *Between people.* Chicago: Science Research Associates.

Miller, G. R., & Sunnafrank, M. J. (1982). All is for one but one is not for all. In F. Dance (Ed.), *Human communication theory* New York: Harper and Row.

Mischel, W. (1965). Predicting the success of Peace Corps volunteers in Nigeria. *Journal of Personality and Social Psychology, 1,* 510-517.

Morris, R. T. (1960). *The two way mirror: National status in foreign students' adjustment.* Minneapolis: University of Minnesota Press.

Murphy, H.B.M. (1973). The low rate of hospitalization shown by immigrants to Canada. In C. Zwingemann & M. Pfister-Ammende (Eds.), *Uprooting and after.* Heidelberg: Springer-Verlag.

Murray, J. P., & Kippax, S. (1979). From the early window to the late night show: International trends in the study of television's impact on children and adults. In L. Berkowitz (Ed.), *Advances in experimental social psychology* (Vol. 12). New York: Academic Press.

Naiman, N., Frohlich, M., Stern, H., & Todesco, A. (1978). *The good language learner.* Toronto: Ontario Institute for Studies in Education.

O'Driscoll, M., & Feather, N. (1983). Perception of value congruence and interethnic behavioral intentions. *International Journal of Intercultural Relations, 7,* 239-252.

Padilla, A. M. (1980). The role of cultural awareness and ethnic loyalty in acculturation. In A. Padilla (Ed.), *Acculturation: Theory, models, and some new findings.* Boulder, CO: Westview Press.

Padilla, A. M., Wagatsuma, Y., & Lindholm, K. (1985). Acculturation and personality as predictors of stress in Japanese and Japanese-Americans. *Journal of Social Psychology, 125,* 295-305.

Parks, M., & Adelman, M. (1983). Communication networks and the development of romantic relationships. *Human Communication Research, 10,* 55-80.

Pettigrew, T. (1978). Three issues in ethnicity. In J. Yinger & S. Cutler (Eds.), *Major social issues.* New York: Free Press.

Rose, T. L. (1981). Cognitive and dyadic processes in intergroup contact. In D. Hamilton (Ed.), *Cognitive processes in stereotyping and intergroup behavior.* Hillsdale, NJ: Lawrence Erlbaum.

Rothbart, M., Dawed, R., & Park, B. (1984). Stereotyping and sampling biases in intergroup perception. In J. Eiser (Ed.), *Attitudinal judgment.* New York: Springer-Verlag.

Ruben, B. D. (1983). A system-theoretic view. In W. Gudykunst (Ed.), *Intercultural communication theory.* Newbury Park, CA: Sage.

Schuetz, A. (1944). The stranger. *American Journal of Sociology, 49,* 599-607.

Selltiz, C., Christ, J. R., Havel, J., & Cook, S. W. (1963). *Attitudes and social relations of foreign students in the United States.* Minneapolis: University of Minnesota Press.

Sherif, M. (1966). *Group conflict and cooperation.* London: Routledge and Kegan Paul.

Simard, L. (1981). Cross-cultural interaction. *Journal of Social Psychology, 113,* 171-192.

Simmel, G. (1950). The stranger. In K. Wolff (Ed. & Trans.). *The sociology of Georg Simmel.* New York: Free Press.

Snyder, M. (1974). Self-monitoring of expressive behavior. *Journal of Personality and Social Psychology, 30,* 526-537.

Snyder, M., & Ickes, W. (1985). Personality and social behaviors. In G. Lindzey & E. Aronson (Eds.), *The handbook of social psychology* (3rd ed., Vol. II). New York: Random House.

Sodetani, L. L., & Gudykunst, W. B. (1986) The effects of surprising events on intercultural relationships. Manuscript submitted for publication.

Stephan, W. G. (1985). Intergroup relations. In G. Lindzey & E. Aronson (Eds.), *The handbook of social psychology* (3rd ed., Vol. II). New York: Random House.

Stephan, W. G., & Stephan, C. W. (1984). The role of ignorance in intergroup relations. In N. Miller & M. Brewer (Eds.), *Groups in contact* (pp. 229-257). New York: Academic Press.

Stephan, W. G., & Stephan, C. W. (1985). Intergroup anxiety. *Journal of Social Issues, 41*(3), 157-176.

Taft, R. (1966). From stranger to citizen. London: Tavistock Publications.

Tajfel, H., & Turner, J. C. (1979). An integrative theory of intergroup conflict. In W. Austin & S. Worchel (Eds.), *The social psychology of intergroup relations.* Monterey, CA: Brooks/Cole.

Taylor, D. M., & Jaggi, V. (1974). Ethnocentrism and casual attributions in a South Indian context. *Journal of Cross-Cultural Psychology, 5,* 162-171.

Torbiörn, I. (1982). *Living abroad: Personal adjustment and personnel policy in overseas settings.* Chichester, England: John Wiley.

Triandis, H. C. (1980). Values, attitudes, and interpersonal behavior. In M. Page (Ed.), *Nebraska symposium on motivation 1979* (Vol. 27). Lincoln: University of Nebraska Press.

Wagner, U., & Schonbach, P. (1984). Educational status and prejudice. In N. Miller & M. Brewer (Eds.), *Groups in contact.* New York: Academic Press.

Whyte, W. F., & Holmberg, A. R. (1956). Human problems of U.S. enterprise in Latin America. *Human Relations, 15,* 1-40.

Wilder, D. A., & Allen, V. L. (1978). Group membership and preference for information about others. *Personality and Social Psychology Bulletin, 4,* 106-110.

Witkin, H. A., & Berry, J. W. (1975). Psychological differentiation in cross-cultural perspective. *Journal of Cross-Cultural Psychology, 6,* 4-87.

Yum, J. O., & Wang, G. (1983). Interethnic perceptions and the communication behavior among five ethnic groups in Hawaii. *International Journal of Intercultural Relations, 7,* 285-308.

6

Cross-Cultural Adaptation and Perceptual Development

MUNEO JAY YOSHIKAWA ● *University of Hawaii*

The cross-cultural adaptation process is presented as a creative process that shares an analogous structural relationship with the scientific discovery process and the religious enlightenment process. Five stages of development are described with observations of changes in the individual's modes of perception. Successful cross-cultural adaptation is conceived as a result of the individual's transcendence of binary perception of the world.

The process of cross-cultural adaptation is not a simple phenomenon. It involves the life history of a person, transcending the substitution of one culture for another. It involves the conscious as well as the unconscious changes in the individual. The adaptation process has often been described in terms of developmental stages.

Thomas and Znaniecki (1958) classify the individual variation in response to social conditions into three types: (1) the "philistines," who are inclined to accept the given condition as it is and whose chief propensity is their desire for stability; (2) the "bohemians," whose chief motive is to seek new experiences because they are not content with the given condition; and (3) the "creative," who bring forth a redefinition of the coflicting situations and harmonize the philistines' desire for stability and the bohemian's desire for new experience.

These personality types correspond with Rank's (1945) three types of human character: (1) the "adapted," who are contented with the given condition; (2) the "neurotic," who are discontented with their condition; and (3) the "creative," who are at peace with society as well as with themselves and with others. These characterizations of adjustment are similar to Riesman, Glazer, and Denny's (1961, pp. 206-207) three types of adjustment: (1) the "adjusted," (2) the "anomie," and (3) the "autonomous."

Lifton (1969) and Adler (1975) take these three basic personality types and apply them to their analysis of the process of human transformation. Lifton classifies the process into three stages: "confrontation," "reordering," and "renewal." The "confrontation" stage refers to the stage when the ordinary person, who is well adjusted to his or her society, questions the pattern of his or her existence. The "reordering" stage is the stage when one reorders one's conflicting perception of the world, the self and the other. Lifton views the "reordering" stage as the period of "symbolic emptying" and absorption during which new ideas, new forms of human relationship, and creative expression are attempted. In the final stage of "renewal," the individual attains a new sense of harmony.

To describe the individuals' cross-cultural transitional experience, Adler (1975, p. 39) expands Lifton's notion of the three stages of human transformation into five stages. He explains such experience in terms of a transitional process that he defines as the "movement from a state of low self- and cultural awareness to a state of higher self- and cultural awareness."

STAGES OF CROSS-CULTURAL ADAPTATION

Synthesizing these and other existing conceptualizations, a model of cross-cultural adaptation is presented below. This model characterizes the stages of the adaptation process as contact, disintegration, reintegration, autonomy, and double-swing.

The First Stage: "Contact"

Despite contact with a different culture, one fails to recognize the new realities. One's original world view persists; one sees one's own reality in the second culture. The differences one sees may not be threatening but intriguing. Some individuals may experience this contact period as a "honeymoon" stage in which everything different is new and exciting. For others, the lack of familiarity may prove to be threatening.

The Second Stage: "Disintegration"

One experiences in this stage bewilderment and conflict due to the discrepant world views of the first and second culture. Being overwhelmed by cultural differences, one experiences "culture shock." Adler classifies this stage as the "disintegration" stage.

The Third Stage: "Reintegration"

This stage is marked by one's attempt to find a solution to a difficult situation. At this stage, cultural similarities and differences are rejected through stereotyping, generalization, and judgmental attitudes.

During this stage some individuals switch back and forth between the first stage and the second stage. They are apt to experience an identity crisis, being caught in two cultures and in search of a sense of belongingness. They experience a sense of nothingness or alienation characterized by the "bohemian" (Thomas & Znaniecki, 1958), "neurotic" (Rank, 1945) or "anomie" (Riesman et al., 1961). In Lifton's (1969) terms, such individuals appear to be in the "confrontation" stage where they question the condition of their existence. Adler (1975) calls this stage the "reintegration" stage.

The Fourth Stage: "Autonomy"

One's outlook becomes increasingly flexible at this stage. One gains the ability to experience new situations in a new way. One begins to stand on one's own two feet and accepts and appreciates cultural similarities and differences. In this "autonomous" state, some individuals begin to develop and identify themselves with the "third culture."

The Fifth Stage: "Double-Swing"

This stage is marked by "attitude, emotions, and behaviors that are independent but not independent of cultural influence" (Adler, 1975, p. 144). One is fully able to accept and draw nourishment from both cultural similarities and differences. One is independent, yet simultaneously interdependent. This paradoxical existence can assume a new identity—the "identity-in-unity" or "duality-in-unity." This is the "independent-interdependent" stage (Adler, 1975) in which one becomes capable of bringing new ways to explore the paradox of human diversity and unity.

The paradoxical existence of the fifth stage may be illustrated by reference to the meaning of human being, which consists of the two Chinese characters:

The first character means "person" and the second character means "inbetweenness." Whereas

means person, it alone does not signify fully a human being in the Japanese language. One becomes a human being only in relation to another person.

This inbetweenness of the fifth stage can be viewed as "double-swing" and can be described pictorially as a Möbius strip

$$\infty$$

It reflects Buber's (1966) idea of the twofold movement, that is, setting at a distance and entering into relations, as well as the Buddhist idea of paradoxical relationships—"not-one, not-two" (Nakayama, 1973). The double-swing signifies an "identity-in-unity," embracing the unity of monism and the separateness of dualism. Both sides represent different realities that are complementary and constantly in interaction. Neither side can be excluded nor combined with the other. In this stage of adaptation, therefore, one does not focus either on the experiences in the original culture or on the experiences in the second culture. Instead, one is able to experience the dynamic and dialogical interaction between them.

PERCEPTUAL PATTERNS OF "DOUBLE-SWING"

In characterizing the perceptual patterns of individuals in the double-swing stage, five perceptual patterns need to be identified. One may be called the "ethnocentric" perception, wherein one experiences the other in one's own image. With the second, "sympathetic" perception, one perceives the other's world from one's perspective, projecting one's own feelings that may not necessarily coincide with the other's. While this "sympathetic" perception is a reaction to the other's perspective, the "ethnocentric" perception disregards the existence of the other's perspective.

The third type, the "empathic" perception, puts oneself in the other's shoes and allows one to see the other's world from the other's perspective. With this perception one *experiences* the other side of the relationship. The fourth type, the "mirror-reflecting" perception, allows one to view one's world through the other's perspective. With his perception, both serve as part of a corrective on the other. The fifth may be called the "metacontextual" perception. This perception enables one to perceive the concrete process and context in which the two individuals interact. With this perception, one becomes aware simultaneously of events outside the framework of the "double-swing" movement.

The double-swing perception encompasses all of these five types of perception. It moves in and out and up and down these five perceptual modes. When the double-swing perception is in full swing, one perceives the concrete particulars of physically present individuals as well as the interconnectedness and interdependence of all things in the universe. This holistic perception helps one to seek the hidden dimensions underlying what is presented or experienced. As in the Japanese Noh dance, one can appreciate simultaneously several dimensions of a reality, namely, what is visible and the interaction between the outside and the inside. The perceptual change toward double-swing results in the widening of one's cognitive framework.

As one enters the final stage of development in cross-cultural adaptation, one's capacity for openness, sensitivity, and responsiveness to the world increases. One is increasingly interested in differences and anomalies. At the same time, one becomes more vulnerable because one tries to remain open to what is alien to oneself.

This double-swing open attitude can be viewed as a basic attitude of listening to the other's perception of the world. This openness is different from a "onesided openness," which does not consider the other's needs and feelings. Instead, it is an open attitude based on "existential trust" (Friedman, 1974). To have trust in life is to commit oneself to the changing of being. This commitment enhances one's ability to be surprised at the difference of the familiar.

Further, an individual at the double-swing stage approaches others from a perspective of shared participation in the creation of reality and meaning. Communication is viewed as a creative act in which one participates jointly in the creation of new meaning, adjusting continuously to what happens from moment to moment. One is not limited by given social and cultural realities. Instead, one actively creates one's own stimuli.

A persistent tendency in people in cross-cultural adaptation is to view the new culture as the opposite of one's original culture. The Greek historian Herodotus, for example, described the culture of Egypt (after no more than a four month visit) as being exactly the reverse of the common practice of mankind (Finley, 1959, pp. 68-69). Nineteenth Century Chinese visitors to the West also described their experience in terms of a reverse world (Frodsham, 1974, pp. 148-149).

Binary categorization and its transcendence have been fundamental to the philosophical, scientific, and religious traditions of the world. Examples of fundamental binary categories in science, for example, include: planets-earth in astronomy, arteries-veins in physiology, air-water in chemistry, man-animal in biology, primitive-civilized in anthropology, time-space and mass-energy in physics. In order to create a new paradigm, however, such dualistic thinking has served as a key to the liberation from the human suffering for many religious leaders and to the liberation from the old paradigm for many scientists.

Similarly, the liberation from misplacement for individuals in cross-cultural encounters can be achieved when they transcend the categorization of the old and the new cultures by binary opposites. When they are able to deviate from accepted categories, they may perceive and understand the new reality as it is. As a scientist who takes jarring encounters with anomalies to reach a level of new awareness, an individual takes a leap, a journey, from the binary to the double-swing mode of perceiving the world.

JOURNEY, ENCOUNTER WITH ANOMALY, AND CRISIS

Journey is one of the significant stages people go through to discover or create something extraordinary. In this journey, people have encountered anomalies disturbing enough to shake their existing, customary perceptual foundations. For Darwin, it was the long journey to Galapagos where his thinking was transformed. For Galileo, it was a journey to the planets intermediated by telescope. For Einstein, it was a mental journey (imagination) of riding at the speed of light. For Buddah, it was the short journey from his place to the outside world. In this journey, Buddah encountered anomalies—sick people, old poor people, dying people on the road. His whole existence was shaken by these anomalies.

Kuhn (1970) states that scientific discovery commences with an awareness of anomaly. He further points out the importance of anomaly strong enough to shake the foundation of the existing paradigm. The encounter with anomalies creates crisis. As the Chinese character for crisis is composed of two characters, "danger" and "opportunity," crisis can lead to a great opportunity for growth and discovery. Figure 6.1 shows pictorially the journey into a world of anomalies, and the complete turn in the Möbius strip indicates the crisis they face.

The conflicting value systems and different ways of categorizing realities presented by foreign cultures are anomalies that may create culture shock and crisis for individuals in an unfamiliar cultural milieu. An individual's experiences of these anomalies may propel him or her into higher levels of awareness of self.

Transcendence of Opposites

Transcendence of binary opposites represents enlightenment and the liberation of human condition in Eastern religions. The "coincidentia oppositorium," the unity of the opposites, the mystery of the totality, was a concept employed by Nicholas Cusa to define God (Nakamura, 1975, p. 100). Also, Buddah attained enlightenment when he realized how cultural reality was categorized and constructed. Enlightenment for him meant the transcendence from the web of cultural conditioning factors.

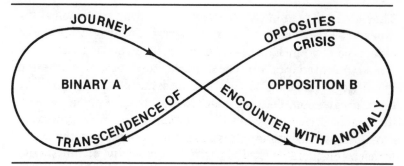

Figure 6.1 Journey Into a World of Anomalies

Mere awareness of the relative nature of reality, however, is not enlightenment. Nor is the view that everything is absolutely relative. It is, instead, another type of binary categorization, of seizing and clinging. It views the division between absolute and relative, the conditioned and the unconditioned, the divided and the undivided, and the permanent and the impermanent (Ramanan, 1966, p. 93).

Thus, not clinging to either absolute reality or relative reality is the "middle way," the way Buddah eventually took. The "middle way" is not a mere compromise position that avoids the two extremes. It is a way of seeing things as they are, recognizing the interdependent and complementary aspects of the seeming opposites. It is a dynamic perception of paradoxical relationship.

This paradoxical relationship is well expressed in the logic of "soku," which is characterized as a logic of "not-one, not-two." This logic emphasizes that the world is neither monistic nor dualistic (Nakayama, 1973, pp. 24-29). The world is viewed as a complementary interplay of categories as well as of noncategories. Enlightenment of "satori," means an understanding of the reality of betweenness that encompasses the mundane (cultural reality) and the ultimate (universal reality)—many and one. Satori is attained when binary opposites are transcended and meaningfully interconnected as the form of the Möbius strip.

CONCLUSION

Individuals who are in the double-swing state are able to accept and draw nourishment from their first as well as second culture.

They are in the realm of inbetweenness, having transcended the binary "we-they" perception of the world. The transcendence of binary perception is considered a key to achieving successful cross-cultural adaptation. The stages in cross-cultural adaptation identified in this chapter may not necessarily follow a straight, linear progression. The fifth stage, double-swing, is not necessarily the final or perfect stage at which one can arrive in the process of cross-cultural adaptation. It is an advanced stage, nonetheless, in which a considerable level of perceptual maturity, openness, and balance has been realized. This perceptual maturity may serve as a guiding light in the long and challenging journey of cross-cultural adaptation.

REFERENCES

Adler, P. (1975). *The boundary experience.* Unpublished doctoral dissertation, Union Graduate School, Yellow Spring, OH.

Buber, M. (1966). *The knowledge of man.* New York: Harper Torchbooks.

Finley, M. (1959). *The Greek historians.* New York: Viking.

Friedman, M. (1974). *Touchstones of reality.* New York: Dutton.

Frodsham, J. (Ed.). (1974). *The first Chinese embassy to the West.* New York: Oxford University Press.

Kuhn, T. (1970). *The structure of scientific revolutions.* Chicago: University of Chicago Press.

Lifton, R. (1969). *Thought reform and the psychology of totalism.* New York: Norton.

Nakamura, M. (1975). *Parallel developments.* Tokyo: Kodansha.

Nakayama, N. (1973). *Mujunteki, sosoku no ronri.* Kyoto: Hyakkaen.

Ramanan, K. (1966). *Nagarjuna's philosophy.* Rutland, VT: Charles E. Tuttle.

Rank, O. (1945). *Will therapy and truth and reality.* New York: Knopf.

Reisman, D., Glazer, N., and Denny, R. (1961). *The lonely crowd.* New Haven, CT: Yale University Press.

Thomas, W., and Znaniecki, F. (1958). *The Polish peasant in Europe and America.* New York: Dover.

II

CURRENT RESEARCH

7

The Psychological Adaptation of Soviet Immigrants in Australia

RONALD TAFT ● *Monash University, Melbourne, Australia*

When people are required to adjust to an unaccustomed sociocultural environment over an extended period, as for immigration, they need to learn new cultural repertoires and competencies. Adaptation to an unfamiliar culture requires changes in cognition, attitudes and behavior, in the absence of which culture shock and acculturative stress are likely. This chapter describes a schema for analyzing the facets of the adaptation process into: adjustment, national and ethnic identity, cultural competence, social absorption, and role acculturation, each of which has an internal and external aspect. These facets and their measurement are illustrated by some results from a study of Soviet immigrants in Australia.

In the course of everyday living, people constantly make adaptations to their environment, which is continually in a state of change between the relatively familiar and the quite unfamiliar. They adapt by using any of four strategies: reconstructing their perception of the environment, adapting their behavior to the demands of the environment, or changing the environment, either by reshaping it or by moving to a more congenial one. In the case of immigrants, each one of these strategies is employed; thus immigrants learn new repertoires, adapt their perceptions and behavior to their new situation, and choose immediate environments that are as appropriate as possible to their needs and competence. Immigrants often move into a new society, which, at the macro level, is radically different from their previous one, and the opportunities for reshaping the environment itself are usually quite limited; however, within the new society an immigrant can usually choose a subsociety—family, neighborhood, ethnic community—that is reasonably congenial. This chapter will outline in detail the conceptualization of the adaptation process in terms of five facets, and will illustrate this conceptualization outlining a study of recent immigrants from the Soviet Union in Australia.

CONCEPTUALIZATION OF ADAPTATION
TO NEW ENVIRONMENTS

Elsewhere I have argued (Taft, 1977, p. 121) that "adaptation to unfamiliar cultures is a special case of responding to a new environmental event, where that event is complex, enduring, and social in nature and where it has a cultural context that is unfamiliar to the actor." A wide range of situations fit this description, of which immigration is only one; some of these situations—immigration, foreign study, diplomatic service, tourism, business, anthropology, to take only some of the examples—involve the person in geographical locomotion as visitors, temporary sojourners, or settlers. There are other situations that may require profound cultural adaptation but do not involve locomotion, for example, social class mobility, marriage, entry into a new vocation; segregated residences such as old-age homes, armed services, hospital and so on; changes in society, such as the rapid crumbling of an indigenous culture, rapid modernization, revolution. Despite their obvious differences, all of these situations have common aspects owing to the initial unfamiliarity of the new culture and that the repertoires and strategies that people normally use to cope with their customary social environment are inadequate for meeting the demands of a new one. One other common feature of these situations is that, with habituation and the achievement of some degree of mastery, an unfamiliar environment can be quickly perceived as familiar. As Rheingold (1985, p. 2) has put it "Learning is a process of the new becoming familiar."

Cultural Learning

All of the unfamiliar situations described above require the person to learn and accept new behavioral norms, and to engage in social contacts with a new set of people, observing and learning new social cues and communicating information by means of unfamiliar signs, symbols and media. This learning may proceed simply by observation plus trial and error on the part of the learner, which is the customary laissez-faire circumstance in most of the situations described above, and a slow and hazardous way of learning in most cases. Sometimes the process can be eased by the presence of a "cultural mediator" (Bochner, 1981), who can act as a model or informant to assist the adapting person to cope with the unfamiliar culture.

The learning of a new culture involves some fairly substantial changes and developments with respect to three large categories of psychological functions (see Brislin, 1981; Taft, 1977)— cognition, dynamic tendencies, and performance. *Cognition* refers to the learning of such culturally defined aspects of behavior as ways of categorizing social observations (see Rosch, 1977) and the rules of social interaction (Kelvin, 1970). *Dynamic* refers to attitudes, goals and values, habits, traits, and expectations. *Performance* refers to role behavior, language and culturally relevant technical and social skills.

Initially, when faced with a gap between the demands of the situation and the resources that they have for coping, people are likely to suffer from feelings of confusion, deprivation, social importance and moral indignation—commonly referred to as "culture shock" when it is associated with a change of culture (Taft, 1977, pp. 139-143). In addition, the sheer effort of having to make substantial psychological changes in order to cope can, in itself, be stressful and the person may need to take steps to reduce the psychological pressure. For example, an immigrant may partially avoid contact with the larger society by withdrawal into the familiar ethnic group. Wherever possible, an immigrant will use existing repertoires of behavior provided this does not impede a reasonable level of successful coping.

Facets of Adaptation

Many studies of the adaptation of immigrants have included one index of integration (or "acculturation" or "assimilation") derived by adding together diverse indicators such as proficiency in English, adoption of citizenship, membership in social organizations, friendship with members of the host population, and so on. This can be misleading since the elements that make up such indices may vary independently of each other and may be determined by different factors; for example, an immigrant's proficiency in English may be the result of the amount of his or her education and may not have any relationship to assimilationist attitudes or behavior. The model of analysis that has been used in my own studies is a multifaceted one consisting of 1) socialemotional adjustment, and 2) four aspects of integration—national and ethnic identity, cultural competence, social absorption, and role acculturation. Each one of the five aspects is looked at from two viewpoints, internal (or "subjective") and external, which are distinguished according to the differences in the methods used to measure them. The internal side is reflected typically in self-judgment and consists of attitudes and perceptions (such as the answer to the question "Would you like to spend the rest of your life as a resident of Australia?"), while the external measures are derived from observable behavior or ratings of the immigrant by outsiders (for example, "How well does he or she speak English?" or "How well does he or she fit into the group?").

The remainder of this chapter will be an elaboration on this multifaceted structure of immigrant adaptation that will be illustrated by a description of a study of immigrants from the Soviet Union who had arrived recently in Australia. Since this study was psychologically oriented, the internal aspects of the immigrants' adaptation was emphasized over the external.

PROCEDURES

The Soviet Subjects[1]

In the years 1974 to 1982 approximately 3,000-4,000 Jews emigrated to Australia from the USSR; although technically they had Jewish nationality in the USSR, few of the older ones and none of the younger ones had any knowledge of Jewish history or traditions and with very few exceptions their normal language was Russian (rather than Yiddish). Almost all came from large cities, and most of the adults were well educated, over half having some post-secondary education. The reasons given by the respondents for their emigration reveal some of the circumstances leading up to it and provide hints as to what they may be seeking in their new country. Their answers to the question "What were your main reasons for emigrating?" provided the following distribution: *political* (including "freedom")—56%, *anti-semitism*—47%, *children's future*—34%, *economic reasons*—14%.

The sample for the study consisted of the entire cohort of families that arrived in Australia in the previous four years, were resident in Melbourne, and included at least one teenage child. This provided 154 adults (73 males and 81 females) and 101 adolescents (52 boys and 49 girls), representing 90 different families. The adults' median age was 44 and the adolescents' was 16. Three quarters of the latter were full-time students, and one quarter were attending a Jewish school full time. The data were gathered by (1) an interview schedule, (2) a battery of personality scales, (3) a semantic differential scale that included a set of concepts related to ethnic and self-identity and (4) the Rokeach Value Survey. The interviews and questionnaires were carefully translated and administered to the respondents in their home or school, in English or Russian, depending on their preference.

Structural Analysis of Adaptation Process

This study approached the adaptation process *functionally*, by looking at the history of the individual's aspirations, expectations, learning and coping strategies, and attitude changes, and *structurally* by analyzing the internal and external status of the immigrant with respect to the five aspects described at the beginning of this chapter. These aspects are set out in Table 7.1.

RESULTS AND DISCUSSION

Socioemotional Adjustment

Adjustment is defined, in terms of its positive pole, as the feeling of being in harmony with one's environment; this is a function of the degree to which the environment fulfills a person's needs and goals and it is reflected directly in feelings of satisfaction with various areas of life. It is a form of integration with the social environment, but, unlike the four facets delineated below, it does not necessarily involve any integration. It is often possible for immigrants to be well-adjusted, by living a full life encapsulated inside one's own ethnic community, with only a minimum of adaptation to the new society. In practice, however, good socioemotional adjustment of immigrants often proves to be a facilitator of movement toward integration with the larger

TABLE 7.1
Analysis of Adaptation of Immigrants

| | Perspective | |
Aspect	Internal	External
A. SOCIO-EMOTIONAL ADJUSTMENT		
	Feelings of satisfaction	Quality of life
	Sense of wellbeing	Mental health
	Emotional comfort	
B. SOCIAL AND PSYCHOLOGICAL INTEGRATION		
I. National and ethnic identity	Self-perceived identity	Citizenship
	Feeling of belonging	Overt social identity
	Ethnic reference group	
II. Cultural competence	Self-perceived competence	Language competence
	Feeling of mastery	Potential for role-performance
III. Social absorption	Favourable attitude to social relations with host group	Interpersonal contact with host group
	Perceived acceptance	Member in organizations
		Social acceptance
IV. Role acculturation	Language preference	Language use
	Attitude to conformity	Behavioral conformity

host society, although it may not necessarily involve at the same time a compensatory movement away from the ethnic community (Richardson, 1961; Taft, 1966).

On the *internal* side, adjustment is represented by expressed feelings of satisfaction, fulfillment, emotional comfort, and sense of well-being. These feelings may be specific to certain areas of life or they may be general. On the whole, studies of satisfaction with particular areas of life among immigrants tend to produce a cluster of highly intercorrelated measures, which suggests that a general satisfaction with life underlies the specific satisfactions. Table 7.1 sets out the findings for the satisfaction areas that were tapped in the study of Soviet parents; the areas chosen for the interviews with their children were similar, but they also included satisfaction with school. The last question, a comparison between satisfaction in the USSR and in Australia, was used as the measure of general satisfaction, although this also could have been measured more directly by a question such as "In general, how satisfied are you with your life in Australia?" The relationship between general and specific satisfactions differs among national groups and may provide an indication of the relative importance of an area to the particular group. For both the adults and the adolescents the highest correlation with general satisfaction was satisfaction (or dissatisfaction) with leisure time activities (0.53 and 0.38 respectively); this finding draws attention to an important but rarely considered aspect of immigrant adjustment—leisure.

External adjustment is reflected in two main ways: (1) the immigrant's participation in social life and the economy, for example, a job or business, membership in organizations, informal social relations, and (2) objective evidence of mental health or disturbance. Subjective satisfaction with aspects of life does not necessarily accord with objective measures of adjustment in those aspects; for example, those immigrants who have a "good" job may not be satisfied with it and, most important, immigrants who are grossly dissatisfied with their life my not show signs of mental disturbance. Unless these aspects are studied separately, a misleading impression may be built of an immigrant's adjustment. Most of the Soviet immigrants had jobs, but dissatisfaction with them was widespread, a not unusual reaction in well-educated refugees, no matter what their background.

In conclusion, let me quote the following description of the interplay between experience and feelings of satisfaction in another group of refugees—Hungarians. "Satisfaction is largely a matter of expectations and aspiration levels; . . . as a short-term perspective gives way to a long-term one, the importance of apparent progress toward ultimate goals increases. On arrival in Australia the refugees mostly felt that they had been granted a breathing spell to reconsider their future aims and aspirations. . . . Whether they considered that Australia would or would not provide such satisfaction was determined by their experience in the first few years after immigration in what could be called a testing period. . . . After the initial period, which had been dominated by a 'sanctuary' mentality, the usual middle-class aspirations for status started to take over" (Taft & Doczy, 1962, p. 32).

TABLE 7.2
Parent's Degree of Satisfaction (percentages)

How satisfied are you with:	Very satisfied[1]	Fairly satisfied	Dissatisfied[1]
Your general standard of living in Melbourne	31.8	54.5	13.6
Your present work	22.7	33.8	43.3
Your housing	35.0	53.9	11.0
Educational prospects of your children	50.7	34.2	15.1
Your children's educational progress	36.4	43.0	20.6
The future for your children in Australia	44.1	48.1	7.7
Number of friends you have here	26.6	40.9	32.5
Health facilities	32.5	54.5	12.9
Leisure time activities	22.0	40.9	37.0
Compared to your life in the U.S.S.R. how satisfied are you with life here?	48.7	39.0	12.3

Note: For simplicity, the "Completely" and "Very" satisfied categories and the "A Little" and "Very" Dissatisfied have been combined.

Social and Psychological Integration

The four facets described below are all relevant to the integration of an immigrant into a new society. For simplicity, the model has been devised to deal with the situation where the immigrant, coming from an alien cultural background, has entered a nation in which there is a predominant ("host") culture with which the immigrant has to come to terms. Brislin (1981) has drawn a distinction between adjustment to a culturally monistic society and adjustment to a pluralistic one and the model set out here is more readily applicable to the former than to the latter, although it can easily fit the former.

National and ethnic identity. Social identity has been defined by Tajfel as "That part of the individuals' self-concept that derives from their knowledge of their membership of a social group (or groups) together with the values and emotional significance attached to that membership" (1981, p. 255). The internal aspect of ethnic identity involves a sense of belonging to, and of sharing the "fate" of the ethnic group, a feeling of pride, shame, depression and so on, according to the situation of the group.

Social identity is complex and multiple and a person's identification with any of his or her several identities may vary in salience according to the context at the time. Thus, immigrants to Australia may in their work context feel their Australian identity preeminently, while at an ethnic music festival they may feel their ethnic identity more strongly. The national and ethnic identity of the Soviet-Jewish immigrants has the additional complication that the USSR consists of multiple official nationalities, of which Jews are one, but they come from a variety of Soviet regions (for example, Ukraine, White Russia, Georgia, or Russia), and may have multiple loyalties as a result. Furthermore, in Australia they tend to be viewed as "Russians" rather than Jews, since the latter identity is regarded more as a religion than as a nationality.

Because of the complicated background to their ethnicity, our studies of the identity of the Soviet immigrants included measures of their identification with Australian and Soviet nationality and with various facets of Jewishness. Two types of measures were used: (1) structured interview questions and (2) a semantic differential scale. In the interview the respondents were asked to rate the degree to which they "feel themselves to be Australian;" the degree to which they "feel at home in Australia;" and the degree to which they had previously "felt at home in the USSR." On the first question, 25% of the adolescents and 9% of the adults claimed to feel themselves to be "very strongly" Australian, while 33% and 38%, respectively, were "not at all" Australian. These figures represent a rapid change in claimed identification for many of the immigrants, especially when we noted that there were no differences between those who had very recently arrived (0-2 years) and the longer-term residents (3-4 years). Youth was a factor in the immigrants' flexibility; the adolescents had higher identification with Australia than did their parents and younger adolescents (12-15 years old) had higher identification than did the older ones (16-19). These results suggest that the reported identification feelings have some construct validity even though they are probably somewhat superficial and easily subject to contextual influences. Confirmation of the above findings was obtained on the question about "feeling at home" in Australia; the typical respondent described him/herself as feeling "fairly much" so, whereas they typically described themselves as having been "not much" at home in the USSR, especially the adolescents. This, of course, is not unexpected in people who have decided to emigrate from their home country because they found life there unpleasant.

One question that has been used as a standard marker in many of the Australian studies of immigrants is "Apart from possible holidays abroad, would you like to spend the rest of your life in Australia?" This question may well be the best single measure of integration because it combines satisfaction with identification and commitment, but the answers are usually dictated by much more than national identity considerations (for example, family reasons, age, impossibility of returning home). Of the Soviet parents, 72% answered "Yes" versus 3% "No;" of the adolescents, the figures were 46% versus 27%, respectively.

Respondents were also asked in the interview to rate the "importance" to them of various aspects of Jewish identity: the Jewish community, friends, the Yiddish language, Israel, religion, emotional participation, the continued maintenance of Jewish identity. With the exception of religion and community, the respondents' identification with their Jewish ethnicity was rather high, especially when it is considered that they were the emigrants from the USSR who elected not to settle in Israel.

The second method of studying ethnic identity, the semantic differential, provided an opportunity to make some more accurate comparisons among the attitudes toward the different ethnic and national concepts. The respondents were asked to rate a number of characteristics using the following concepts: *Myself, Australians, Russians, Jews, Australia, USSR, Israel.* These ratings provided a score on "positive evaluation" of each concept on which they could be compared with one another and with the concept of self. The respondents' positive identification with Australia reported above was confirmed by the fact, for example, that they rated *Myself* more similarly to *Australians* than they did to *Russians* or *Jews*. The semantic differential can produce complicated cognitive patterns that give structure to the internal aspect of identity and its relationship to self-esteem.

Thus a clear picture emerges of immigrants who were not comfortable in their country of origin and who, soon after arrival, declared themselves to be reasonably satisfied with most aspects of their new country and many of whom, especially the younger ones, already are starting to settle in and to change their self-concept with respect to the two countries. The impact of this change is reduced by the possibility for them to retain continuity in their ethnic identity through their Jewishness, which had some common features in both the USSR and Australia.

The external side of identity refers to such observable social characteristics as the immigrant's choice of citizenship and the ethnicity that is attributed to them by others. The first is partly dependent on legal factors such as length of residence, while the second is seldom measured because of the difficulty in doing so, although in some studies the interviewer has made a rating of the ethnic appearance of the respondents. External identity was not measured in the study of Soviet immigrants.

Cultural competence. The ability to perform the necessary skills in order to adapt to a culture is a prerequisite for satisfactory adjustment. Every culture involves a set of technical, social, and above all linguistic competencies that are required for the performance of appropriate role behavior. Acculturation may be represented as the acquisition of the appropriate cultural skills; for instance, the required language, historical knowledge, ability to earn one's living, relevant sporting skills, knowledge of the etiquette of social relations, the recognition of social roles, and so on (Taft, 1977). Clearly cultural competence can best be defined in terms of its external manifestations, and some of the studies of immigrants in Australia (for example, Johnston, 1965; Richardson, 1974; Scott & Stumpf, 1984) have used simple tests of language and other culturally relevant competence, and ratings of various aspects of competence made by observers and informants.

In the Soviet study, no external assessment was made of competence, but the respondents were asked to rate themselves. There is some evidence that self-perceptions of competence in English are not necessarily unrealistic; for example, in a working-class sample of Dutch males in Australia, ratings of quality of spoken English by the respondents correlated 0.70 with those made by the interviewer (Taft, 1966, p. 29). According to the self-ratings of the Soviet respondents, 46% of the adolescents spoke English "quite well" at the time of the interviews, compared with only 6% of their parents; there were similar discrepancies in the ratings of ability to read and write English, presumably due to the combined effect of age and schooling in English. There were marked differences in competence in English between the more recent (0-2 years) and the less recent (3-5 years) immigrants for both adults and adolescents.

The acquisition of the predominant language and other culturally relevant skills is dependent on the personal characteristics of an immigrant and on the opportunities to learn. The latter is reflected in the degree of informal and formal contact with the host group (especially in the person of a spouse, children, or a close friend) and of formal schooling in childhood and of special tuition of the adults. Other personal characteristics related to the acquisition of cultural competence are: age (young), experience with other (third) cultures and languages, amount of relevant cultural competence possessed at the time of arrival, and level of general education. Relevant psychological characteristics are: motivation to learn, intellectual and linguistic aptitude, and such traits as emotional stability, low dogmatism, and having trust in people. (These characteristics, which are found in the results of various empirical studies of immigrants, are summarized in Taft, 1981 and Taft, 1985). In the study of the Soviet immigrants various tests of competence were used (in Russian translation), and it was found to be related to intelligence, education, trust in people, low dogmatism, and greater "personal efficacy" (the test used for the latter was the "personal competence" scale of Campbell, Converse, Miller & Stokes, 1960). "Thus a person whose general personality functioning in his own culture is competent also seems to be more capable of adapting to another one" (Taft, 1981, p. 81).

Social absorption. The establishment of social contacts with the host population has been shown in several studies in Australia to be related positively to all other aspects of adjustment and integration—although it is not a necessary corollary that the maintenance of relations with members of the original ethnic group is negatively related (Taft, 1966). "Social participation with Australians is highly correlated with acculturation; there is probably a mutual interaction effect between these two variables, but social participation seems to lead to acculturation more often than it does the reverse" (Taft, 1966, p. 69). A minimal degree of cultural competence, specifically of the ability to speak the language, is a prerequisite for social interaction with the host group; however, our studies in Australia indicate that being accepted socially stimulates the learning of English as much as the knowledge of English stimulates social relations.

The relevant social interactions may vary greatly in intensity and intimacy; they may range from casual contacts and token membership of nonethnic associations to close friendships and marriage. Since the main determinants of the acquisition of cultural competence are the amount of cultural contact and the opportunity to obtain tuition and guidance in the new culture, intimate contacts through friendship and marriage have been found to be related substantially to other measures of integration (Taft, 1985). The Soviet immigrants were, by definition, either young and unmarried or they were married to other Soviet immigrants. Despite their recent arrival, some of them already had been on reciprocal visiting terms with nonimmigrant Australians and as many as 30% of the adolescents and 20% of the adults claim to have "personal friends" in Australia who were not fellow Russians or other Jews.

An important *external* index of social absorption is the degree to which immigrants are acceptable to formal organizations and informal social groups that are dominated by the majority. This can be ascertained by measures such as social surveys of general ethnic attitudes or sociometric studies of groups such as school classes and work groups to which immigrants belong. The latter method has been used in some studies of immigrant children (for example, Doczy, 1966; Ross, 1977; Taft & Cahill, 1978), but it is difficult to apply to adults and it was not used in the Soviet immigrant study.

On the basis of several studies of immigrant adaptation, the conclusion was reached that perceived acceptance, or at least the perception that they are not rejected, is more significant for the adjustment and integration of immigrants than is actual acceptance (Taft, 1966). In the case of recent, non-English speaking immigrants, such as the Soviet subjects, the internal aspect of social relations, better described as social relations attitudes and intentions, also provides a more meaningful variable than does the external, but, as has already been pointed out, there is some difficulty in interpreting the responses of the Soviet subjects because of their involvement in three paramount ethnonational groups: Russians, Jews, and Australians. Both the adults and adolescents expressed a strong desire to mix with Australians as well as Russians, and 61% of the adults considered that it was important for them to have Jewish friends while the figure for the adolescents was 41%. The semantic differential results, quoted in Table 7.3, show that both the adults and the adolescents evaluate "Australians" more highly than "Jews," and both of these are higher than "Russians."

Role acculturation. This refers to changes in culturally relevant behavior brought about by contact with the new society as well as the adoption of the attitudes, beliefs, and values of the host group. Whereas cultural competence refers to the *potential* for acculturation, role acculturation implies *actual* convergence to the behavior and attitudes that the society regards as appropriate to the roles assumed by the newcomer. This is essentially defined in terms of the external viewpoint. An immigrant who is fully acculturated would be so changed with respect to such behavioral products as dress, eating habits, home decoration, and spoken language that their external identity would be perceived as a member of the dominant group. This is probably a rare occurrence in persons who emigrate as adults. One objective method used to study acculturation has been a specially developed scale of "Australianism," in which an immigrant's responses to opinion items are compared to those of modal Australian and European immigrant respondents (Taft & Putnins, 1976). Similarly, Richardson (1961) developed an Australian Slang test that is sensitive to language acculutration even in those who already know standard English. As a measure of external acculturation, the Soviet subjects were administered a Russian version of the Rokeach Value Survey on which their responses varied notably from comparative Australian ones (Taft & Steinkalk, 1982).

The internal side of role acculturation is attitudinal rather than behavioral and is not necessarily reflected in changes in behavior. In the Soviet study the respondents were interviewed on their general and specific attitudes toward acculturation, including their desire to learn about Australian history and customs, and

TABLE 7.3
Soviet Immigrants
Evaluation of Concepts on Semantic Differential Scale
(Maximum possible score = 56; Minimum score = 8)

Concept	Parents (n = 154)	Adolescents (n = 101)	Significance of Difference (t test)
Myself	44.3	42.8	.08
Jews	38.9	36.9	.07
Australians	42.3	38.4	N.S.
Russians	34.7	36.3	N.S.
Israel	42.4	40.7	N.S.
Australia	45.2	42.5	.01
USSR	22.1	28.6	.01

their preferences in sport, food, and the use of the Russian or English language. The results for the latter, set out in Table 7.3, indicate that already there has been a strong transfer from a preference for speaking Russian to a preference for English in the adolescents, but not in their parents. The transfer is considerably greater with respect to written language than spoken, and even a third of the parents stated that they preferred to read in English over Russian, presumably in order to learn the language in view of the much greater instrumental need for English. The adults with more education (more then 10 years versus less) expressed a greater desire to learn English and other aspects of the "Australian way of life." A rapid change to a preference for speaking English among the adolescents is typically found in studies of immigrant school children in Australia and, in fact, the Soviet adolescents are more reluctant to change from Russian to English than are those of most other nationalities. Another interesting finding was that the preference for speaking English did not increase with time in either the parents or the adolescents, but it must be remembered that they were all comparatively recent immigrants.

CONCLUSION

This concludes the sketchy account of a particular example of a study of a very complex social phenomenon - the movement of people, in this case Soviet immigrants, from a familiar sociocultural environment to a relatively unfamiliar one and the consequential adaptation process. While there are several clear-cut findings from the study of defined immigrant groups, such as the Soviet immigrants in Australia, few federal principles about adaptation that can be applied with any confidence to immigrants without respect to their background and their circumstances can be derived at this stage from the findings, although there are some that relate to the characteristics of the immigrants and the support that they are given in the host community. We are still developing an understanding of some of the psychological processes involved and of working out a framework for analysis together with methods of measuring the dependent variables. This chapter has demonstrated some of the possible directions in which future research might go.

A satisfactory approach to the study of this topic requires the combined resources of a number of social sciences; the obvious ones are demography, history, sociology, education, as well as social psychology. Communication experts should have much to contribute in view of the important role of language, interpersonal relations, education, and communication through the media in the adaptation of immigrants (Argyle, 1982). Unfortunately, it is rare in studies of immigrant groups for representatives of two or more of these social science disciplines to cooperate. The understanding of the process of immigrant adaptation still has a long way to go and it may be enhanced by interdisciplinary cooperation if the researchers can agree on their conceptual framework. The multifaceted schema presented in this chapter represents a modest attempt to provide such a framework for one portion of the topic, that which lends itself to a psychological approach.

NOTE

1. The research on which this report is based was carried out by the late Elka Steinkalk at Monash University in 1978 under the supervision of the author (Steinkalk, 1983).

REFERENCES

Argyle, M. (1982). Inter-cultural communication. In S. Bochner (Ed.), *Cultures in contact: Studies in cross-cultural interaction.* Oxford: Pergamon.

Bochner, S. (Ed.), (1981). *The mediating person: Bridges between cultures.* Cambridge: Shenkman.

Bochner, S. (Ed.), (1982). *Cultures in contact: Studies in cross-cultural interactions.* Oxford: Pergamon.

Brislin, R. W. (1981). *Cross-cultural encounters: Face-to-face interaction.* Elmsford, NY: Pergamon.

Campbell, A., Converse, P. E., Miller, W. E., & Stokes, D. E. (1960). *The American Voter.* New York: Wiley.

Doczy, A. G. (1966). *The social assimilation of adolescent boys of European parentage in the metropolitan area of western Australia.* Unpublished doctoral dissertation, University of Western Australia, Perth.

Johnston, R. (1965). *Immigrant assimilation.* Perth, Western Australia: Paterson Brokensha.

Kelvin, P. (1970). *The bases of social behavior.* London: Holt, Rinehart & Winston.

Rheingold, H. L. (1985). Development as the acquisition of familiarity. *Annual Review of Psychology, 36,* 1-17.

Richardson, A. (1961). The assimilation of British immigrants in a Western Australian community: A psychological study. *Research Group for European Migration Problems (REMP), 9,* 1-75.

Richardson, A. (1974). *British immigrants and Australia: A psycho-social inquiry.* Canberra: Australian National University Press.

Rosch, E. (1977). Human categorization. In M. Warren (Ed.), *Studies in cross-cultural psychology* (Vol. 1), London: Academic Press.

Ross, U. (1977). *The integration of immigrant children in the school.* Unpublished master's thesis, Monash University, Melbourne, Australia.

Scott, W. A., & Stumpf, J. (1984). Personal satisfaction and role performance: Subjective and social aspects of adaptation. *Journal of Personality and Social Psychology, 47,* 812-827.

Steinkalk, E. (1983). *The adaptation of Soviet Jews in Victoria: A study of adolescent immigrants and their parents.* Unpublished doctoral dissertation, Monash University, Melbourne, Australia.

Taft, R. (1966). *From stranger to citizen.* London: Tavistock.

Taft, R. (1977). Coping with unfamiliar cultures. In N. Warren (Ed.), *Studies in cross-cultural psychology* (Vol. 1). London: Academic Press.

Taft, R. (1981). The role and personality of the mediator. In S. Bochner (Ed), *The mediating person: Bridges between cultures.* Boston: G. K. Hall.

Taft, R. (1985). The psychological study of the adjustment and adaptation of immigrants in Australia. In N. T. Feather (Ed.), *Survey of Australian Psychology: Trends in research.* Sydney: Allen & Unwin.

Taft, R., & Cahill, D. (1978). Education of immigrants in Australia. In J. Bhatnager (Ed), *Educating immigrants.* London: Croom Helm.

Taft, R., & Doczy, A. G. (1962). *The assimilation of intellectual refugees in Western Australia.* The Hague: Research Group for European Migration Problems.

Taft, R., & Putnins, A. L. (1976). The Australianism scale revisited: A review of recent data. *The Australian Psychologist, 11,* 147-151.

Taft, R., & Steinkalk, E. (1982). The values of Soviet Jewish immigrants in Australia. In R. Rath, H. S. Asthana, D. Sinha, & J.B.H. Sinha (Eds.), *Diversity and unity in cross-cultural psychology*. Amsterdam: Swets & Zeitlinger.

Tajfel, H. (1981). *Human categories*. Cambridge: Cambridge University Press.

8

Culture Barriers as a Social Psychological Construct
An Empirical Validation

INGEMAR TORBIÖRN ● *University of Stockholm*

A culture barrier has been defined as a bicultural and monodirectional reactional phenomenon, reflecting psychological limitations in the ability or willingness to understand, accept, or adopt the norms of a foreign culture. Through the aggregation of information on individual reactions to the country level, constellations of own culture versus foreign culture were established for Swedish expatriates in 26 countries. A cluster-analysis produced groupings of countries grossly in line with requirements of the culture-barrier hypothesis; that is, countries similar in objective dimensions of culture and cluster profiles tending to differ in the hypothesized direction across reactional domains were isolated. Results were interpreted in support of the theory, although need of more refined criteria to portray several cultures objectively was stated.

The purpose of this chapter is to clarify theoretically the concept of culture barrier as a psychological construct, and to offer some empirical validation of cultural barriers as a psychological phenomenon. Generally, cultural barriers refer to individual reactions in situations of cross-cultural contact where cultural differences negatively affect an individuals' ability, willingness to understand, accept, adhere to, or adopt the norms of a foreign culture.

Empirical evidence of barriers arising from cultural differences, cultural distance, and so on, is ample. However, as Church (1982) points out in a thorough review of sojourn literature, most of the studies relate reactions by persons of various cultural backgrounds to a single host culture. From the point of view adopted here, these studies discuss cultural barriers in a sociological rather than a psychological sense owing to lack of control of the "psyche," that is, the cultural background of subjects. Church (1982, p. 560) holds that "There is a notable absence of studies that compare adjustment of sojourns of a given nationality in different host cultures."

Problems in intercultural communication are often described as resulting from culture barriers. Since cultural differences are often conspicuous in situations of international contact, they may be taken at face value for causes of various outcomes of such situations, when, in fact, behaviors or reactions do not depend on the cultural backgrounds of the persons involved. The causes may be found instead among strictly personal or situation-specific factors that are not representative of the culture of any part involved (Brislin, 1981; Pedersen & Pedersen, 1985).

This chapter attempts to demonstrate the relevance of culture alone as a mediator of reactions that may express cultural barriers. Furthermore, this chapter assumes that international communication does not necessarily involve two or more persons, but does involve at least one person, and that culture barriers manifest themselves in the reactions of this individual to persons, objects, or conditions representing a different culture, that is, the reactions are mediated through psychological mechanisms.

OBJECTIVE AND INTERNALIZED CULTURE

Culture, in an "objective," sociological sense, can be defined as a set of norms, according to which things are run, or simply "are" in a particular society or country, and to which most members of the society adhere in values, attitudes interpretations, and behaviors. Such a definition purposely is wide and vague, but should contain the essence of the concept of culture as it is outlined by several writers (for example, Hofstede, 1980; Kluck-hohn, 1951; Triandis, 1972) and it should be sufficient for linking the "objective" side of culture to a subjective side in terms of widely used psychological concepts. If one is well adjusted to one's own culture, one should have internalized many cultural norms into the frame of reference; that is, one conceives of these norms as representing what is normal in the sense of being usual, rational, logical, understandable, appropriate, preferable, and so on. In other words, any individual shows a considerable degree of overlap between, on the one hand, elements in the frame of reference (represented by values, attitudes, cognitive structures and norms for behaviors and interpretations) and, on the other hand, those norms that constitute their own culture (Grove & Torbiörn, 1985). This does not mean that people are exclusively the products of their cultures, as these latter will not provide "cultural norms" for every situation an individual faces. Even in contexts where cultural norms exist, a person might in many instances apply other norms, for example, of some specific ethnic group or of some organization, or adhere to strictly personal, individual norms.

Any two national cultures will differ to some extent. This could be stated in terms of similarity or the degree of overlap within the sets of norms defining each culture. Such differences or similarities among cultures may be described roughly along single dimensions or aspects of several cultures, for example, in terms of aggregate structural characteristics such as GNP per capita, or a common or similar history, location, climate, and so on. As soon as behavioral matters so central to the concept of culture are involved, however, differences or similarities among cultures, although easy to observe and describe, are difficult to interpret one-dimensionally, especially for multicultural comparisons. This traditional dilemma of cross-cultural research is implied in the behavioral or psychological component in the phenomenon of culture. This is so because objective culture, as internalized by people, affects psychological processes and reactions.

Thus two people socialized to different cultures may react to a situation differently because of differences in internalized conceptions of the content of the situation, of what is normal, what is appropriate, and so on. Although this creates problems for cross-cultural research, it may also help to clarify the psychological role of culture in international communication, as it implies that an individual will react to the same or corresponding situation in two or several foreign cultures differently on the understanding that the latter also differ. This should apply insofar as one's own culture prescribes the meaning of what is normal in the situation at hand, but it can be tested empirically only if the difference among the three or more cultures involved are assessed in terms of objective culture.

CULTURE BARRIERS IN
INTERCULTURAL COMMUNICATION

A situation of intercultural communication in this context does not denote person-to-person relations in particular, but person-environment relations in general. Furthermore, reactions on the part of an individual are not restricted to behavior alone but include evaluative interpretations and the formation of private opinions regarding various aspects of the environment. Also, culture is only one of the factors that may affect reactions and outcomes of intercultural situations. If personal or situation-specific factors are the sole determinants of reactions, the situation would still be intercultural, although cultural factors are irrelevant to the outcomes. In other instances, reactions result from interactions between situation-specific, or personal factors, and cultural aspects of situations.

This chapter deals with the somewhat more clear-cut case, where cultural background, through a person's frame of reference, interacts with cultural aspects of the situation. In the latter instance the reaction of the individual shall be termed culture-dependent. This broad term covers but does not necessarily imply the presence of a cultural barrier, as the latter construct presupposes certain characteristics regarding the direction and strength of reactions.

Cultural barriers as used here should be reflected through an individual's reaction to a foreign culture and in terms of reactions representing negative evaluations rather than positive evaluations, dislike rather than like, avoidance rather than approach, and so on. This should be so because aspects of the new culture deviate from the norms of evaluative standards to which the individual is acculturated (LeVine & Campbell, 1972; Ehrenhaus, 1983). Thus aspects of the other culture may appear as less normal, less familiar, less good, and so on, whereby reactions tending to the negative are more "logical" than positive reactions. This is not owing to aversion or hostility versus the other culture, nor is it necessarily an expression of pronounced ethnocentrism. It is rather, as LeVine and Campbell (1972, p. 14) put it, the effect of a more general "naive phenomenal absolutism."

In addition to a direction of reactions, a cultural barrier, in order to be "cultural," requires that the degree to which the reactions occur should be more pronounced the more different two cultures are; that is, the most dissimilar, foreign, strange, a situation appears, the more negative the attitudes, the stronger the tendencies to avoid or withdraw from the situation. Such a monodirectional and monotonous relation between reactions and perceived cultural differences is consistent with a number of sociopsychological theories (for example, Rokeach, 1960; LeVine & Campbell, 1972; Brewer & Campbell, 1976; Ellingsworth, 1983).

The above theoretical picture also suggests that culture barriers are nonreciprocal. Thus in a psychological meaning, the concept can be applied only to the relation between two specified cultures or groups of cultures, and this can be done in only one direction as defined from a focal person to a foreign culture. A cultural barrier between countries A and B need not be so high as that between B and A. The relevant situational context might affect values, opinions, and cultural commitments that differ in centrality to members of cultures A and B. The content of the situation may be interpreted or attributed differently, may be associated with different reactional aspects among members of A and B, and so on (Altman & Chemers, 1980; Detweiler, 1978). That cultural barriers are nonreciprocal does not exclude the possibility that the barrier on the part of A versus B reflects the reaction of B upon A.

As the concept of culture barrier is defined here in terms of the individual's reaction upon some specific aspect of the foreign culture, a barrier should not be manifested uniformly or to the same extent across the whole range of possible reactions. A cultural barrier may thus appear "lower" in regard to strictly psychological reactions, for example, of an attitudinal nature, than in regard to overt behaviors. Furthermore, the notion of centrality suggests that any cultural difference, large or small, may constitute a high or even "absolute" barrier if it touches on a fundamental and central aspect of the individual's own culture and of the individual as a member of that culture. Thus it seems that the concept of cultural barrier needs specification not only as to which aspect of another culture confronts the individual, but also as to how central that aspect is to the individual and which type or level of reaction is called for by the situation.

Finally, a cultural barrier also concerns an individual's reaction to a cultural difference as perceived at a particular moment. Both cultures and an individual's perception (of what is normal, appropriate, and so on) change, although the past in many instances remains present in both culture and individual (Berry, 1980; Triandis, 1980a). For a person who is engaged in a certain intercultural experience the barrier will tend to become "lower" as time passes (Torbiörn, 1982).

METHOD

As the psychological meaning of cultural barriers seems to be rather complex, the present chapter aims only at an approximate empirical validation of the construct. This requires three things: information on reactions in situations of intercultural contact, information about objective cultures, and a method to relate the two types of information to each other. These three components should also be used in a way that satisfies assumptions regarding cross-cultural equivalence; for example, as laid out by Hui and Triandis (1985).

Reactional Information

In this study, information about reactions to foreign cultures is based on mail questionnaires in the Swedish language completed by 1,115 Swedes (641 men and 474 women married to the male respondents) who were assigned to long-term duty abroad for Swedish companies in 1972. Data on attitudes, feelings, behaviors, and adjustment in various respects that relate to host and home cultures have been analyzed at the level of individuals (Torbiörn, 1982) and are further analyzed here, using cultures or countries as the unit of analysis. Attitudinal scores used in the analysis are averages for 26 countries or groups of countries. Percentages of the respondents in each country engaging in various host-country related activities are used as criteria of behaviors. This is done to eliminate within-group variance from the analysis, that is, possible effects from person- or situation-specific factors, and to achieve scores as representative as possible of reactions from people with a certain cultural background to conditions in a given host culture. It should be remembered, however, that the original answers to the questionnaire items are about the respondents' personal conditions as they related to the host culture and not statements about the culture per se. Evidence of cultural barriers will thus be sought in reactional information from persons with, as far as culture is concerned, a common background, but who live in a variety of foreign cultures.

As noted at the outset, such an approach should favor the validation of the psychological meaning of culture barriers as the alternative. Studying people from various cultures in regard to reactions to one single host culture should be of less cross-cultural equivalence owing to differences in centrality, perceptions, attributions, and interpretations.

Classification of Cultures

In attempting to classify cultures in objective terms, the task is one of relating several cultures to each other along one dimension at a time, and of ordering the cultures from greatest to smallest similarity. For the 26 countries or groups of countries included in the present study, this can be achieved only by using highly general or aggregate descriptive dimensions. On the one hand, there is the problem that broad and general aspects of cultures describe very imprecisely the situations facing sojourners. On the other hand, a few basic aspects of culture may have great impact upon norms and ways of living and be manifest in multifarious ways in those situations without this being explicitly recognized. This study shall consider three such dimensions: religion, language, and technological level.

Religion here includes not only the actual dogma of a particular faith, but also the general manifestations of a particular fundamental religious view that pervades society, as well as the living patterns and general outlook and mentality of its members. Similarly, by language is meant more than the purely technical code of communication, including nonverbal codes and other features of thought and behavior patterns that stem from the structure and expressive modes of particular language. Technological level refers to conditions of societal infrastructure as reflected in rough criteria of material welfare such as per capita GNP or gross electricity consumption per capita. Concerning religion and language, classifications are based on those predominating or official in the several countries. Some descriptions, therefore, are rather approximate. Technological levels were assessed through the UN Statistical Yearbook as broad descriptive dimensions. Rankings of countries use averages as weighted according to each countries population in those instances where several countries are grouped together as units of analysis (Torbiörn, 1982).

The basis of the rankings along the above dimensions should be the conditions of the respondents background culture: Sweden. From the statement that Sweden is a Christian, Protestant, highly industrialized culture with an Indo-European, Germanic language, the following conclusions regarding relations or rankings of other cultures can be drawn:

(1) Regarding religion, the closest kinship is with other Protestant countries, and after that with other Christian (in this case Catholic) countries. There is least kinship with countries whose culture is dominated by non-Christian religions such as Islam, Hinduism, Buddhism, and so on, which cannot be ranked among themselves according to their "kinship" with Christianity.

(2) Linguistic kinship is greatest with other Germanic languages. Among these, English can perhaps be ranked above German, since this is the first language taught in Swedish schools and the one that Swedes know best. The Germanic languages are followed by other Indo-European languages, in this case the Romance languages, which again, cannot be ranked among themselves. Last come countries with non-Indo-European languages.

(3) Regarding the level of technological development, Sweden, being among the top nations with the criteria used, could be easily classified in relation to the other cultures from UN statistics.

Classifications by similarity or cultural kinship along these crude dimensions could be made only at an ordinal level; even so classifications offer few categories and, consequently, several ties when many countries are rank ordered. This problem, as well as the problem of high intercorrelations between ranks along the three cultural dimensions, will remain unsolved until more refined criteria for the objective ranking of several cultures are applied. The dimensions and criteria used thus lack a certain explanatory potential, although they should match the present purpose of merely establishing cultural barriers as a phenomenon.

Relating Objective Culture to Reactions

Although cultural barriers possibly could be due to interaction from cultural differences in several dimensions, the analysis will try to establish the phenomenon as accounted for by single cultural dimensions. The theoretical model assumes that the individual's reaction reflects the difference between background culture and host culture. A test of the model in regard to the extent of the reaction thus requires comparisons including more than one culture foreign to the individual. The more cultures involved, the more reliable and valid, for explanatory purposes, will be the evidence extracted from comparisons. Although the concept of culture barrier is defined biculturally, multicultural comparisons should, as a first step, help to determine whether reactions are culture dependent along the lines of the theoretical discussion above. A criterion of whether this is the case would be the rank correlation between reactional information at country level and rankings of countries as objectively classified in terms of similarity or kinship with Sweden. (Kendall's rank correlation will be used here as more appropriate when rankings contain several ties.)

It is important to note that a high rank correlation in this context indicates only the degree to which reactions may be culture dependent. Such dependency is a prerequisite for a barrier in that it tells that culture plays a role for the individual's reaction. A high rank correlation, however, implies only that the directional requirement from the theory is met. Whether a barrier is high or low depends instead on the character, degree, or strength of the reaction itself, for example, as inferred from the level, value, or position on the scale used for measuring the reaction. It follows that statements about differences in height on one culture's barriers toward two or more foreign cultures require that reactions are at distinct or different scale levels for the cultures compared, and so in the direction prescribed by the theory.

The first step of analysis will thus be to identify, by means of rank correlations, reactional aspects that are culture dependent along single dimensions of objective culture. Secondly, variables will be grouped together by a factor analysis as representing more general reactional domains. In order to isolate such domains the third step shall try to identify differences among groups of countries in regard to the reactional items selected for each domain. Such differences should reflect escalations in culture barriers between the respondents' home culture and various host cultures if the latter differ from each other in a manner consistent across the item profile of a reactional domain and if the differences are in accordance with the directional assumptions.

In order to test such a hypothesis, one could inspect the profiles of a priori designed groupings of countries being culturally similar or related, a principle that was in fact applied in step one of the analysis. One could also use cluster analysis, which is more mechanistic, but in regard to the culture barrier hypothesis, a more impartial method. Hypothetically, the groupings of cultures resulting from such an analysis should be culturally homogeneous in regard to the objective dimension associated most strongly with the reactional domain under study. Cluster analysis shall be performed here according to Ward's (1963) hierarchical method, as recommended by Griffeth, Hom, DeNisi, and Kirchner (1985).

RESULTS

Culture-Dependent Reactions

Table 8.1 gives the results from steps one and two of the analysis. Regarding culture dependency, most of the host culture related variables are associated significantly with all of the objective cultural dimensions, although more strongly to either the religion-language aspects (which give almost identical rankings of countries) or to the criteria of technological level, (which are also correlated strongly among themselves).

Variables dealing with reactions that reflect the individuals' relation less directly to the host culture show low rank correlations, that is, are not culture dependent in regard to the objective dimensions of Table 8.1. This holds for the items on family solidarity, perceived social isolation, and housing and material

TABLE 8.1

Correlations Between Rankings of Reactional Data at Country Level and Cultural Kinship
in Objective Dimensions (Kendalls r; p < .01 for r = .33), and Variable Groups from Factor Analysis

Reactional Domains	Cultural Dimensions		Technological Level	
= Items	Religion	Language	GNP per capita	Electricity Consumption per capita
= Items				
Social contact (Factor 1)				
= knowledge of host country language (men)	.60	.62	.35	.42
= knowledge of host country language (women)	.57	.58	.33	.38
= knowledge of news and topical events (men)	.54	.53	.43	.42
= knowledge of news and topical events (women)	.57	.55	.42	.42
= host country companionship groups	.78	.73	.55	.60
= professional skills of host country colleagues	.38	.31	.44	.44
= feeling as "ambassador" of home country	.32	.28	.08	.11
Societal comfort (Factor 2)				
= orderliness, safety in public places (men)	.29	.30	.44	.40
= orderliness, safety in public places (women)	.40	.39	.56	.52
= communications, transports	.35	.36	.45	.44
= culture and entertainment (men)	.47	.49	.54	.52
= culture and entertainment (women)	.42	.44	.54	.52
= health and medical care	.48	.47	.38	.40
Assimilation (Factor 3)				
= adoption of local customs and lifestyle (men)	.65	.63	.53	.54

= adoption of local customs and lifestyle (women)	.59	.61	.50	.51
= children's use of host-country language in the home	.49	.50	.39	.47
= adults use of host-country language off the job	.58	.58	.47	.48
= adults use of host-country language in family	.39	.39	.45	.44
= "family solidarity benefits from overseas stay"	.00	.01	−.07	−.08

Close comfort (Factor 4)

= food standard (quality, hygiene, choice) (men)	.53	.56	.66	.65
= food standard (quality, hygiene, choice) (women)	.52	.52	.67	.60
= general satisfaction (men)	.54	.50	.33	.25
= general satisfaction (women)	.37	.34	.27	.24
= material living standard (men)	.14	.09	.13	.08
= material living standard (women)	.13	.10	.13	.07
= housing standard	.08	.08	.13	.15

Open-air environment (Factor 5)

= climate conditions (temperature, humidity, air pollution)	.19	.24	.03	.01
= opportunities for sports and open-air activities	.11	.17	−.10	−.09

Insights into host-society (Factor 6)

= knowledge of host-country's development, traditions and cultural background (men)	.20	.26	.15	.13
= knowledge of host-country's development, traditions and cultural background (women)	−.14	−.13	−.03	.00
= knowledge of host-country's social and political conditions (men)	.43	.45	.23	.27
= knowledge of host-country's social and political conditions (women)	.09	.11	.04	.10
= perceived social isolation	.05	.01	.15	.91

living standard, where the latter two variables should reflect conditions of personal material welfare as provided for by the Swedish employer.

Although it is difficult to tell which objective dimension accounts for culture dependent reactions, the results so far tend to support the culture-barrier hypothesis, both concerning which variables are culture dependent, and in regard to the direction of such dependencies. It should, however, be noted that the results do not tell whether culture dependent variables also imply the existence of cultural barriers of any practical significance. For some variables, this is most likely so, for example, social contact for which the percentage of Swedes with host country companionship groups off-the-job varies among countries from zero percent (Liberia) to 85 percent (England).

Regarding the reactional aspects showing low correlations, the results tell only that they are not culture dependent in the objective respects studies here. This applies to items that do not relate to the host culture, but also to some that do; for example, the items about knowledge of host country development and traditions and of social and political conditions. This might possibly imply that they are culture dependent in some "unknown" objective dimension. This, in fact, seems to be the case for the items on climate conditions and opportunities for open-air activities, which constitute a separate factor. These items show significant negative rank correlations ($r = -.43$; $r = -.41$) with population density, measured as the number of inhabitants per square kilometer. The more densely populated the host country, the less positive are evaluations in these two respects.

Reactional Domains

Table 8.1 also gives the results of a varimax rotated factor analysis. Six factors held eigenvalues greater than 1.5. These factors are interpreted as reactional domains, denoting areas of experience as captured by the overseas Swedes' reactions in terms of judgments, attitudes, and behaviors.

According to Table 8.1, the three first factors contain items that show consistently higher rank correlations with one of the two main dimensions of objective culture, religion-language, and technological level. The reactional domains, tentatively labeled social contact and assimilation, seem to be associated with religion-language, whereas societal comfort seems to be associated more with technological level. Factors 4-6 are tentatively labeled: close comfort, open-air environment, and insights into the host society. They show no consistent pattern across items that related to one of the objective dimensions, or they are composed of items not associated significantly with either dimension.

In the third step of analysis, some of the items of Factors 1-3 shall be omitted because of nonsignificant correlations with the objective culture dimensions, or because of correlations deviating from the dominant pattern among items in a factor. This is done to achieve reactional domains that relate more clearly to only one objective dimension, as required for the present purpose of evaluating the culture barrier hypothesis. For Factors 4-6, this hypothesis does not apply, and all items shall be used in the third step of analysis since there is no theoretical ground for omitting some. Here, interpretations can be made only through a search procedure by inspection of the results.

Country Clusters for Reactional Domains

A cluster is a set of points characterized by nearness in a multidimensional space. For the present purposes the items of each reactional domain form the dimensions of such a space and each of the 26 countries or regions used here is a point in that space. Ward's (1963) hierarchical method, as applied here, starts out with 26 "clusters" and ends with one cluster, through merging in successive steps those two clusters that result in the smallest increase in within-cluster variance; that is, for each step it merges those clusters that are closest to each other in the multidimensional space. Results from the cluster analysis were established by selecting the solution yielding the number of clusters, after which a further step in the merging process would display a radical rise in within-cluster variance. Such a strictly mechanical criterion is reasonable, since the matter of which countries cluster together is central to the culture-barrier hypothesis. Table 8.2 specifies, for each country, the number of the cluster to which it was allotted in each of the six reactional domains.

TABLE 8.2

Country Clusters for Six Reactional Domains (cluster no.)

Country/Country-Group: (Number of Clusters)	Social Contact (6)	Assimilation (4)	Societal Comfort (3)	Close Comfort (3)	Insights into Host-Society (4)	Open-Air Environment (4)
USA	1	1	1	1	1	1
Canada	2	1	1	1	2	2
Australia & New Zealand	1	2	2	1	2	1
England	3	2	1	1	3	3
West Germany	2	2	1	1	1	2
Austria	3	2	1	1	2	2
Switzerland	3	4	1	1	4	3
Holland	3	2	1	1	1	3
Belgium	2	3	1	1	4	1
France	2	2	2	1	4	3
Italy	4	2	1	1	1	1
Spain	5	2	1	1	4	2
Portugal	5	2	2	1	2	1
Mexico	4	2	2	1	3	4
Brazil	4	3	2	1	2	2
Argentina & Uruguay	3	2	2	2	3	2
Chile & Peru	5	2	3	1	1	3
Colombia, Ecuador, & Venezuela	2	4	3	3	1	3
India & Pakistan	5	4	3	3	1	3
South East Asia	5	4	2	1	2	3
Japan	6	4	1	2	4	4
Middle East	6	4	3	2	4	1
North Africa	6	4	3	3	1	1
East Africa	6	4	3	2	4	1
Liberia	6	4	3	2	2	2
South Africa	3	2	2	1	1	2

Social Contact

For social contact, countries should cluster, hypothetically, according to kinship in the religion-language aspect. Cluster 1 is predominantly Protestant and English-speaking. Clusters 2 and 3 are formed by countries with Germanic or Romance languages (Indo-European) and with Christian religions (exceptions: India and Pakistan). Clusters 4 and 5 could be more clearly termed Latin clusters containing Catholic cultures with Romance languages. Cluster 6 contains countries or regions with non-Christian religions and non-Indo-European languages.

Although with some "misallocations," clusters, in regard to social contact, seem to contain, at large, countries with some common traits regarding religion-language. Figure 8.1 gives profiles (t-values) across items for five reactional domains. Concerning social contact (Fig. 8.1), country cluster profiles tend to differ in level across items, so that clusters made up of cultures that are less closely related to the Swedish respondents' home culture show less positive evaluations. This is in support of the directional assumption regarding culture dependency, but it also confirms that, from a Swedish perspective, there are differences in the height of a social contact culture barrier between at least Cluster 1 and Clusters 5 and 6, and between Clusters 2 and 3 and Cluster 6.

Assimilation

This domain of reactions represents a more personal and active involvement in the host society. Countries should cluster, hypothetically, according to religion-language kinship. The results from Table 8.2 and Figure 8.2 are similar to those regarding social contact; that is, one English-speaking, predominantly Protestant cluster (1) of relatively good assimilation, two mixed clusters (Cluster 2—filled symbol; Cluster 3—unfilled), which are intermediate in assimilation and are formed by Western European and Latin American cultures. Cluster 4, of relatively poor assimilation, contains Africa, Asia and Holland.

Societal Comfort

This reactional domain is taken to reflect experiences of societal facilities and service, forming part of the infrastructure of

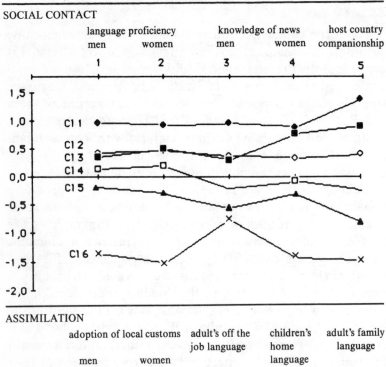

SOCIAL CONTACT

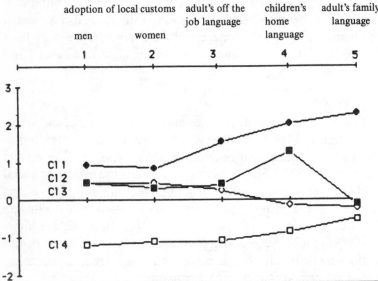

ASSIMILATION

Figure 8.1–8.5 Cluster Prefixes of Five Reactional Domains (Standardized Variable Means)

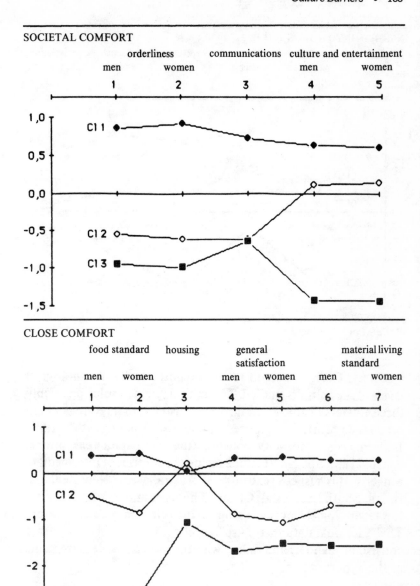

Figure 8.1-8.5 Continued

INSIGHTS INTO HOST-SOCIETY

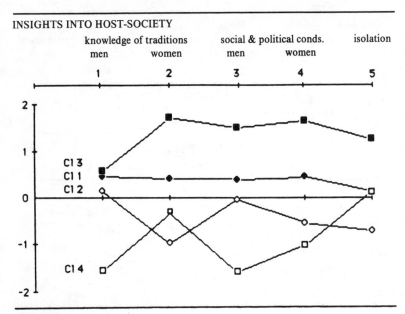

Figure 8.1-8.5 Continued

a society. Clusters should reflect, hypothetically, technological levels of the cultures studied. The analysis yields a solution of only three clusters (Table 8.2; Fig. 8.3). Cluster 1, of a relatively high societal comfort, is composed of countries ranging, at the time, 1-11 in gross electricity consumption per capita (exceptions: Portugal and Spain). Cluster 2 includes countries of intermediate range in this respect (exceptions: Australia and New Zealand, Brazil, South East Asia). Cluster 3 holds countries of a relatively low technological level, ranging 18-26 in electricity consumption. The reactional data of Figure 8.3 reflect these levels in a rather consistent manner, and in line with the directional requirements of the hypothesis.

Non-Culture-Dependent Domains

The remaining reactional domains, labeled: close comfort, insights into host society, and open-air environment, contain items with no- or low-rank correlations in the objective dimensions used. Thus, there can be no hypothesis as to which countries should cluster together, or in regard to consistency or direction of differences in profile levels. For the domain of close comfort, almost all countries are included in Cluster 1 (Table 8.2). This should reflect that, for the category of expatriates studied here, good personal, material living conditions are provided by the Swedish head offices, balancing variations in host-country conditions. Still, Figure 8.4 shows differences in level of profiles between Cluster 1 and Clusters 2 (Chile and Peru, Middle East, East Africa, Liberia) and Cluster 3 (North Africa, India and Pakistan).

The psychological meaning of the factor "insights into host society" is unclear since it implies that good knowledge of host country traditions and cultural background and of social and political conditions is combined with a high degree of social isolation as perceived by the women of the study. The country composition of the four clusters (Table 8.2) and the profiles of Figure 8.5 do not make much sense. Since three of the clusters tend to differ in profile level, however, the possibility should not be ruled out that there may be some "unknown" dimension of culture behind these results.

The reactional domain termed open-air environment, as formed by only two reactional items, produced a four-cluster solution (Table 8.2) with profiles at different levels (not illustrated). Cluster 2, containing rather sparsely populated countries, holds the most positive profile, whereas Cluster 1 is close to average. Cluster 3 holds a less positive profile and consists mainly of highly industrialized Central European countries. Cluster 4, formed by Japan and Argentina and Uruguay, displays strongly negative evaluations.

CONCLUSION

This chapter has presented a theoretical specification and a limited validation of the culture barrier construct. Through the aggregation of information on individual reactions to the country level, constellations of own culture versus foreign culture were established regarding Swedes living in a great number of countries. A clear-cut validation of the culture barrier hypothesis as laid out here, thus required that within-country variation in reactional variables owing to person- or situation-specific factors be disregarded, and that variations among countries owing to such factors be assumed away. These are, of course, far-reaching simplifications of real situations of intercultural communication. Furthermore, reactions at the item level were tested for culture dependency of only single dimensions of culture, which were operationalized in very approximate and rough terms. This was also done at the level of reactional domains through the mechanical application of cluster analysis.

At each step of such a validation procedure there is, of course, a number of methodological issues that can be raised and discussed. For the present, I shall, however, jump to the somewhat risky conclusion that the results at large are in support of the culture-barrier hypothesis. It should be remembered though, that because of the bicultural and monodirectional character of culture barriers, the results could not be generalized. Still, they confirm the relevance of the phenomenon as such.

One basic assumption of the theory and analysis presented is that an individual's reaction in a situation of intercultural contact is based on a psychological "transformation" of the objective foreign culture into a subjective foreign culture reflecting the individual's own culture. Thus the reaction does not tell about the foreign culture per se. The comparisons in this chapter of reactions to conditions of several cultures fill the function only of illustrating one aspect of the psychological role of culture, or in Price-Williams (1980) terms, of how a certain psychological mechanism is meshed into culture.

From the above, it is also evident that descriptive dimensions of objective culture should not be derived from reactional measures of people from cultures other than the one to be described, if such dimensions are to serve as objective criteria against which the psychological role of culture shall be understood. Nor would the means to reach such an understanding be the further refinement of psychological criteria besides those already available, at least not in the first place. This does not imply a denial of the need for theorizing on intercultural communication issues; for example, as stated by Gudykunst (1983). Rather, it emphasizes the need of adequate criteria for the validation of theories. Thus there is a need to find and elaborate descriptive dimensions of objective culture, dimensions that manifest themselves at a sociological level, for example, of the context (Hall, 1959) or structural tightness (Boldt, 1978). Such dimensions should be applicable generally, yet precise enough to discriminate beyond dichotomies, and they should capture in a more subtle way aspects of objective culture that may be relevant for the purposes of psychology.

Such criteria are even more needed if, as suggested by Triandis (1980b) and Pedersen and Pedersen (1985), personal and situational factors are included in the psychological study of intercultural communication. Regarding the situational context, psychological research in general faces a corresponding need of taxonomies (Magnusson, 1984). Although in intercultural communication, the cultural aspect may also be seen as a special instance of the situational context, an important problem in both fields of research is to find objective correlates to match already subtle psychological criteria in order to provide valid psychological interpretations of person-environment interaction.

REFERENCES

Altman, I., & Chemers, M. (1980). Cultural aspects of environment-behavior relationships. In H. Triansis & R. Brislin (Eds.), *Handbook of cross-cultural psychology*. Boston: Allyn & Bacon.

Berry, J.W. (1980). Social and cultural change. In H. Triandis & R. Brislin (Eds.), *Handbook of cross-cultural psychology*. Boston: Allyn & Bacon.

Boldt, E. (1978). Structural tightness and cross-cultural research. *Journal of Cross-cultural Psychology, 9*(2), 151-165.

Brewer, M., & Campbell, D. (1976). *Ethnocentrism and intergroup attitudes*. New York: Halsted.

Brislin, R. (1981). *Cross-cultural encounters*. Elmsford, NY: Pergamon.

Church, A. (1982). Sojourner adjustment. *Psychological Bulletin, 91*(3), 540-572.

Detweiler, R. (1978). Culture, category width and attributions. *Journal of Cross-cultural Psychology, 9*(3), 259-284.

Ellingsworth, H., (1983). Adaptive intercultural communication. In W. Gudykunst (Ed.), *Intercultural communication theory: Current perspectives*. Newbury Park, CA: Sage.

Ehrenhaus, P. (1983). Culture and the attribution process: Barriers to effective communication. In W. Gudykunst (Ed.), *Intercultural communication theory: Current perspectives*. Newbury Park, CA: Sage.

Griffeth, R., Hom, P., DeNisi, A., & Kirchner, W. (1985). A comparison of different methods of clustering countries on the basis of employee attitudes. *Human Relations, 38*(9), 813-840.

Grove, C., & Torbiörn, I. (1985). A new conceptualization of intercultural adjustment and the goals of training. *Intercultural Journal of Intercultural Relations, 9,* 205-233.

Gudykunst, W. (1983). Theorizing in intercultural communication. In W. Gudykunst (Ed.), *Intercultural communication theory: Current perspectives.* Newbury Park, CA: Sage.

Hall, E. (1959). *The silent language.* New York: Doubleday.

Hofstede, G. (1980). *Cultures consequences: International differences in work-related values:* Newbury Park, CA: Sage.

Hui, H., & Triandis, H. (1985). Measurement in cross-cultural psychology: A review and comparison of strategies. *Journal of Cross-cultural Psychology, 16,* 131-152.

Kluckhohn, C. (1951). The study of culture. In D. Lerner & H. Lasswell (Eds.), *The policy sciences.* Stanford, CA: Stanford University Press.

LeVine, R., & Campbell, D. (1972). *Ethnocentrism: Theories of conflict, ethnic attitudes and group behavior.* New York: Wiley.

Magnusson, D. (1984). On the situational context in psychological research. In K. Lagerspetz & P. Niemi (Eds.), *Psychology in the 1990s.* Amsterdam, North Holland: Elsevier.

Pedersen, A. & Pedersen, P. (1985). The cultural grid: A personal cultural orientation. In L. Samovar & R. Porter (Eds.), *Intercultural communication: A reader (fourth edition).* Belmont, CA: Wadsworth.

Price-Williams, D. (1980). Toward the idea of a cultural psychology. *Journal of Cross-cultural Psychology, 11*(1), 75-88.

Rokeach, M. (1960). *The open and closed mind.* New York: Basic Books.

Torbiörn, I. (1982). *Living abroad: Personal adjustment and the personnel policy in the overseas setting.* New York: Wiley.

Triandis, H. (1972). *The analysis of subjective cultures.* New York: Wiley.

Triandis, H. (1980a). A theoretical framework for the study of bilingual-bicultural adaptation. *International Review of Applied Psychology, 29,* 7-16.

Triandis, H. (1980b). Reflections on trends in cross-cultural research. *Journal of Cross-cultural Psychology, 11*(1), 35-58.

Ward, J. (1963). Hierarchical grouping of optimizing an objective function. *Journal of the American Statistical Association, 58,* 236-244.

9

Locus of Control and Communication Patterns of Immigrants

JUNE O. YUM • *State University of New York at Albany*

The general purpose of the study is to explore the effect of a psychological construct, locus of control, on the intercultural communication patterns of immigrants. The construct, internal versus external control of reinforcement, refers to the extent to which an individual feels in control over the reinforcements that occur relative to one's own behavior. High levels of intercultural communication require active participation in a new social system. Therefore, the level of belief of one's control over the environment and events should influence such interaction. Four different types of intercultural communication, such as intercultural interpersonal contacts, intercultural friendship, participation in ethnically mixed organizations, and exposure to English language newspapers, were measured among five different ethnic groups in Hawaii. The results of the study revealed that locus of control had statistically significant, but weak, relationships with participation in ethnically mixed organizations and intercultural interpersonal contacts, but no significant relationship with intercultural friendship patterns.

INTRODUCTION

In recent years there has been an increasing number of studies that focus on ethnic groups and their communication patterns. The majority of immigration research, however, is still conducted by sociologists and anthropologists focusing on demographic variables to explain immigrants' assimilation, economic accomplishments, acculturation, and adjustment. Variables, such as level of education, occupational status, age, sex, income, and so forth, are the most commonly applied explanatory variables. Demographic variables, however, are not sufficient to explain the differential patterns of communication. For instance, demographic variables alone do not adequately explain why immigrants of the same socioeconomic status have different communication patterns. The major purpose of this study was to explore the effect of a psychological construct, locus of control, on the intercultural communication patterns of immigrants vis-à-vis sociodemographic variables.

Intercultural communication patterns, whether interpersonal communication or mass communication, have been studied three different ways: as independent variables that affect acculturation or adjustment, as variables that intervene between socioeconomic variables and acculturation, or as the ultimate dependent variables, very often as indexes of acculturation. A few recent studies (Y. Kim, 1977; J. Kim, 1980; Nagata, 1969) have employed intercultural communication both as an independent variable (channel availability, for instance, as interaction potential) and as an intervening variable between exogenous variables and acculturation. Yum's (1982) study focused on the diversity of communication, that is, whether immigrants depend upon only a few communication sources or evenly distribute their time over several communication sources. Communication diversity was found to intervene between the social and psychological capacity of immigrants and the level of information they have.

In this study, intercultural communication patterns were considered as indicators of the degree that ethnic members were informationally integrated into their host society consisting of other ethnic groups. Thus, communication patterns serve as an index of the second stage of acculturation (Taft, 1957), known as structural acculturation (Gordon, 1964).

Most studies explain the intercultural communication patterns of just one ethnic group rather than of several ethnic groups at the same time. Comparisons across ethnic groups are rare. In this study, the ethnic variability of locus of control and intercultural communication patterns were tested with five major ethnic groups in Hawaii.

THEORY

Locus of Control

One of the psychological constructs with great potential for understanding ethnic group members' intercultural communication patterns is locus of control. The internal-external locus of control construct has received increasing attention since it was introduced by Rotter (1954) in his social learning theory. Locus of control is defined as "the degree to which the individual perceives that reward follows from, or is contingent upon, his own behavior or attributes versus the degree to which he feels the reward is controlled by forces outside of himself and may occur independently of his own actions" (Rotter, 1966, p. 1). This construct, internal versus external control of reinforcement (I-E control), refers to the extent to which an individual feels that they have control over the reinforcements that occur relative to their own behavior. Internals tend to feel that they control their own destiny and are effective agents in determining the occurrence of reinforcements. Externals, however, tend to see forces beyond their control as being the essential factors in determining the occurrence of reinforcements (such forces as fate, chance, powerful others, the complexity or unpredictability of the world, and so forth). Whether one perceives that they have some control over the environment and external events will influence their interaction with and participation in a new social system. The perception of this causal relationship is not necessarily a dichotomous distinction, but can be expected to vary in degree along a continuum from low internal control to high internal control.

Tiffany, Shontz, and Woll (1969) developed a general model of control that (1) reformulates the controversy between freedom versus determinism of human behavior, and (2) integrates contemporary theories of personality and behavior. They posit two dimensions in place of the traditional one-dimensional conceptualization of freedom-determinism: (a) freedom to non-freedom (control *over* the environment), and (b) determinism to indeterminism (control *from* the environment). The inclusion of objective control through one's competence, mastery, and autonomy and subjective control experienced as a sense of internal-external control, efficacy, powerlessness, and so forth, refines simple S-R (stimulus-response) learning theory by emphasizing the importance of reinforcement in situations that the individual perceives as dependent upon one's own behavior.

In reviewing cross-cultural research on locus of control, Hui (1982) was concerned about the cross-cultural conceptual and functional equivalence of the construct and its dimensionality. He suggested that "while we can defend the construct's unidimensionality at least partially for a single culture, extending it to other cultures reflects insensitivity to cultural differences" (p. 315).

Gurin, Gurin, Lao, and Beattie (1969) also found that internal control was not a single dimension in attitude structure of Black college students. Instead, internal control was found to be multidimensional and based on two key distinctions. The first, a distinction between self and other, highlights the fact that people may feel they are in control of their own life, yet believe that people in general are not; second, more likely for poor people or victims of discrimination, they may feel that most people control their destinies, although they do not.

In the case of immigrants, the measurement scale of locus of control should be carefully prepared so that both control by an individual and control in conjunction with others can be measured. To those who are from a traditional or extended family society, pluralistic control may have more meaning than does individual control.

Locus of control and communication behavior. There have been several studies that relate perceived locus of control to communication behavior, information-seeking, acquisition, and retention. Seeman and Evans (1962) matched groups of internals (high perceived control) and externals (low perceived control), who were hospitalized in a tuberculosis hospital, on socioeconomic and hospital experience variables. The results indicated that internal patients possessed more objective information concerning their illnesses, were rated by the hospital staff as having more knowledge of their illnesses, and were less satisfied with the information they received in the ward.

A study by Davis and Phares (1967) demonstrated differences between internals and externals in terms of how actively they sought additional relevant information. In an experimental study, subjects were led to believe that their task was to influence the attitude of another person toward the war in Vietnam during the 1960s. During the procedure, they were given the opportunity to acquire information about the other person and about the Vietnam issue. Under ambiguous conditions internals sought more information than did externals. Under chance conditions internals and externals did not differ in information-seeking behavior. Under skill conditions externals sought significantly less information than did internals. Phares (1968) also demonstrated that those with high perceived control were more effective in the use of information.

Danowski (1975) found that a person with high perceived control over the environment used more interpersonal communication to maintain an optimal level of uncertainty than did a person with low control. Referring to the concept of effort, he explained that a person with high control would perceive changing the interpersonal communication component as requiring less effort than would a person with low control.

Dye (1975) found that alienation-powerlessness was related to differential patterns of participation in community decision making among six ethnic groups in the lower socioeconomic classes of Hawaii. The alienation-powerlessness measures used in this study were the Dean Powerlessness Scale, the Rotter Internal-External Control (I-E) Scale, and the Alienation-Powerlessness Semantic Differential (ASPD) Scale. The findings showed statistically significant differences among the six ethnic groups, ranged on the continuum of high to low alienation-powerlessness: the Filipinos, the Samoans, the Puerto Ricans, the Portuguese, the Hawaiians, and the Japanese. The six ethnic subsamples also ranged from inactive to active in community participation: the Samoans, the Filipinos, the Puerto Ricans, the Portuguese, the Hawaiians, and the Japanese.

Intercultural Communication

In this study, three types of intercultural communication were explored: interpersonal, organizational, and mass communication. Interpersonal-intercultural communication was defined as the set of individuals in one's communication or friendship networks (Rogers & Kincaid, 1981) who were from ethnic groups different than the respondent's and with whom one had communication on an informal level. The networks established by interpersonal communication play two important functions in the life of immigrants; an instrumental function and an affective function (Yum, 1982, 1983). That one's network is extended beyond one's own ethnic boundary implies that one is acculturated; it also signifies that one has a wider (or more heterogeneous) range of information sources (Kincaid & Yum, in press).

Organizational behavior is viewed in the literature as playing a significant role in the acculturation process of ethnic groups. Whether an immigrant belongs to ethnic organizations or host-society organizations and the level of activity in such organizations have been used as measures of acculturation. On the other hand, it was also found that the longer an immigrant stays in the host society, the more he or she participates in organizational activities regardless of the ethnicity of the organizations (Y. Kim, 1976; Ujimoto, 1973).

Following the tradition of the functional approach, the mass media use of immigrants, along with their interpersonal networks and organized behavior, has been studied mainly as an index of acculturation or as a mediating variable between personal characteristics of immigrants and their acculturation. In general, exposure to the mass media of the host society is regarded as functional for the acculturation of the immigrants to the society. A number of empirical studies have demonstrated that host-language media exposure functions as an intervening variable between socioeconomic status variables and acculturation (De-Fleur & Cho, 1957; Dunn, 1973; Y. Kim, 1977; J. Kim, 1980; Rivera, 1971). In a study of Canadian immigrants, Richmond (1967 pp. 138-139) reported that newspapers and magazines explicitly and implicitly "convey a knowledge of Canadian norms of behavior and social institutions, without which the immigrant will remain incompletely absorbed into the Canadian way of life." Gans's (1962) study of Italian immigrants of the West End of Boston showed that to Italian immigrants, the mass media constituted a major tie to the outside world.

Of the mass media variables used, some require more initiative and active behavior then others. Reading host language newspapers, for example, is an active media behavior compared to watching television or listening to the radio. This type of active media use would require a belief system that one has some control over the outcome, while a passive media use would not necessarily require such a belief system. Therefore, in this study; English newspaper reading was used as an indicator of intercultural mass communication behavior.

Prior studies have shown that participation in intercultural communication varies by demographic characteristics such as age, sex, education, and occupation. Besides these standard demographic variables, such structural variables as the unit of settlement (J. Kim, 1980), number of children (DeFleur & Cho, 1957), completeness of ethnic institutions in a community (Breton, 1964), and channel availability (mass communication or interpersonal) (Anderson, 1971; J. Kim, 1980; Y. Kim, 1977) were found to be significant. For non-English speaking immigrants, English fluency has been found to be significantly related to participation in intercultural communication (Y. Kim, 1977; Pool, 1965; Richmond, 1967). The study of psychological variables in conjunction with intercultural communication is relatively rare. Y. Kim (1977) included acculturation motivation as an explanatory variable of interpersonal-intercultural communication and host-culture mass communication use. In a study of six ethnic groups in Hawaii, Dye (1975) found that alienation-powerlessness, which was partially measured by the Rotter's Internal-External Control Scale (Rotter, 1966), was significantly related to differential patterns of participation in community activities. In developing a multivariate model of acculturation, Dyal and Dyal (1981) included a feeling of control as an important intrapersonal characteristic that influences acculturation.

Participating in intercultural communication requires special effort from the immigrant's point of view. The extra cost is sometimes a material one, such as time or money, but more importantly a psychological one. One needs to have a certain confidence that one can control the situation and that the reward is based upon one's own action before venturing into a new field of interaction. Previous research has maintained that seeking a member of one's own ethnic group as a communication partner is not so much a sign of prejudice as a result of a comfort factor (McCandles & Hoyt, 1961; Ogawa, 1979). To overcome the complacent, psychological comfort of being with one's own kind requires a belief system that one is one's own causal agent.

The individual's concept of control originates in his or her structural milieu and socialization experiences. Rosenberg (1969) suggested that one's sense of control is a deeply entrenched attitude that is related more to fundamental social conditions than it is to ephemeral social interaction. Most first generation immigrants have passed through their early socialization processes in their own home cultures. The experience of immigration may have some effect on their concept of control. Each ethnic group, however, would have a different level of belief in internal control, owing to cultural differences in their initial position on the internal-external continuum.

Even though the results were not always consistent, previous researchers have found ethnic/racial differences in control orientation. For example, Black children were found to be more external than were White children (DuCette, Wolk, & Friedman, 1972) and Black and Puerto Rican children were more external than were Jewish children (Pehazur & Wheeler, 1971). Among the adult samples (Anglo-Americans, Spanish-Americans, and American Indians), Spanish-Americans showed the most external orientation, followed by American Indians (Jesser, Graves, Hanson, & Jessor, 1968). Chinese and Japanese students were found to be more external than were American students (Bond & Tornatzky, 1973; Krampen & Wieberg, 1981) while Indians were found to be more internal than were Japanese, Western, and Middle-Eastern respondents (Parsons & Schneider, 1974). These differences may be partially dependent upon whether a cultural group has a value pattern of mastery over nature, such as Anglo-Americans, or a value pattern of subjugation to nature or group norms, such as Japanese (Hui, 1982).

Following the above discussion, two research questions were explored: first, whether each ethnic group has a significantly different level of locus of control, and second, whether locus of control has a significant influence on intercultural communication patterns measured by intercultural interpersonal communication, intercultural organizational participation, and English-language newspaper reading.

Socioeconomic Variables and Language Fluency

Socioeconomic variables such as age, income, occupational status, length of stay in the United States, and English fluency were included in the study as control variables. These variables were found to be related to the level of intercultural communication in previous empirical research. In this study, the effect of locus of control was investigated, controlling for these conventional variables; that is, it was tested whether or not locus of control had effects over and above these variables.

METHODOLOGY

Samples

Hawaii is an ethnically heterogeneous state. According to the 1980 population census of Hawaii, 33.3% were Caucasian; 24.8%, Japanese; 12.0%, Hawaiian or part Hawaiian; 11.3%, Filipino; 5.8%, Chinese; 1.9%, Korean; 1.8%, Black; 1.5%, Samoan; and 0.4%, Vietnamese. Hawaii has not only the highest ratio of Asian descendants in the population, but it has become the home for many new Asian immigrants in recent years. From 1978 to 1979, a survey was conducted to investigate the communication patterns, locus of control, interethnic perceptions, and information acquisition of five ethnic groups in Hawaii. Three of the major immigrant groups in Hawaii were interviewed: 401 Koreans, 208 Filipinos, and 199 Samoans. Two major ethnic groups of the host population were also interviewed for purposes of comparison: 203 local Japanese and 200 Caucasian-Americans.

The Korean sample was randomly selected from the Oahu telephone directory. From the directory, all Korean surnames were selected using an exhaustive list of 249 Korean surnames from the 1975 Korean census. In the Oahu telephone directory, 78 different Korean surnames were found. This lengthy list of about 4,200 names was numbered, then names were selected using a systematic sampling procedure with a random starting point (Glass & Stanley, 1970). Face-to-face interviews were conducted at residences after a brief telephone interview to screen disconnected numbers and non-Koreans and to check the age eligibility (18 years or older).

The Caucasian and Filipino samples were selected by means of a three stage cluster technique, beginning with census tracts randomly selected in proportion to the known probability of members of those ethnic groups residing within them. Then households were selected systematically from random starting points following a serpentine path through the tract. Finally, each selected household became the starting point for clusters, which were identified by means of the Hawaii Telephone Crossreference Directory for Oahu. Potential respondents were then telephoned for screening according to the following eligibility requirements: resident of Hawaii, at least 18 years old, member of the required ethnic group, and willingness to participate in the study.

The Japanese sample was selected by the same procedures followed for the Korean sample: randomly selected Japanese surnames from the 1978 Honolulu telephone directory, pre-screened by telephone for eligibility and willingness to participate. The Samoan sample was selected first with a random selection of known Samoan surnames from the Honolulu telephone directory. Each name drawn was visited at home and, if the person met the eligibility requirements and was interviewed, he or she was asked to identify up to 15 other Samoan households in the same neighborhood for interviewing before the interviewer moved on to the next neighborhood cluster. Although the Samoan sample represents the major subgroup of Samoans on Oahu, it does not qualify strictly as a probability sample.

For the immigrant groups, only the first generation of immigrants (those who were born in the country of origin) were included in the sample. Of the Japanese respondents, 93% were born in Hawaii. The Caucasian-Americans have lived in Hawaii for an average of 10 years. For all samples, face-to-face interviews were conducted by native interviewers using native-language questionnaires, which were finalized after double translation procedures.

MEASUREMENT

Interpersonal communication. Two types of interpersonal communication relevant to the study of ethnic groups were studies: their general communication contacts and their friendship contacts. General communication contacts were defined as the set of individuals with whom one talks most frequently during the week, either face-to-face or over the telephone. The friendship contacts were elicited by asking respondents to name their best friends in the United States, in order of importance. The total number of different ethnic members in each type of contact were used as indexes of interpersonal intercultural communication, and intercultural friendship.

Organizational communication. To make sure that respondents named the total number of organizations to which they belonged, a list of organizational types was read aloud by the interviewer. The respondents were asked to name any organization to which they belonged corresponding to each type of organization. After the names of specific organizations were elicited, the respondent was asked if the membership of each organization was just for one ethnic group or for other ethnic groups as well. The total number of members in mixed ethnic organizations was used as an index of organizational intercultural communication.

Exposure to English-language newspapers. Each respondent was asked what newspapers (English and ethnic) they subscribed to and read regularly. For all newspapers mentioned, the frequency of reading and the average amount of time spent reading was asked. For those who mentioned English newspapers or both English and ethnic newspapers, the time spent reading English newspapers during the average day was also asked. Frequency of reading of the two main English newspapers in Honolulu was summed as an indicator of exposure to English-language newspapers.

The range of each of the measures of intercultural communication was from 0 to 10. Therefore, they were summed to create an overall index of intercultural communication. The analysis was done with each intercultural communication index as well as with the overall index.

Locus of control. Locus of control was measured by adapting some items from Rotter's (1966) scale and an alternative version developed by Gurin et al. (1969), reworded to make them more appropriate for the study of immigrants. Seven Likert-type items were created, four that measured perceived control over individual matters leading to personal success or failure, and three that measured perceived control as a result of participation in the political process. The five items that loaded on the principal axis of the factor analysis were chosen for the locus of control scale. The internal reliability check suggested, however, that two items were not intercorrelated. Therefore, only the remaining three items were summed to create an index of locus of control. Internal reliability was different from ethnic group to ethnic group, with the Samoan group being the highest (0.81) and the Filipino group the lowest (0.44). The average reliability for all ethnic groups was 0.57, as measured by Cronbach's alpha.

English fluency and socioeconomic variables. Education was measured by the number of years of formal education that each respondent had completed. Occupational status was measured by asking the respondents to give the specific name of their job rather than the general area or place of work. Occupation was coded for occupational prestige using the Treiman (1977) scale. Length of stay was measured by asking respondents how many years they had lived in the United States. English fluency was measured by the respondents' subjective evaluation of their English fluency and by the use of a five-point Likert-type scale for each of the following items: difficulty in understanding an English-speaking native, hesitation in using the telephone because of the language problem, and evaluation of their own English ability compared to the average native speaker. The internal reliability was 0.87 as measured by Cronbach's alpha. The mean scores and standard deviations for each variable for each ethnic group is reported in Table 9.1.

RESULTS

To test ethnic variability, the locus of control and intercultural communication variables were analyzed employing one-way analysis of variance with ethnicity as the independent variable. The results revealed statistically significant ethnic variability for locus of control ($F = 50.94$; $df = 4/1009$; $p < .001$). Caucasians showed the highest level of internal control ($M = 10.43$), followed by the Koreans and Japanese ($M = 9.42$ and $M = 9.41$, respectively). The Samoan group showed quite a drop ($M = 7.87$) and the Filipino group showed the lowest control orientation ($M = 7.33$). The results were consistent with Dye's (1975) findings for Filipinos and Samoans using the alienation-powerlessness scale. He found that the Japanese had the lowest powerlessness orientation (Dye's study did not include Koreans or Caucasians).

TABLE 9.1
Means and Standard Deviations of Intercultural Communication and Locus of Control of Five Ethnic Groups

	Intercultural Communication		Intercultural Friendship		Intercultural Organizations		English Newspaper		Total Intercultural Index		Locus of Control	
	M	SD	M	SD	M	SD	M	SD	M	SD	M	SD
Korean	.76	1.38	.35	.94	.31	.78	1.54	2.37	2.96	3.97	9.42	3.00
Filipino	.60	1.33	.56	1.26	.56	1.26	3.46	2.96	5.16	3.81	7.33	1.74
Samoan	.94	1.67	.97	1.61	.97	1.61	3.19	3.59	5.46	5.62	7.87	2.88
Caucasian	1.72	1.63	1.01	1.23	1.01	1.23	5.55	2.4	9.94	4.14	10.43	2.16
Japanese	.94	1.23	.74	1.08	.74	1.08	4.05	2.64	6.92	3.90	9.58	2.34

All five intercultural communication variables were also significantly different across ethnic groups: intercultural communication size ($F = 20.62$; dr = 4/1206; $p < .001$), intercultural friendship size ($F = 17.57$; df = 4/1206; $p < .001$), intercultural organizational membership ($F = 65.78$; df = 4/1206; $p < .001$), and English newspaper consumption ($F = 39.87$; df = 2/805; $p < .001$). Caucasians had the highest scores for both intercultural communication and intercultural friendship size, followed by the Japanese and Samoans. Filipino immigrants had the smallest intercultural communication contacts and Korean immigrants had the smallest intercultural friendship contacts.

To test the bivariate relationships between locus of control and intercultural communication patterns, Pearson correlations were calculated for all five ethnic groups. These results are reported in Table 9.2.

The results showed that locus of control had small but statistically significant and positive correlations with the degree of intercultural interpersonal communication among Koreans ($r = .14$, $p < .01$) and Filipinos ($r = .14$, $p < .05$). Locus of control was also statistically significant and correlated positively with the total number of intercultural organizations to which one belongs among all ethnic groups except Samoans. The size of the correlations were: Koreans ($r = .12$, $p < .01$), Filipinos ($r = 13$, $p < .05$), Caucasians ($r = .17$, $p < .001$), and Japanese ($r = .17$, $p < .001$). Locus of control had no significant relationship with the level of intercultural friendships among any of the five ethnic groups. Pearson correlations also revealed that locus of control had statistically significant and positive correlations with the total index of intercultural communication among Koreans ($r = .22$, $p < .001$), Filipinos ($r = .15$, $p < .05$), and Japanese ($r = .17$, $p < .01$).

In the final stage of analysis, multiple regression was used to analyze the unique contribution of locus of control on intercultural communications controlling for the effects of English fluency and socioeconomic variables. For the Caucasians and Japanese, locus of control had significant effects on the number of memberships in intercultural organizations after controlling for the effects of sociodemographic variables. Tables 9.3 and 9.4 display these results.

TABLE 9.2

Zero-Order Correlations of Locus of Control with Intercultural Communication Patterns
of Five Ethnic Groups

	Intercultural Communication	Intercultural Friendships	Intercultural Organizations	English Newspapers	Total Intercultural Index
Korean (401)	.14**	.06	.12**	.17***	.18***
Filipino (208)	.14*	.10	.13*	.04	.15*
Samoan (199)	−.02	−.02	.10	−.10	−.00
Caucasian (200	.01	.02	.17**	.06	.11
Japanese (203)	−.06	−.08	.24***	.17**	.17**

Note: *p < .05; **p < .01; ***p < .001.

205

TABLE 9.3

Results of the Multiple Regression of the Memberships in
Intercultural Organizations among Caucasian Respondents

Independent Variable	Multiple R	CR^2 Change	Zero-order Correlation	Beta	F
Income	.35	.12	.35	.26	13.77**
Age	.39	.03	.25	.17	6.01*
Locus of Control	.41	.02	.16	.13	3.87*
Education	.42	.01	.20	.10	2.39

Note: *p < .05; **p < .01.

The contribution of locus of control in explaining the member-ships in intercultural organizations was not so big as other sociodemographic variables, but it was still statistically significant beyond the 0.05 level for both Caucasians and Japanese; it was not significant among the other three ethnic groups. The contribution of locus of control in explaining other intercultural communication patterns was not significant for any of the five ethnic groups.

DISCUSSION

Internal-external locus of control has received increasing attention since it was introduced by Rotter (1954) because of its function in the learning process. High levels of intercultural communication require active participation in a new social system. Therefore, the level of belief of one's control over the environment and events should influence such interaction. The results of the current study revealed that locus of control had statistically significant, but weak, relationships with participation in ethnically mixed organizations and intercultural communication contacts, but no relationship at all with intercultural friendship patterns.

Considering that friendship is fundamentally an affective relationship while membership in organizations is an instrumental relationship, it is logical that the notion of control would play a significant role in organizational memberships, but not in intercultural friendship formation. In other words, friendship may not be expected to yield any other reward beyond the

TABLE 9.4

Results of the Multiple Regression of the Membership in
Intercultural Organizations among Japanese Respondents

Independent Variable	Multiple R	R^2 Change	Zero-order Correlation	Beta	F
Education	.39	.15	.39	.43	39.94**
Age	.45	.05	.01	.25	15.55**
Income	.48	.03	.30	.17	7.13*
Locus of Control	.49	.01	.24	.11	3.59*

Note: *p < .05; **p < .01.

friendship itself. Therefore, the concept of control of the outcome does not play an important role. Joining organizations whose membership includes both one's own ethnic members and other ethnic members requires more purposeful initiation and the specific expectation about further outcomes of such memberships beyond their social function.

Samoans were different from other ethnic groups in that the relationships between locus of control and intercultural communication patterns were almost zero. The instrumental distinction of communication patterns just made, may not apply to the Samoan culture. Among the five ethnic groups, Samoan culture has the strongest notion of communal life. Traditional Samoan culture is organized as a large community under a *matai* (community chief). All material things were shared communally and individual ownership was not accepted. Under such a cultural norm, many types of relationships may have nothing to do with one's personal control over the environment. An ethnographic exploration of the development of communication relationships and the concept of control over one's environment would be a fascinating and necessary step to determine exactly why locus of control has no relationship with any type of intercultural communications among Samoans.

Among the three immigrant groups—Koreans, Filipinos, and Samoans—the effect of locus of control was not significant when English fluency and other socioeconomic variables were controlled. It seems likely that, for immigrants, English fluency was almost a necessary precondition for intercultural communication. When English fluency was controlled, the effects of other variables were weakened or disappeared. Also, length of stay in the United States had strong effects suggesting that to become enmeshed into a new society simply requires time per se (or direct experience). Since these two variables—English fluency and length of stay—were not relevant for the two host ethnic members (Caucasians and Japanese), multiple regression was conducted without these variables. Under these conditions, locus of control was found to have a statistically significant relationship with intercultural organizational behavior.

The results imply that to be engaged in intercultural communication, one has to meet necessary conditions, such as language competency and a certain length of residence, but that once these prerequisites are satisfied, one's personal psychological orientation will have some effects on intercultural communication.

One of the methodological problems was the low reliability for the measurement of locus of control, and that may be the reason why the size of the observed correlations were rather small. Even though Rotter's I-E scale has been found to be reliable, it may not be very relevant to a specific locale such as Hawaii, with its own idiosyncratic political situations. Even with its low reliability, however, the results were consistent with previous studies and theoretically meaningful. With a better measurement of the construct in these cultural environments, we may be able to observe a stronger relationship between locus of control and intercultural communication.

Another reason why the correlations were small may be because of the very nature of intercultural communication. Despite the wishful thinking of melting-pot theorists, the absolute level of intercultural communication was found to be very low in this study. The percentage of respondents who replied that they had no intercultural communication contacts was astonishingly high. For intercultural communication contacts, the percentage of respondents with no contacts were: Koreans, 68%; Filipinos, 76%; Samoans, 66%; Caucasians, 28%; and Japanese, 50%. The percentage of the respondents with zero intercultural friendships were: Koreans, 83%; Filipinos, 75%; Samoans, 64%; Caucasians, 47%; and Japanese, 58%. The percentage with no intercultural organization memberships were: Koreans, 77%; Filipinos, 59%; Samoans, 75%; Caucasians, 31%; and Japanese, 39%. The frequency distributions were skewed positively because of the large number of zeros, reducing the overall variance considerably. A severely truncated range of a variable makes it difficult to observe its relationship with other variables.

The discovery of such a low incidence of intercultural communication was a significant finding in itself. On the other hand, to test the explanatory power of a construct such as locus of control, it would be desirable to study a social system with adequate levels of immigration where the incidence of intercultural communications is more frequent and, thereby, amenable to empirical analysis.

REFERENCES

Anderson, G. M. (1971). *The channel facilitators model of migration: A model tested using Portuguese blue-collar immigrants in metropolitan Toronto.* Unpublished doctoral dissertation, University of Toronto.

Bond, M. H., & Tornatzky, L. G. (1973). Locus of control in students from Japan and the United States: Dimensions and levels of response. *Psychologia, 16,* 209-213.

Breton, R. (1964). Institutional completeness of ethnic communities and the personal relations of immigrants. *American Journal of Sociology, 64,* 264-271.

Danowski, J. A. (1975). *An information theory of communication functions: A focus of information aging.* Unpublished doctoral dissertation, Michigan State University.

Davis, W. L., & Phares, E. J. (1967). Internal-external control as a determinant of information-seeking in a social influence situation. *Journal of Personality, 35,* 547-561.

DeFleur, M. L., & Cho, C. S. (1957). Assimilation of Japanese-born women in an American city. *Social Problems, 4,* 244-257.

DuCette, J., Wolk, S., & Friedman, S. (1972). Locus of control and creativity in Black and White children. *Journal of Social Psychology, 88,* 297-298.

Dunn, E. W. (1973). *A factor analysis of communication habits and attitudes among Mexican Americans in Austin and San Antonio, Texas.* Unpublished doctoral dissertation, University of Texas at Austin.

Dyal, J. A., & Dyal, R. Y. (1981). Acculturation, stress, and coping: Some implications for research and education. *International Journal of Intercultural Relations, 5,* 301-328.

Dye, L. D. (1975). A study of alienation-powerlessness and differential patterns of participation in community decision making among six ethnic groups in the lower socio-economic class in Honolulu, Hawaii. Unpublished doctoral dissertation, Western Reserve University.

Gans, H. J. (1962). *The urban villagers: Group and class in the life of Italian Americans.* Glencoe, IL: Free Press.

Glass, G. V., & Stanley, J. C. (1970). *Statistical methods in education and psychology.* Englewood Cliffs, NJ: Prentice-Hall.

Gordon, M. M. (1964). *Assimilation in American life.* New York: Oxford University Press.

Gurin, P., Gurin, G., Lao, R., & Beattie, M. (1969). Internal-external control in the motivational dynamics of Negro youth. *Journal of Social Issues, 25*, 29-53.

Hui, C. H. (1982). Locus of control: A review of cross-cultural research. *International Journal of Intercultural Relations, 6*, 301-323.

Jesser, R., Graves, T. D., Hanson, R. C., & Jessor, S. L. (1968). *Society, personality, and deviant behavior*. New York: Holt, Rinehart & Winston.

Kim, J. K. (1980). Explaining acculturation in a communication framework: An empirical test. *Communication Monographs, 47*, 155-179.

Kim, Y. Y. (1977). Communication patterns of foreign immigrants in the profess of acculturation. *Human Communication Research, 4*, 66-77.

Kim, Y. Y. (1976). *Communication patterns of foreign immigrants in the process of acculturation: A survey among the Korean population in Chicago*. Unpublished doctoral dissertation, Northwestern University.

Kincaid, D., & Yum, J. (in press). A comparative study of Korean, Filipino, and Samoan immigrants to Hawaii: Socioeconomic consequences. *Human Organizations*.

Krampen, G., & Wieberg, H. W. (1981). Three aspects of locus of control in German, American, and Japanese university students. *Journal of Social Psychology, 113*, 133-134.

McCandles, B. R., & Hoyt, J. M. (1961). Sex, ethnicity, and play preferences of preschool children. *Journal of Abnormal and Social Psychology, 62*, 680-695.

Nagata, G. (1969). *A statistical approach to the study of acculturation of an ethnic group based on communication oriented variables: The case of Japanese Americans in Chicago*. Unpublished doctoral dissertation, University of Illinois.

Ogawa, D. M. (1979). Communication characteristics of Asian-Americans in urban settings: The case of Honolulu Japanese. In M. Asante et al. (Eds.), *Handbook of intercultural communication*. Newbury Park, CA: Sage.

Parsons, O., & Schneider, J. M. (1974). Locus of control in university students from Eastern and Western societies. *Journal of Counselling and Clinical Psychology, 35*, 30-37.

Pehazur, L., & Wheeler, L. (1971). Locus of perceived control and need achievement. *Perceptual and Motor Skills, 33*, 1281-1282.

Phares, E. J. (1968). Differential utilization of information as a function of internal-external control. *Journal of Personality, 36*, 649-662.

Pool, I. D. (1965). Effects of cross-national contacts on national and international images. In H. Kelman (Ed.), *International behavior: A social-psychological analysis*. New York: Holt, Rinehart & Winston.

Richmond, A. H. (1967). *Post-war immigrants in Canada*. Toronto: University of Toronto Press.

Rivera, G. F. (1971). *El barrio: A sociological study of acculturation in a Mexican American community*. Unpublished doctoral dissertation, State University of New York at Buffalo.

Rogers, E. M., & Kincaid, D. L. (1981). *Communication networks: Toward a new paradigm for research*. New York: Free Press.

Rosenberg, M. L. (1969). An experiment to change attitudes of powerlessness among low-income Negro youths. Unpublished doctoral dissertation, Western Reserve University. *Dissertation Abstracts International, 30*, 397.

Rotter, J. B. (1954). *Social learning and clinical psychology*. Englewood Cliffs, NJ: Prentice Hall.

Rotter, J. B. (1966). Generalized expectancies for internal versus external control of reinforcement. *Psychological Monographs, 80* (1, Whole No. 609), 1-28.

Seeman, M., & Evans, J. W. (1962). Alienation and learning in a hospital setting. *American Sociological Review, 27,* 772-783.

Taft, R. (1957). A psychological model for the study of social assimilation. *Human Relations, 10,* 141-156.

Treiman, D. J. (1977). *Occupational prestige in comparative perspective.* New York: Academic Press.

Triffany, D. W., Schonz, F. C., & Woll, S. B. (1969). A model of control. *Journal of General Psychology, 81,* 67-82.

Ujimoto, K. V. (1973). *Post-war Japanese immigrants in Canada: Job transferability, work, and social participation.* Unpublished doctoral dissertation, University of British Columbia.

Yum, J. O. (1982). Communication diversity and information acquisition among Korean immigrants in Hawaii. *Human Communication Research, 8,* 154-169.

Yum, J. O. (1983). Social network patterns of five ethnic groups in Hawaii. In R. Bostrom (Ed), *Communication yearbook 7,* Newbury Park, CA: Sage.

10

Cross-Cultural Adaptation and Diversity: *Hispanic Americans*

LORAND B. SZALAY ● *The Institute of Comparative Social and Cultural Studies, Bethesda, MD*

ANDRES INN ● *The Chinese University of Hong Kong*

How similar are Mexican Americans, Puerto Ricans, Cubans, and other Latin American immigrants in their views and values of mainstream Americans' way of thinking? What do the similarities and differences show in the psychocultural meanings and their ability to relate to their U.S. environment? These questions were addressed in two large nationwide studies that involved the comparison of 10 Hispanic- and 3 Anglo-American regional samples (n = 100). The similarities and levels of adaptation were measured by the Associative Group Analysis (AGA) method. The results offer insights into the scope and major domains of life. The overall distances measured bear on educational and management policies and the findings on the key issues bear on effective communication as well as on mental health to bilingual education.

This chapter focuses on the homogeneity or diversity of Hispanic-American cultures and their relation to the Anglo-American. How similar are Mexican-Americans to Anglo-Americans? How similar are Puerto Ricans in San Juan to Puerto Ricans in New York? How much does the psychocultural distance measured between the groups depend on the specific domains involved in the comparison? We are not speaking of similarities in language or of physical attributes such as skin color or body size; our focus is on people's views, on their shared psychocultural dispositions.

The findings on psychocultural distance will be examined to discuss such theoretical and practical issues as (a) the homogeneity of Hispanic-American populations, (b) the effects of culture change or acculturation on Hispanic-Americans (for example,

AUTHORS' NOTE: *The research results presented in this chapter are drawn from studies sponsored by the National Institute of Mental Health and the Office of Naval Research. The authors are thankful of their financial support. The views expressed herein are independent from those of the sponsors. An earlier version of this chapter was presented at the convention of the American Psychological Association in Montreal.*

Mexican-Americans, Puerto Ricans, and Cubans), and (c) the variation in cultural distances in the specific domains examined. Since findings are based on a method that extends measurements into new dimensions, generally deemed too subjective or too personal to be quantifiable, an operational definition of the present concept of psychocultural distance and a brief summary of the measurement procedure are offered first.

SUBJECTIVE CULTURE:
A SYSTEM OF SHARED REPRESENTATIONS

Psychologists have tended to approach culture through the empirical study of subjective meaning (Osgood, Suci, & Tannebaum, 1957; Miller, 1967). Triandis and Vassilou (1967) have pointed to the close relationship between people's subjective meanings and their behavior, observing that the system of cognitions constitutes a map of the ways in which individuals conceive of the environment, and that different cultural maps offer the key to understanding different cultural behavior.

There is considerable convergence of psychological and anthropological interest in this area, which has been identified by anthropologists as "implicit culture" and by psychologists as "subjective culture." As Campbell (1963) observes, the diversity of labels should not cloud the fact that they have essentially the same referent, that is, behavioral disposition or behavioral organization. Some of the best known concepts include "subjective lexicon" (Miller, 1967), "meaning systems" (Osgood et al., 1957), "sociocultural premises" (Diaz-Guerrero, 1982), "cognitive map" (Tolman, 1948), "mazeways" (Wallace, 1956), "worldview" (Black, 1973), "belief systems" (D'Andrade, Quinn, Nerlove, & Romney, 1972), "thought world" (Whorf, 1956), and "ethnographic dictionary" (Werner, 1969).

Subjective culture is viewed in this study as a system of culturally characteristic views of individuals, that is, a "system of subjective representations" developed and shared by members of a particular group with the same background and similar experiences. This system of subjective representations is passed on from generation to generation in the process of socialization and enculturation. Also, the comparative analysis of two cultures can be conceived of as a comparison between two systems of representations or cognitive maps. In speaking of cognitive mapping, psychologists (Tolman, 1948; Triandis & Vassilou, 1967) do not mean anything like cartographic mapping; it is not a duplicative, photographic process. Cognitive maps, instead, refers to what Downs and Stea (1973) call "complex, highly selective, abstract, generalized representations."

The elementary "units" of representation are subjective meanings and images that are learned by experience, representing important elements of the environment that can readily be given verbal labels. We call these "themes." Based on the clustering of semantic relationships, individual themes are organized into larger units identified as "domains." For example, such themes as "father," "mother," and "children" form the domain of "family." Subjective culture is further conceived then, as a system of subjective representations; an important part of the system is given by the organized totality and structure of themes and domains. Within this system three main "themes" are identified: "dominance," the relative importance of themes and domains; "affinity," the relatedness of representational units;" and "affect loading," the intensity of positive/negative evaluations of representational units.

Following this conceptualization, an analysis of subjective culture involves a reconstruction of its basic *units* and its main *dimensions* (Szalay & Maday, 1973). In such an analysis, the distance between two cultures can be gauged by measuring the distances or similarities between corresponding units and dimensions of two systems of subjective representations. The measurement of cultural distance further necessitates the identification of comparable *themes* of high dominance to two or more culture groups, measuring the degree to which such comparable, translation-equivalent themes have similar (or different) subjective meanings.

CHARTING SYSTEMS OF SUBJECTIVE REPRESENTATIONS

The Associative Group Analysis (AGA) approach follows the methodological orientation of such psychologists as Osgood et al., (1957), Triandis and Vassilou (1967), and Miller (1967) who study culture by assessing subjective meanings. AGA is an unstructured inferential research technique that does not ask for people's judgments or opinions but, instead, reconstructs their subjective meanings from the distribution of their free word associations (Szalay & Brent, 1967; Szalay & Deese, 1978). This AGA approach is a logical extension of the trends in psycholinguistics that emphasize the role of meaning in mediating associations. Noble (1952), for example, introduced a measure of meaningfulness based on the number of associations obtained in one minute. A variety of other measures also have been derived to quantify the relationship for stimulus words based on shared responses (Cofer, 1957; Deese, 1962). Deese has defined associative meaning operationally as "the distribution of response" obtained in free verbal association tasks. He demonstrated that factor analysis of associative overlap index matrices (derived from the overlap of response distributions) offers an identification of main meaning components. Investigations comparing word association, semantic differential, and factor analysis of similarity judgment found close correspondence among the measures (Szalay & Bryson, 1974).

Thus a systematic mapping of subjective representations requires an analysis of the dominant themes and domains of the culture groups compared. Such a strategy is available through a three-step procedure of stimulus selection (Szalay & Maday, 1973). Following this procedure, the systems of subjective representation of two or more culture groups are reproduced based on a comparable number (10-15) of the most dominant domains chosen from each culture. The relationship, or distance of, these systems can then be measured along their three major dimensions: subjective priorities or dominance, perceptual/semantic representation, and subjective organization or affinity structure. Applied to the comparative study of Black and White American samples, the distance measures obtained on these three dimensions demonstrated a high degree of consistency (Szalay & Bryson, 1973).

An application of this distance measure to a variety of culture groups (Anglo-Americans, Hispanic-Americans, Filipinos, Koreans) has shown the importance of culture as a source of perceptual and motivational differences compared to other variables, such as socioeconomic background or gender (Szalay & Maday, 1983). The measure of psychocultural distance has been found to be useful in tracing various types of changes, including the effects of acculturation (Szalay & Deese, 1978), as well as the effects produced by cultural contacts or ideological influences on culturally characteristic subjective views or representations (Szalay & Kelly, 1982). The mean test-retest reliability of this distance coefficient varied between 0.89 and 0.96 depending on the size of the groups compared (Szalay & Deese, 1978; Szalay & Bryson, 1973).

Although there are no criterion measures available to test the validity of the measure of psychocultural distance, the internal consistency of the results can be compared with our commonsense expectations. For instance, Puerto Ricans who live in New York among Anglo-Americans would show more similarity with Anglo-Americans than would those who live among themselves on the island of Puerto Rico. The findings of the present study consistently confirm this expectation not only at the level of overall distances (see Figure 10.2) but at the level of specific domains (see Table 10.3).

PSYCHOCULTURAL DISTANCE MEASURED BY RESPONSE DISTRIBUTIONS

The Associative Group Analysis (AGA) in this study involved the analysis of hundreds of responses to stimulus themes presented in the respondents' native language. The free association task was administered in written form and the respondents (usually samples of 100, 50 males, and 50 females) were asked to write as many ideas in relation to each theme as they could think of in one minute. The responses were weighted on the basis of their ranking, that is, whether they were given as a first response, as a second response, and so on. The weights assigned, beginning with the first in the sequence, are 6,5,4,3,3,3,3,2,2,1,1,1. These weights were derived empirically from the differential stability of rank place assessed by the test-retest method in previous investigations (Szalay & Brent, 1967).

Each response constituted a mosaic element in the group's subjective image of the stimulus theme such as "mental illness" (see Table 10.1). The importance of each of these mosaic pieces in the group's subjective image was indicated by the response score. The response lists a detailed description of each group's subjective image through the proportional reproduction of all its salient mosaic elements. These extensive lists (in which each response is characterized by a numerical score) provide an empirical basis for comparing groups with regard to their subjective views of selected themes, domains, or the entire system of subjective images.

Since the distribution of free association reveals people's subjective meanings, the similarity of these distributions offers an empirical measure of the similarity of subjective meanings. The more identical the high frequency responses of one group are with the high frequency responses of the other group and the more similar their low frequency responses, the more similar are subjective images between the two groups. Pearson's product moment correlation (r) offers a measure for the numerical expression of these intergroup similarities. To measure distance, (r_d), the inverted value of the similarity coefficient (r_s) is used by subtracting it from 1 ($r_d = 1 - r_s$). Thus higher values indicate greater distance between groups in their subjective images. Using the above formula, it was found that Mexican-Americans were closest to Anglos (0.17) while Puerto Ricans in San Juan were furthest from Anglos (0.41) and Mexican-Americans (0.47).

TWO COMPARATIVE STUDIES OF ANGLO- AND HISPANIC-AMERICANS

Samples

Two independent studies were conducted involving in-depth comparative analysis of Hispanic and Anglo-American cultural samples. Each study used samples of 100 respondents of matching sociodemographic composition. The first study (sponsored by the National Institute of Mental Health) compared five Hispanic-American samples (Puerto Ricans from San Juan, Puerto Ricans from New York, Mexican-Americans from El Paso, Mexicans from Los Angeles, and Cubans from Miami) with Anglo-Americans (from New York and Los Angeles). Each of these seven samples were users of mental health service programs (25%)

TABLE 10.1
Twenty Highest Scoring Reactions by Selected Groups
to the Stimulus Theme MENTAL ILLNESS

Anglo Americans (New York)		Mexican Americans (Los Angeles)		Puerto Ricans (New York)		Puerto Ricans (San Juan)	
Response	Score	Response	Score	Response	Score	Response	Score
sick,ness	183	sick,ness	139	crazy	124	madness	193
hospital	123	help	184	hospital	112	crazy	176
help	71	hospital	87	sick,ness	95	hospital	176
doctor	67	doctor	91	help	70	psychiatrist	143
therapy	57	crazy	72	doctor	65	doctor	137
sad	50	sad	49	nerves,ous	61	ill,ness	100
health	48	bad	48	psychiatrist	57	medicine	50
mind	47	people	40	sad,ness	52	problem,s	43
crazy	37	mind	31	problem,s	33	asylum	40
psychology	36	drugs	29	depression	29	psychologist	40
depression	35	head	24	madness	38	mind	35
psychologist	28	medicine	24	drugs	38	health	30
psychosis	28	retarded	24	people	24	treatment	28
retarded	28	depression	19	emotional	22	bad	28
breakdown	26	therapy	19	retarded	22	drugs	22
psychiatrist	19	eccentric	18	treatment	22	nerves	21
people	19	clinic	15	therapy	18	therapeutic	20
schizo	19	brain	17	solitude	17	help	20
Ph.D.	17	problems	17	nurse	15	obsession	18
problems	17	treatment	13	mind	15	brain	18

and their family members and friends (75%). There were equal numbers of males and females, young and old age groups, and lower and higher income groups.

The second study (sponsored by the Office of Naval Research) involved five Hispanic-American male-student samples, again from five regions of the United States (Puerto Ricans from New York and from San Juan, Mexican-Americans from El Paso and Tempe, and Cubans from Miami) and an Anglo-American student samples from New York and from Washington, D.C. The student samples consisted of junior and seniors in high schools from these locations.

Procedures

The association tasks were administered following a standard procedure designed to elicit multiple responses. This written form was administered in group sessions. The subjects received a pile of randomly ordered cards, each of which showed one stimulus theme. They were asked to write their free associations in the language of their choice and were given one minute to each card. Following this task they completed a background questionnaire regarding the relevant economic and sociodemographic character- istics of the subjects.

Rather than statistically representing all Mexican-Americans or all Anglo-Americans an in-depth cultural analysis was per- formed relying only on culturally comparable and representative samples. Samples consisted of Hispanic-Americans who identify themselves as such. By applying the same criteria, matching samples were drawn, comparable in age, sex, and other relevant characteristics.

Acculturation (operationally defined here as a process of psychocultural adaptation) is accompanied by a shift in language use—a shift from Spanish to English. Since the measure of psychocultural distance relies on free association, it is important to ask to what extent is the measure dependent on language. This subject has been explored in several past studies (for example, Szalay & Windle, 1968). As the findings indicate, there is a complex relationship, the discussion of which goes beyond the scope of this chapter. The observed changes in distance among groups of the same language, however, indicate the sensitivity of the measure to assess psychocultural distance independently of the language used in the assessment.

In the present studies, a large number of stimulus themes (up to 120) were selected to represent 10 to 15 high priority domains. In the main analysis, subjective images were reconstructed from the distribution of the free word associations. Psychocultural distances were calculated by using the previously described distance measures based on several hundred thousand responses to the strategically selected stimulus themes.

FINDINGS

Differences in Subjective Meanings

The Hispanic-American studies (sponsored by the National Institute of National Health) address the problem that, compared to Black and White Americans, Hispanic-Americans take limited advantage of mental health services as nationwide statistics show. Leading mental health professionals of Hispanic background have indicated that cultural differences, including differences in the cultural views of mental illness and mental health, are a major factor responsible for this low usage. In support of the widely stated need to adapt both the content and style of therapeutic communications to the cultural frames of reference of Hispanic clients (Acosta & Sheehan, 1976; Boulette, 1972; Miranda, 1976), this research has produced extensive information on relevant cultural images and meanings (Szalay, Ruiz, Lopez, Turbyville, & Strohl, 1978; Szalay, Diaz-Royo, Miranda, Yudin, & Brena, 1983) of various Hispanic-American samples.

Thus present analysis of cultural distances is limited to the theme "mental illness." The cultural samples, subjective images of mental illness, measured by the free word associations, have been grouped into 8-12 main semantic clusters. These main clusters and the score values show the main patterns of perceptions and evaluations characteristic of the groups' subjective meaning of a particular theme.

The results show that Anglo-Americans have a stronger disposition to view mental illness as sickness and as a reason to seek treatment or therapy. Such disposition reflects a tendency to view mental illness as largely a reflection of emotional instability and as a problem of mind and nerves that can be treated (see Table 10.2). On the other hand, Puerto Ricans, particularly the group from San Juan, show a strong tendency to view mental illness as a more extreme state of madness. Accordingly, these groups think more of the extreme consequences, more of medical treatment and hospitalization, and relatively little of prevention or psychotherapy.

Similar findings are observed consistently in other related theme areas of mental health, such as images of the psychiatrist, reflecting their understanding of these problems and determine what they are inclined to do about them.

Distances Between Mexican-American, Puerto Rican, and Cuban Regional Samples

The studies provide a broad empirical database from which to examine the relative distances between the 10 regional Hispanic-American samples. Figure 10.1 shows the relationship between Hispanic-American student samples and between Hispanic-American adult samples as measured by the coefficient of psychocultural distance. As the bars of varying length indicate, there is broad variation in intra-Hispanic distances. The intra-group heterogeneity value of 0.1, shown on the left, conveys the value that should be discounted in construing the actual distances between groups. This value was obtained by randomly splitting the cultural samples into two equal halves, and calculating the distances between the split-half groups. While the heterogeneity coefficients did show some variation from culture group to culture group, the value of 0.1 is a mean coefficient calculated for Hispanic- and Anglo-American samples across the board.

As the distance coefficients among the various Hispanic student groups indicate, the Mexican-American samples show the closest relationship to each other; their distance from the Puerto Ricans in New York is small as well. These Hispanic-American regional samples have lived longer in the U.S. cultural environment, which may explain their close similarity. In contrast, the Puerto Ricans from San Juan, show the largest distances from the samples living in the continental United States. It is interesting to note that the Puerto Ricans from New York are

TABLE 10.2
Content Analysis Revealing the Main Components of
Perceptions and Evaluations of MENTAL ILLNESS

Perceptions and Evaluations by:	Anglo Americans	Mexican Americans	Puerto Ricans New York	Puerto Ricans San Juan
Main Components	Percentage of Total Score			
Sick, Ill	18	14	10	8
Treatment, Help	18	20	16	12
Unstable, Sad	20	16	22	7
People, Family	4	5	4	1
Crazy, Madness	10	9	16	26
Doctor, Psychiatrist	14	11	14	24
Hospital, Institution	10	13	12	14
Bad, Death	4	9	6	5
Miscellaneous	3	3	1	1
Total Scores	1509	1115	1096	1508

closer to the Mexican-Americans than they are to the Puerto Ricans in San Juan.

The distances measured between the Hispanic-American adult samples show similar interrelationships. Again, the Mexican-American adult samples are the closest to each other, and the Puerto Rican adults in New York are closer to the Mexican-Americans than they are to the Puerto Ricans from San Juan. The Puerto Ricans in San Juan show a sizable distance from the Mexican-Americans. In the case of the Cubans, however, the adults appear to be quite distant from the Mexican-Americans, while the Cuban students were found to be relatively close to the Mexican-Americans and to the Puerto Ricans from New York.

As a general trend it appears that there are two main clusters. The first cluster consists of those Hispanic-Americans who have lived in the U.S. cultural environment for an extended time. The second, smaller cluster is formed of the Puerto Ricans in San Juan and of the adult Cuban immigrants whose primary background is from Cuba. While the distances within these two clusters are relatively small, the distances between their representatives are relatively large. This trend suggests that living in the United States, that is, the time spent in the U.S. cultural environment, may be an important factor influencing inter-Hispanic similarities and differences. A comparison with the

DISTANCES BETWEEN HISPANIC AMERICAN STUDENTS

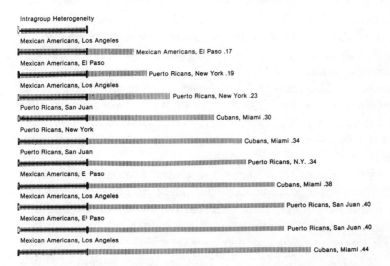

DISTANCES BETWEEN HISPANIC AMERICAN ADULTS

Figure 10.1 Distances Between Hispanic-Americans (Students and Adults)

NOTE: Distance (including intragroup heterogeneity) = 1 − r (coefficient of similarity). Distance is conceived to include the intragroup heterogeneity measured by split half method, which was found to vary around the value of 0.1.

Anglo-American regional samples offers an opportunity to explore the actual value of this observation.

Similarities and Differences Between Hispanic- and Anglo-American Samples

Distances between Anglo- and Hispanic-Americans are presented in the order of increasing distance in Figure 10.2. The Anglo-American regional samples are shown on the left and the Hispanic-American samples are shown on the right, starting with the Hispanic groups showing the least distance from the Anglos and ending with those with the greatest distance. The distances measured between the student samples and the distances measured between the adult samples are shown together. As the bars of varying length indicate, these Anglo-/Hispanic-American distances show a particularly broad range of variation. The Mexican-American and the New York Puerto Rican students are closest to the Anglo-Americans while the Puerto Rican students from San Juan are the most distant. The Cuban students in Miami occupy an intermediary position between the above two clusters of Hispanic samples. The Cubans were somewhat more distant (0.32) than were the Mexican-American groups (0.13, 0.19) and the Puerto Ricans in San Juan have shown the largest distance (0.47).

The two Mexican-American groups were found to be about as similar to the Anglo-Americans (0.13, 0.19) as they were similar to each other (0.20). This small distance of Mexican-Americans from Anglo-Americans indicates a relatively high level of acculturation to the U.S. cultural environment.

In the case of the Cubans, the students show a much closer similarity with the Anglo students than do the adults. This may be explained by the circumstance that these students arrived at a younger age and have been more influenced by their new environment than have their parents who came to the United States as adults. As is rather natural, young people are more receptive to the influences of a new cultural environment than are adults.

The Puerto Ricans in New York also seem to be affected by cultural adaptation. The Puerto Rican students in New York were closer to Anglo-Americans (0.26) than were the Puerto

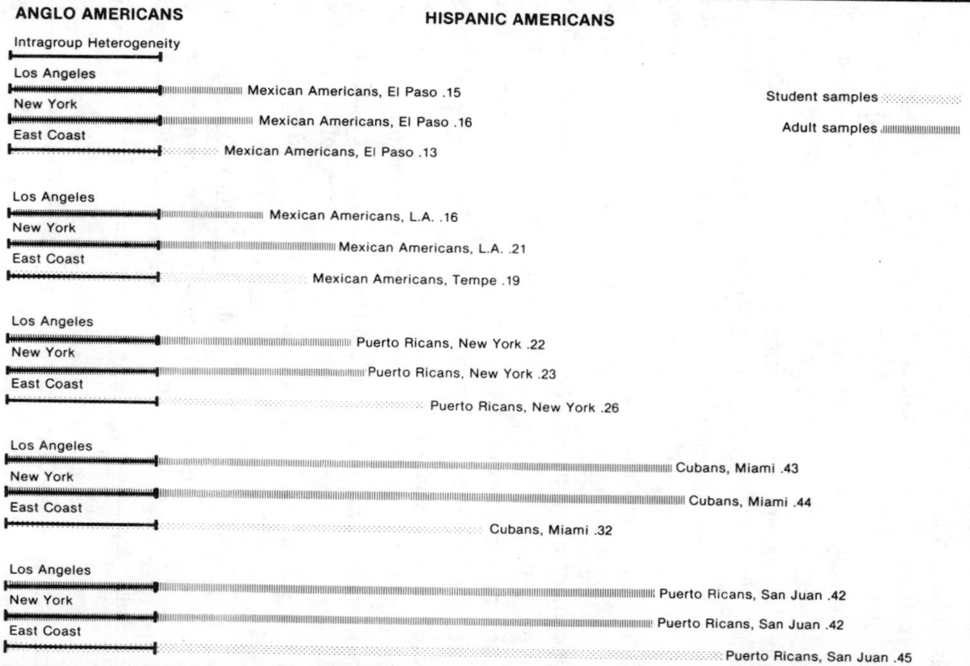

Figure 10.2 Distances Between Anglo-American and Hispanic-American Groups

NOTE: Distance (including intragroup heterogeneity) = 1 – r (coefficient of similarity). Distance is conceived to include the intragroup heterogeneity measured by split half method, which was found to vary around the value of 0.1.

225

Ricans tested in San Juan (0.47). The Puerto Rican students in New York were actually further away from the Puerto Rican students in San Juan (0.36) than they were from the Anglo-American students in New York (see Figure 10.3).

Acculturation is conceptualized as a process by which people who come from a different country or culture gradually adapt to the views and values of the host culture; however, the process of growing similar to the host culture could not occur without eventually increasing the distance from the native cultural environment. The Puerto Rican students from New York, in a progressed stage of acculturation, show more similarity with people in the new environment than they do with people in the original cultural environment.

It is tempting to think of cultural adaptation, frequently labeled acculturation, as a linear process of progressive adaptation moving toward zero distance from the new cultural environment, absorbing elements of the new environment at the same rate as they gradually modify or eliminate old views and attitudes that were part of the original culture. The results suggest, however, that the New York based Puerto Rican group does not follow a direct linear transition from the traditional Puerto Rican environment to the Anglo-American environment of New York. While this group does progress toward the Anglo-American group, at the same time it also moves sideways. This indicates that adaptation is not merely a simple gradual substitution of Hispanic-American with Anglo-American perceptions and evaluations, but that it results in the development of new views and attitudes. This suggests that, while the Puerto Ricans in New York are nearly as far away from their Puerto Rican brothers in San Juan as the Anglo-Americans on the East Coast are from the San Juan sample, the New York Puerto Ricans are still separated by a rather sizable distance from the Anglo-Americans.

Distances Between Hispanic and Anglo-Americans in Specific Domains of Life

The findings presented previously bear on overall distances between the groups compared. The following comparison shows how the distance between selected groups varies across the 10

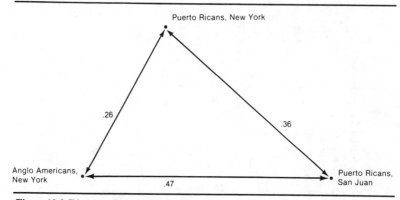

Figure 10.3 Distances Between Anglo-American and Puerto Rican Groups

domains examined in the framework of the present study. The results in Table 10.3 support some of the previous observations. The distances measured between Anglo-Americans in New York and in Los Angeles are very small, particularly if we consider that the distances measured encompass an average of 0.1 internal heterogeneity. If we subtract this value from the distances actually obtained, we find actually no distance. This seems to be the case in several domains such as "religion, morality" or "economic, money." In other words, the distance actually measured here is largely a consequence of internal heterogeneity. The smallest distance between the Hispanic- and Anglo-American groups in this study was between the Anglo-Americans and the Mexican-Americans in Los Angeles, while the greatest distance was between the Puerto Ricans in San Juan and the Anglo-Americans in New York.

There is, again, a high degree of consistency in the findings on distance across the domains. Without a single exception, the previously observed differences are maintained within each particular domain. The distance between the two Anglo-American groups was, in all domains, smaller than was the distance between the Mexican- and the Anglo-American groups compared. The distance between the Mexican- and the Anglo-American groups was in all domains smaller than was the distance between the New York based Puerto Rican and Anglo-American groups. And again, the distance between the New York based Puerto Rican and Anglo-American groups was in all domains smaller than was

TABLE 10.3
Distances Between U.S. and Hispanic-American Groups Measured in Selected Domains

Domain	Puerto Ricans, San Juan / Anglo Americans, New York	Puerto Ricans, New York / Anglo Americans, New York	Mexican Americans, Los Angeles / Anglo Americans, Los Angeles	Anglo Americans, New York / Anglo Americans, Los Angeles
Family, Self	.45	.20	.15	.10
Friendship, Understanding	.62	.39	.26	.16
Community, Society	.56	.26	.18	.16
Love, Sex	.51	.26	.19	.14
Religion, Morality	.31	.15	.12	.10
Economy, Money	.27	.15	.15	.09
Work, Achievement	.35	.25	.14	.14
Education, Upbringing	.39	.22	.14	.11
Health, Well-Being	.35	.28	.12	.10
Human problems	.51	.23	.19	.11
Overall Mean coefficients	.42	.23	.16	.12

Note: The mean coefficients were calculated by the formula $d = 1 - r$. The mean r values (Pearson's coefficient) are based on response distributions obtained for twelve themes per domain including about 2,000 pairs of observations. Z transformation was used to calculate the means.

the distance between the Anglo-Americans in New York and the Puerto Ricans in San Juan.

At the same time, interesting variations in the distances were observed for particular domains. There were above average distances in the domain of "friendship, understanding" and "community, society," while there were small distances in the domains of "economy, money" and "religion, morality" (that is, above average similarities) across all groups compared. There could be two main explanations for this type of consistency of variations. One reason is that intragroup heterogeneity varies from word to word and from domain to domain as well. It is lower in well-defined domains, which include concrete themes such as money or church, and it is higher in domains where the themes have less clearly defined referents such as understanding or freedom. Where the intragroup heterogeneity is lower, one can expect the intergroup distances to be less, where intragroup heterogeneity is higher, one can expect the distances to be relatively greater. Another reason for these variations is that in certain domains such as "religion, morality," two Christian cultures have more in common than, for instance, the domain of "friendship, understanding," which involves interpersonal relations. With regard to Anglo- and Hispanic-Americans, the dominant social nexus shows greater variation.

The consistency observed across domains reveals an important trend. It suggests that the groups more intensively adapted to the U.S. environment (for example, Mexican-Americans) differ from the Anglo-Americans in a similar pattern as do the relatively little accultured Puerto Ricans in San Juan. The differences are a matter of degree. Using a somewhat different formulation, one may conclude that the differences between Anglo-Americans and the various Hispanic-American groups show similar patterns but differ in the intensity or articulateness of these patterns. The relatively unaccultured Hispanic-American groups show these patterns in more articulate forms, while in the case of the more culturally adapted groups, these patterns are less accentuated, less articulate.

CONCLUSIONS

The investigations reported in this chapter represent an attempt to approach the question of inter-Hispanic cultural diversity on the basis of some new empirical results obtained through an unstructured, open-ended method of analysis. The results support a few conclusions.

(1) The results show broader inter-Hispanic differences than were initially anticipated. There are particularly sizable differences between Hispanic-American regional groups who have lived in the U.S. cultural environment over an extended period of time and those regional groups characterized by more traditional Hispanic/Latin-American backgrounds.

(2) The comparison of Hispanic-American regional samples with Anglo-American samples shows the critical role of cultural adaptation as the main factor responsible for the inter-Hispanic differences observed.

(3) The importance of subjective culture as a system of subjective representation receives considerable empirical support from the findings. Cultural background was found to control more perceptual and attitudinal variance than did major socio-demographic variables, such as level of income.

(4) The comparison of distance measures obtained across specific domains demonstrates the systemic nature of culture. These and other findings support the conceptualization of culture as a system of representation determined intrinsically by dominant cultural perspectives.

The broad scope of the above studies and the consistency of the results emerging from 13 independent regional samples provide a foundation for the main trends registered above in the domain of Hispanic-American cultural adaptation. In view of the implications of the findings for education, mental health, personnel management, and other important areas, we hope that the results will stimulate investigations aiming at a deeper and better understanding of this process of cultural adaptation as it effects the largest and fastest growing minority population in the United States, characterized by its own language and culture and plagued by a host of social and economic problems pressing for close individual attention.

REFERENCES

Acosta, F. X., & Sheehan, J. G. (1976). Preferences toward Mexican American and Anglo American psychotherapists. *Journal of Consulting and Clinical Psychology, 44,* 272-279.

Black, M. (1973). Belief systems. In J. J. Honigmann (Ed.), *Handbook of social and cultural anthropology* (pp. 509-579). Chicago: Rand McNally.

Boulette, T. R. (1972). Determining needs and appropriate counseling approaches for Mexican American women: A comparison of therapeutic listing and behavioral rehearsal. Doctoral dissertation, University of California, Santa Barbara.

Campbell, D. T. (1963). Social attitudes and other acquired behavioral dispositions. In S. Koch (Ed.), *Psychology: A study of a science* (pp. 94-172). New York: McGraw Hill.

Cofer, C. N. (1957). Associative commonality and ranked similarity of certain words from Haagen's list. *Psychological Reports, 3,* 603-606.

D'Andrade, R., Quinn, N., Nerlove, S. B., & Romney, A. K. (1972). Categories of disease in American-English and Mexican-Spanish. In A. K. Romney, N. Shapard, & S. G. Nerlove (Eds.), *Multidimensional scaling: Theory and application in the behavioral sciences: Vol II* (pp. 9-54). New York: Academic Press.

Deese, J. (1962). On the structure of associative meaning. *Psychological Review, 59,* 161-175.

Diaz-Guerrero, R. (1982). The psychology of the historic-sociocultural premise, I. In R. Diaz-Guerrero (Ed.), *Spanish-language psychology* (pp. 383-410). Amsterdam: North-Holland.

Downs, R. M., & Stea, D. (Eds.), (1973). *Image and environment: Cognitive mapping and spatial behavior.* Chicago: Aldine.

Miller, G. A. (1967). Psycholinguistic approaches to the study of communication. In D. Arm (Ed.), *Journeys in science* (pp. 22-73). Albuquerque: University of New Mexico Press.

Miranda, M. R. (Ed.), (1976). *Psychotherapy with the Spanish-speaking: Issues in research and service delivery* (Monograph No. 3). Los Angeles: Spanish Speaking Mental Health Center.

Noble, C. E. (1952). An analysis of meaning. *Psychological Review, 59,* 421-430.

Osgood, C. E., Suci, G. J., & Tannanbaum, P. H. (1957). *The measurement of meaning.* Urbana: University of Illinois Press.

Szalay, L. B., & Brent, J. (1967). The analysis of cultural meanings through free verbal associations. *Journal of Social Psychology, LXXII,* 161-187.

Szalay, L. B., & Bryson, J. A. (1973). Measurement of psychocultural distance: A comparison of American Blacks and Whites. *Journal of Personality and Social Psychology, 26,* 166-177.

Szalay, L. B., & Bryson, J. A. (1974). Psychological meaning: Comparative analyses and theoretical implications. *Journal of Personality and Social Psychology, 30,* 860-870.

Szalay, L. B., & Deese, J. (1978). *Subjective meaning and culture: An assessment through word associations.* Hillsdale, NJ: Lawrence Erlbaum/Wiley.

Szalay, L. B., Diaz-Royo, A. T., Miranda, M. R., Yudin, L. W., & Brena, M. N. (1983). *Comparative analysis of Mexican American, Puerto Rican, Cuban, and Anglo American psychocultural dispositions.* Washington, DC: Institute of Comparative Social and Cultural Studies.

Szalay, L. B., & Kelly, R. M. (1982). Political ideology and subjective culture: Conceptualization and empirical assessment. *American Political Science Review, 76,* 585-602.

Szalay, L. B., & Maday, B. C. (1973). Verbal associations in the analysis of subjective culture. *Current Anthropology, 14,* 151-173.

Szalay, L. B., & Maday, B. C. (1983). Implicit culture and psychocultural distance. *American Anthropologist, 85*(1), 110-118.

Szalay, L. B., Ruiz, P., Lopez, R., Turbyville, L., & Strohl, J. (1978). *The Hispanic American cultural frame of reference: A communication guide for use in mental health, education, and training.* Washington, DC: Institute of Comparative Social and Cultural Studies.

Szalay, L. B., & Windle, C. (1968). Relative influence of linguistic versus cultural factors on free verbal associations. *Psychological Reports, XII,* 43-51.

Tolman, E. C. (1948). Cognitive maps in rats and men. *Psychological Review, 55,* 189-208.

Triandis, H. C., & Vassilou, V. A. (1967). A comparative analysis of subjective culture (Technical Report). Urbana: University of Illinois, Department of Psychology.

Wallace, A.F.C. (1956). Mazeway resynthesis: A bio-cultural theory of religious inspiration. *Transactions of the New York Academy of Sciences, 18,* 626-638.

Werner, O. (1969). The basic assumptions of ethnoscience. *Semiotica, 1,* 329-338.

Whorf, B. G. (1956). *Language, thought, and reality.* New York: Technological Press/Wiley.

11

Changes in the Lateralization Pattern of Two Immigrant Groups in Sweden

EDITH MÄGISTE ● *University of Uppsala, Sweden*

Developmental changes of cerebral hemispheric involvement were followed in 80 German-Swedish high school students and in 28 Polish-Swedish adults who came as political refugees from Poland to Sweden. By using a cross-sectional approach with length of residence in Sweden as the main independent variable, second language proficiency in Swedish was found to vary from zero to native-like competence. Various linguistic measures in two languages were taken on the work level for tachistoscopic tests and on both word and sentence level for dichotic listening. The results across modalities provide evidence for decreasing left-hemisphere involvement with increasing bilingualism. The gradual shift to the right hemisphere occurred in both early and late bilinguals to the same extent and in Language 1 and 2 (L1 and L2) for similar languages. For dissimilar languages, a marginally significant effect was obtained for L2 only. The results were discussed in terms of current hypotheses of laterality and provide evidence against the stage hypothesis.

The purpose of the present study was to follow the developmental changes in the lateralization pattern of the brain in two immigrant groups. A detailed analysis of this development for Language 1 (L1) and Language 2 (L2) has not been made previously. Such a study could be expected to cast further light on the confusing picture that characterizes present research on cerebral lateralization of language in normal bilinguals. About a dozen studies indicate that bilinguals use the right hemisphere to a greater extent than do monolinguals. This has been shown for L1 (Gordon, 1980), L2 (Hynd, Teeter, & Stewart, 1980; Sussman, Franklin, & Simon, 1982), or both languages (Genesee, Hamers, Lambert, Mononen, Seitz, & Starck, 1978). But there are at least as many studies where no laterality differences were found based

AUTHOR'S NOTE: *The material in this chapter was presented at the Second Biennial Minority Assessment Conference, November 6-9, 1985, in Tucson, AZ.*

on bilingualism (for example, Galloway & Scarcella, 1982; Piazza & Zatorre, 1981).

The absence of any laterality differences in certain studies might be the result of an inadequate control for gender. There is actually a great number of studies that consistently show that hemispheric involvement seems to differ between the sexes, with men shown as being more lateralized than women. For verbal stimuli, for example, left-hemisphere dominance is generally more pronounced among men, while women show more bilateral involvement (see McGlone, 1980; Earle & Pikus, 1982). Gender seems to be an important factor that may override parameters of bilingualism. However, the chief determinant of the lateralization pattern in the human brain is certainly handedness (Bryden, 1982; Hugdahl & Andersson, 1984; Hugdahl & Franzon, 1985), followed by several other factors such as proficiency level and familiarity with a task, gender, bilingualism, age, and context of acquisition of L2. These factors seem to interact in one way or another (Vaid, 1983).

At least three main hypotheses have been proposed to account for the differential lateralization pattern in bilinguals. First, the age hypothesis, according to which a language acquired after puberty will be less lateralized owing to a greater functional independence between L1 and L2 when L2 is acquired later in life. Second, the stage hypothesis, according to which the right hemisphere will be maximally involved in language processing at the beginning of L2 acquisition and then a gradual shift to the left hemisphere will take place as proficiency in L2 increases. According to Schneiderman (1986), this should be due to processing differences between the competent language performer and the language learner. The early acquirer, with an undifferentiated knowledge of novel linguistic data, relies to a greater extent on holistic strategies, the characteristic mode of the right hemisphere (RH). The active speaker, on the other hand, perceives the complex linguistic elements in a more differentiated way and thus uses an analytical-sequential approach characteristic of the left hemisphere (LH). Finally, there is the second-language effect hypothesis, according to which a second language, learned once a first has been acquired, will have greater representation in the right hemisphere.

An ideal test of these hypotheses would require a developmental assessment of learners at increasingly advanced levels of second language proficiency. An excellent opportunity to follow the developmental changes in bilingual proficiency is provided by the German School in Stockholm, which offers German-Swedish bilingual schooling from preschool to high school levels. What makes this school especially interesting is that each grade includes students with a wide range of residence times in Sweden, from some days up to years or birth in Sweden, so that all degrees of bilingual proficiency can be found. It is also a great advantage to study a small language like Swedish as no instruction exists in Swedish as a foreign language in public schools outside Scandinavia. This means that the students from German-speaking countries are all in the same situation on arrival in Sweden: They do not know any Swedish; they start from zero so that residence time in Sweden becomes an important variable for L2 proficiency. Generally, students from this school show a native proficiency in German and Swedish languages after 4-6 years of residence in Sweden (Mägiste, 1979, 1980, 1984a).

By using a cross-sectional approach with length of residence in Sweden as the main independent variable, the differential laterality pattern was studied in the auditory modality for both words and sentences. The hypotheses give rise to the following predictions: (1) With increasing bilingualism the LH dominance in German-Swedish high school students will decrease for Swedish (L2) when compared to German (L1), that is, late bilinguals should show a lateralization pattern that differs from monolinguals and early bilinguals. (2) Early German-Swedish bilinguals should show a lateralization pattern that is similar to German monolinguals. (3) Both early and late bilinguals should show less pronounced LH dominance for L2 as compared with L1.

EXPERIMENT 1: DICHOTIC LISTENING FOR WORDS AND SENTENCES

Method

Subjects. Only right-handed subjects (25 males, 25 females) in the age range 15-17 years participated against payment. All were normal-hearing students from the German School in Stockholm that offers German-Swedish bilingual schooling. Residence time in Sweden varied between 5 months and 16 years.

Material. Handedness was assessed by the Edinburgh Handedness Inventory (Oldfield, 1971), language proficiency in German and Swedish by self-ratings on 5-point scales regarding reading, writing, speaking, and listening comprehension. The dichotic listening tasks consisted of words and sentences in both German and Swedish languages. Forty pairs of nouns like "Koter-Kater" (German) and "lampa-limpa" (Swedish) were presented binaurally across two channels and heard through a stereo headset at 85 dB with a noise ratio of 60 dB. The pairs of nouns differed only by the vowel in the middle of the word. Likewise, 24 abstract five-word sentences were presented in German and Swedish. One example of a German sentence was "Das Gesetz bedeuted das Ende der freien Meinung." Only high-frequency nouns were used. The sentences presented binaurally were matched on surface structure and were semantically similar. They were recorded in the same voice and with the same precautions to control for variations in intensity, pitch, and timing.

Procedure. The subjects were tested individually. Each subject started the session by filling in the questionnaire about handedness and language background. The dichotic listening tasks were presented on four different tapes, two for each language. Each of the 20 dichotic word pairs was presented twice, the second time with the assignment of stimuli-to-ears reversed. There was a total of 80 word pairs. Two pairs of words were presented successively with a 20-second interstimulus interval. Subjects were instructed to repeat the four words from both ears, if possible, and to name first the word within each pair that they perceived best. Subjects had 10 seconds for their answers, which were tape recorded.

In the case of the sentences, subjects listened to two pairs of sentences successively with the instruction to repeat two of the sentences presented to one ear as correctly as possible in any order during 20 seconds. For half of the sentences, subjects were instructed to concentrate on the right ear, for the other half on the left ear. There was a total of 48 sentences. Conditions and languages were counterbalanced across subjects. At the start of a new condition, subjects were given some practice trials. Subjects with a short residence in Sweden had, of course, difficulties with the Swedish tasks. They were encouraged to repeat the stimuli anyway, which often was accomplished on a phonetic basis with poor comprehension of the meanings of the words and sentences.

Scoring of the data. For each language, the laterality scores were calculated as a function of length of residence in Sweden. Laterality scores are correct right-ear responses minus correct left-ear responses divided by the number of stimuli. A right-ear advantage means LH dominance, a left-ear advantage means RH dominance. The data were treated by regression analysis, and the regression lines were drawn separately for boys and girls. Each point represents a different individual.

Results

Figure 11.1 shows the laterality scores for words in Swedish. Most subjects with a recent arrival in Sweden identified more words correctly heard in the right ear than in the left ear, indicating LH dominance. With increased proficiency in Swedish, the LH dominance decreases, and was more pronounced for girls than for boys. The slope of the regression line is significant for girls, t (23) = 2.95, p < .005, significant for boys, t (23) = 1.96, p < .05, and significant for boys and girls taken together, t (48) = 3.31, p < .005.

A corresponding development was obtained for words in German, the subjects' first language. As indicated by Figure 11.2, there is a slight LH dominance for most subjects with a short residence in Sweden. After 14-16 years in Sweden, about half the subjects show LH dominance, the other half RH dominance. The slope of the regression line is significant for girls, t (23) = 2.26, p < .02, but not for boys, t (23) = 0.77, p > .05. The slope for boys and girls taken together, however, reaches significance, t (48) = 2.13, p < .02.

When subjects were asked which word from either ear they recognized best, both boys and girls showed a clear LH preference in German and Swedish languages, as can be seen in Figures 11.3 and 11.4. It is interesting to note that there was no subject with a residence time in Sweden of four years or less who recognized words better in the left ear. Such a left-ear advantage is quite

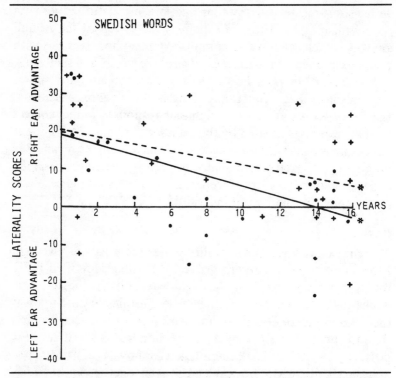

Figure 11.1 Laterality Scores for Words in Swedish as a Function of Length of Residence in Sweden (+ --- = boys, • = girls, * sign = sign).

usual in bilingual subjects with a longer residence in Sweden. Generally, LH dominance decreases continuously for both languages with increasing bilingualism as a long lasting effect in early as well as in late bilinguals. Despite great individual variations, the slope of the regression lines is clearly significant for boys in German, $t(23) = 3.32$, $p < .005$, and Swedish, $t(23) = 2.53$, $p < .01$, as well as for girls in German, $t(23) = 2.79$, $p < .01$, and Swedish, $t(23) = 2.21$, $p < .02$. Girls show less pronounced LH dominance than do boys at all stages.

The results for repeating Swedish sentences are in line with the results obtained for words: The preference for the LH decreases with increasing bilingualism as indicated by Figure 11.5. The slope of the regression lines is significant for girls, $t(23) = 1.71$, $p < .05$, insignificant for boys, $t(23) = 1.14$, $p > .05$; however, it is significant for boys and girls taken together, $t(48) = 2.55$, $p < .01$.

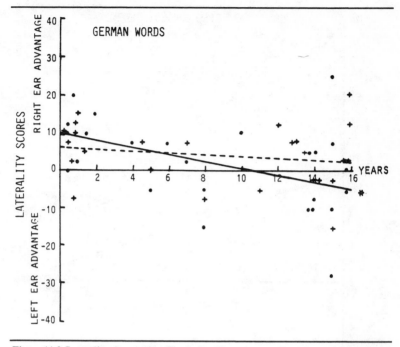

Figure 11.2 Laterality Scores for Words in German as a Function of Gender and Residence in Sweden.

Repeating German sentences was the only condition that did not lead to a change in the laterality pattern (Figure 11.6) and under which girls showed a slight tendency to more LH dominance than did boys. The slopes of the regression lines for both boys, t (23) = 0.93, p > .05, and girls, t (23) = 1.70, p > .05, did not reach significance.

EXPERIMENT 2: TACHISTOSCOPIC WORD IDENTIFICATION

To find out whether results in the visual modality follow the laterality pattern obtained in the auditory modality, a tachisto-scopic study was carried out with words varying in degree of verbal information. Three types of words were chosen and were expected to result in decreasing LH lateralization. With the verbal centers located mainly in the LH, the most marked LH dominance was predicted for abstract words, as these words

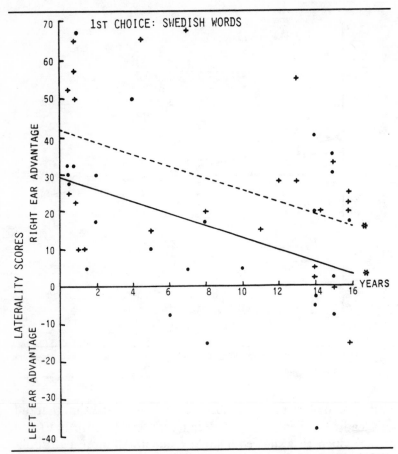

Figure 11.3 Laterality Scores for Swedish Words Best Recognized in One Hemisphere. For both Boys and Girls Decreasing LH Dominance with Increasing Bilingualism.

contain verbal information in its purest form. Less marked LH dominance was predicted for concrete words because of the dual code entailed in these words—the verbal and the imagery. Least marked LH dominance was expected for preverbal coding, a condition leading to a motor response that should also involve the RH.

If the results in the visual study follow the pattern obtained in the dichotic listening study, early as well as late German-Swedish bilinguals should show less LH participation when compared to

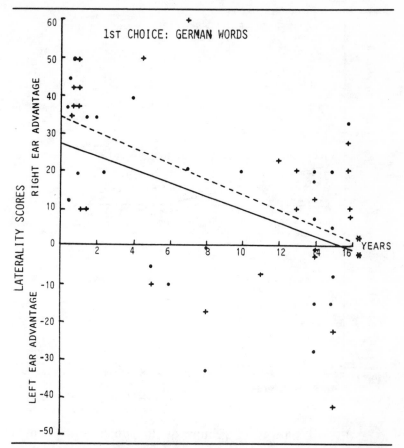

Figure 11.4 Laterality Scores for German Words Best Recognized in One Hemisphere. With Increasing Bilingualism more RH Involvement for both Boys and Girls.

monolinguals. Decreasing LH involvement was also predicted for both L1 and L2 and it was predicted to be most clearly pronounced in the processing of abstract words. To allow further testing of the age hypothesis and to include languages more dissimilar than German and Swedish, an adult group of immigrants to Sweden from Poland was included in the visual study.

Method

Subjects. Thirty right-handed subjects (15 males, 15 females) in the age range 15-17 years participated against payment. They

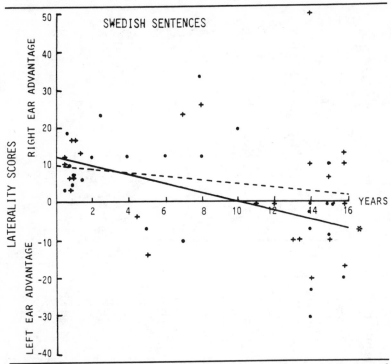

Figure 11.5 Laterality Scores for Swedish Sentences as a Function of Gender and Residence in Sweden.

were divided into three groups of 10 subjects: a German monolingual group with a stay of 1-5 months in Sweden, a German-Swedish late bilingual group with 2-7 years length of residence in Sweden, and a German-Swedish early bilingual group who had resided in Sweden from 14-17 years, most of whom were actually born in Sweden. For both bilingual groups the language at home was German. Swedish was acquired outside the home in a natural context, that is, the languages were acquired in both informal environments and in formal teaching situations in school. These rather exclusive groups have achieved a very high degree of proficiency in their two languages. On 5-point scales most of these subjects rated their skills in German and Swedish as about equal in terms of reading, writing, speaking, and listening comprehension. As to age, social, and language background, the

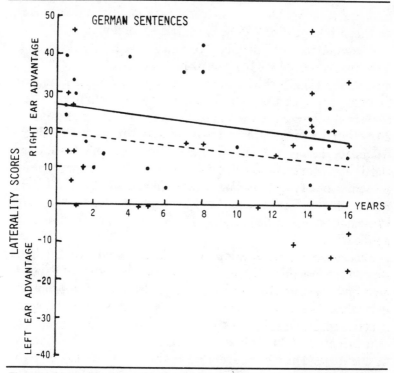

Figure 11.6 Laterality Scores for German Sentences. No Significant Change in the Laterality Pattern Owing to Bilingualism.

three groups may be considered homogeneous. The groups differ mainly in length of residence in Sweden.

Furthermore, 28 Polish right-handed subjects (14 males, 14 females) aged 20-40 years participated against payment. They were divided into two groups of 14 subjects: a Polish monolingual group with a stay between 1-5 months in Sweden and a Polish-Swedish bilingual group with a residence time of 3-16 years in Sweden. Compared to the German-Swedish bilingual groups, this group is very heterogeneous as to age, social, and language background. Workers as well as university professors participated. These subjects do not handle Swedish with the competence of a native speaker. When they came to Sweden as political refugees, they were adults and, apart from a short course in Swedish upon their arrival, they have not received any formal bilingual training. They use Swedish in their daily work, however, and their bilingualism can be considered functional.

Material. In each language (German, Swedish, Polish) there were two conditions: (1) identification of 20 abstract 4-5 letter nouns, and (2) identification of 20 concrete 4-5 letter nouns. In German and Swedish, a third condition was included where preverbal coding was expected by the subjects' motor response to 20 4-5 letter nouns representing objects and animals. Only high-frequency nouns were used, chosen from Eaton's (1961) and Battig and Montague's (1969) word norms. The tachistoscope for presentation of the stimuli was a three-field model G 1132 T-3 B 2 Serial 38301. The luminance was kept constant as 12 lux. Presentation time varied between 150-320 ms and was individually applied.

Procedure. Corresponding to the dichotic study, each subject started the session by filling in the questionnaires about handedness and language background. To find the most appropriate individual presentation times, each subject was given some practice trials and a short session of 12 words. When a subject was able to identify 8-10 of these words, the exposure time was judged as adequate. The words occurred randomly in the left or right visual field relative to a fixation point in the center. Each word was 2 or 2.5 cm long, 7 mm high, and written in block capital letters. The distance of each word from the fixation point in the center was 3.5 cm, which subtended a retinal angle of approximately 2.30°.

All words were repeated twice in mirror/reversed order, first in one language, then in the other, with a short rest between languages. The German and Polish monolingual groups, however, were given words in their first language only. Subjects were instructed to concentrate on the fixation point in the center and to press a button that elicited stimulus presentation. By pressing the button, subjects decided themselves when they were ready to identify a word. Subjects started with the motor-response condition for concrete nouns where they were asked to demonstrate the answer: Clapping both hands indicated that the stimulus was an animal, stamping the feet on the floor indicated that the stimulus was not an animal, and remaining silent indicated that the subject could not identify the stimulus. Then the abstract and concrete nouns were presented in counterbalanced order. Subjects were instructed to answer verbally by saying the word loudly.

Results

Table 11.1 shows the mean percentages of words identified correctly in the left and right hemisphere and the mean differences between the hemispheres. On these differences, separate analyses of variance were carried out for each language. A $3 \times 2 \times 3$ mixed ANOVA was used with three groups (monolinguals, early bilinguals, late bilinguals), two sexes (boys, girls), and three conditions (abstract, concrete, demonstration).

When Swedish was the language of response, the ANOVA revealed a significant main effect of groups, $F (2, 24) = 3.41, p < .05$, indicating that bilingualism affected the laterality pattern. In both early and late bilingual subjects, the laterality differences are clearly less pronounced than they are in German monolingual subjects. This decreasing LH involvement is evident in all conditions and is most marked in identification of abstract words. Whereas monolingual subjects identified 41% more abstract words in the LH, the corresponding percentages for the two bilingual groups were 20% and 18%, respectively.

In line with the hypotheses, the abstract condition led to most pronounced laterality differences in all three groups as also indicated by a significant main effect of conditions, $F (2,48) = 11.2, p < .005$. According to comparisons with Tukey's post hoc test, other differences between the concrete and the demonstration conditions did not reach significance in any group. The main effect of gender was significant $F (1,24) = 5.75, p < .05$, which means, since no interaction effects were found, that the girls in all groups and conditions showed relatively more bilateral involvement than did boys.

A similar effect of decreasing lateralization with increasing bilingualism was observed when German, L1, was the response language as indicated by a significant main effect of groups, $F (2,24) = 4.13, p < .05$, and conditions, $F (2,48) = 17.8, p < .01$. The decreasing LH dominance is found in both bilingual groups to about the same degree, with no particular effect for the abstract condition. The main effect of gender was highly significant, $F (1,24) = 14.58, p < .001$, but there is no simple relation as indicated

TABLE 11.1
Percent Correctly Identified Words in the LH and RH and
Mean Percent Difference Between the Hemispheres
as a Function of Group and Task

	German Monolinguals			Early Bilinguals			Late Bilinguals		
	LH	RH	Diff.	LH	RH	Diff.	LH	RH	Diff.
German words									
Abstract	76.0	35.0	41.0	76.5	53.0	23.5	78.0	49.5	28.5
Concrete	71.0	50.5	20.5	70.5	62.0	8.5	68.5	58.5	10.0
Demonstrative	75.0	56.5	18.5	76.0	72.5	3.5	69.0	67.5	1.5
Swedish words									
Abstract				80.0	60.0	20.0	74.0	56.0	18.0
Concrete				72.0	66.5	5.5	68.0	56.0	12.0
Demonstrative				77.0	67.5	9.5	77.5	70.5	7.0

by a significant triple interaction of group X sex X condition, F (4,48) = 2.9, p < .05. Whereas girls in all groups show a less marked LH dominance than do boys for abstract words, the pattern is the reverse for the concrete and demonstration conditions, with boys showing less LH involvement on these tasks than did girls.

Table 11.2 shows the results for the Polish-Swedish adult groups that were analyzed by a 2 X 2 X 2 ANOVA. In line with German monolingual subjects, Polish monolinguals show a clear LH preference for concrete and abstract words. This pattern does not change due to bilingual proficiency: In Polish, Polish-Swedish bilinguals show about the same LH dominance on the two tasks as do Polish monolinguals.

In Swedish, L2, the differences between the two hemispheres are less pronounced. However, the percentages of correctly identified words in the LH are clearly much lower compared with the percentages for Polish words in both the monolingual and bilingual group, indicating that Swedish is the bilinguals' weaker language. The laterality differences between the monolingual and bilingual group were marginally significant, F (1,24) = 3.58, .10 > p < .05, and the main effects of conditions were insignificant in both languages. The main effect of gender significance in both Polish, F (1,24) = 6.1, p < .05, and Swedish, F (1,24) = 5.84, p < .05, indicating more bilateral involvement in females than in males on all tasks.

TABLE 11.2
Percent Correctly Identified Words in the LH and RH and
Mean Percent Difference Between the Hemispheres
as a Function of Group and Language

	Polish Monolinguals			Polish-Swedish Bilinguals		
	LH	*RH*	*Diff.*	*LH*	*RH*	*Diff.*
Polish words						
Abstract	81.8	45.0	36.8	75.0	40.7	34.3
Concrete	79.6	53.9	25.7	73.9	46.1	27.8
Swedish words						
Abstract				59.6	41.4	18.2
Concrete				63.2	47.1	16.1

DISCUSSION

The results of the two developmental studies provide evidence that the RH participates in the linguistic functioning of bilinguals to a greater extent than it does in monolinguals. Upon arrival in Sweden, young immigrants from Germany showed a clear LH dominance for different language tasks in both the visual and auditory modality. With increasing bilingualism resulting from bilingual teaching programs and informal settings, the LH dominance decreased continuously whereas RH participation increased. This was a long-lasting effect observed in both early and late bilinguals and to the same extent in both languages.

On the basis of the present results, there appears to be no evidence for the stage hypothesis, which suggests that RH involvement is more likely in the beginning than in the advanced stages of second language acquisition. Inspection of the individual data of the dichotic study indicates the opposite, namely, that proficient bilinguals show more RH involvement than do non-proficient bilinguals. Further evidence against the stage hypothesis is also provided by the results of the Polish-Swedish adult group. With Polish as the dominant language and Swedish as the weaker language, these are typical nonproficient bilinguals who should show marked RH participation. Actually, their laterality pattern in Swedish shows less RH involvement than it does in the proficient German-Swedish bilingual groups with equivalent performance in their two languages.

The marginally significant laterality effect found for L2 in the Polish-Swedish group partly supports the age hypothesis. All subjects in this group were clearly beyond puberty when they learned Swedish. The differences in the state of brain maturation during first versus second language acquisition are probably greater in this group than they are in German-Swedish late bilinguals who acquired L2 around or shortly after puberty. Thus less functional independence between German and Swedish should explain why the languages are equally lateralized in the student group. The picture is, however, more complicated because of performance and contextual differences among the groups in the acquisition conditions. While L2 in the German-Swedish group was acquired in both informal and formal teaching situations, L2 exposure in the Polish-Swedish group was mainly informal.

Likewise, it seems reasonable to assume that bilinguals show a comparable pattern of hemispheric involvement across their two languages the more similar the languages are, as with German and Swedish. Conversely, the more dissimilar the languages, as in Polish and Swedish, the greater the likelihood that the pattern of hemispheric involvement will differ across the two languages. Such a differential participation of the two hemispheres determined by degree of similarity between languages could also explain other phenomena in connection with second language learning. It is well known that related languages are much easier to learn at receptive levels than are unrelated languages (Mägiste, 1984b), while at productive levels related languages may cause considerable irritation as a result of interference (Ringbom, 1985). These special difficulties could be a result of greater proximity in cerebral representation for similar languages.

The expectations outlined in the third hypothesis in the introductory section are confirmed only partly, since differential hemispheric effects were obtained in the bilingual groups. If language similarity accounts for these differences, the present results have to be replicated in future research across varying age groups and languages. It also would be of great interest to use other measures of lateralization such as EEG and conjugate lateral eye movements in response to verbal, spatial, and emotional tasks.

That bilinguals to a greater extent than monolinguals use the RH, in which the emotional centers are located, might help to explain other research findings in connection with bilingualism. Carringer (1974), Lambert (1973) and Ruke-Dravina (1971) found a greater flexibility and originality in creativity tests in part of a group of bilinguals as compared to monolinguals. Genesee, Tucker, and Lambert (1975) found greater sensitivity to communicative needs; Cohen, Tucker, and Lambert (1967) found a greater level of perceiving new sounds. Knowledge of two or more languages implies a constant confrontation with different language and norm systems. It would be strange if this continual challenge did not lead to positive transfer effects.

There are, nonetheless, wide individual differences in the number of bilinguals showing the expected asymmetry as compared to monolinguals. In the present study 8-11% of the variance is explained by bilingualism, 10-15% by gender. Sex is an important factor and may override parameters of bilingualism. Nevertheless sex has not been controlled adequately in nearly a third of the studies dealing with bilingual laterality.

As a method, the identification and repetition of single words from both ears does not seem to be very sensitive to laterality differences. The LH preference for most monolingual subjects with a short residence in Sweden is only slight, operating at a little better than chance level, especially and most surprisingly in German (L1). A more sensitive measure of lateralization in the present sample was to ask subjects which word from both ears they recognized best. Despite great individual variations, a clear LH preference for both languages was found in all subjects with a short stay in Sweden. In the case of sentences, it has to be kept in mind that apart from the difficulties in constructing equivalent sentences in two languages, the memory load in repeating sentences is great. The task places demands on concentration and motivational factors that do not exist in the repetition of single words.

In summary, this developmental perspective advances our knowledge in the following ways: (1) The notion of differential hemispheric effects for each language cannot be upheld. The results obtained for German-Swedish students support the idea that similar languages are equally lateralized. (2) No RH-superiority was found in tasks requiring perceptual effort of which processing a new language is one example. In the present experiment, both bilingual groups used more RH-based strategies at any stage of language proficiency than did monolinguals. Since leaning to the right was not a temporary effect, there is not much evidence for the stage hypothesis. This finding somewhat reduces the controversy in connection with the lateralization of language in bilinguals. (3) An interesting observation is the slightly better performance of German-Swedish students on the tachistoscopic tasks as can be seen in Table 11.1. In either language, these students identified more words from both hemispheres than did monolingual German students in one language. This result indicates the success of the bilingual program that the students have been following from preschool to high school levels. The high standards of these students in either language will be no guarantor for a good adaptation in Swedish as well as in German-speaking countries. However, this is a rather privileged group of young people who have many opportunities to train in both languages in formal and informal settings. Usually, no bilingual training is offered to immigrants. The performance level in either language often is lower when related to monolingual performance, which in the present study becomes evident when comparing the results of Polish monolinguals and Polish-Swedish bilinguals.

REFERENCES

Battig, W. F., & Montague, W. E. (1969). Category norms for verbal items in 56 categories: A replication and extension of the Connecticut category norms. *Journal of Experimental Psychology Monography, 80,* 1-46.

Bryden, M. P. (1982). *Laterality: Functional asymmetry in the intact brain.* New York: Academic Press.

Carringer, D. (1974). Creative thinking ability of Mexican youth: The relationship of bilingualism. *Journal of Cross Cultural Psychology, 5,* 492-504.

Cohen, S. P., Tucker, G. R., & Lambert, W. E. (1967). The comparative skills of monolinguals and bilinguals in perceiving phoneme sequences. *Language and Speech, 10,* 159-168.

Earle, J.B.B., & Pikus, A. (1982). The effect of sex and task difficulty on EEG alpha activity in association with arithmetic. *Biological Psychology, 15,* 1-14.

Eaton, H. S. (1961). *An English-French-German-Spanish word frequency dictionary.* New York: Dover.

Galloway, L., & Scarcella, R. (1982). Cerebral organization in adult second language acquisition: Is the right hemisphere more involved? *Brain and Language, 16,* 56-60.

Genesee, F., Hamers, J., Lambert, W. E., Mononen, L., Seitz, M., & Starck, R. (1978). Language processing in bilinguals. *Brain and Language, 5,* 1-12.

Genesee, F., Tucker, G. R., & Lambert, W. E. (1975). Communication skills of bilingual children. *Child Development, 46,* 1010-1014.

Gordon, H. W. (1980). Cerebral organization in bilinguals: Vol. I. Lateralization. *Brain and Language, 9,* 255-268.

Hugdahl, K., & Andersson, L. (1984). A dichotic listening study of differences in cerebral organization in dextral and sinistral subjects. *Cortex, 20,* 135-141.

Hugdahl, K., & Franzon, M. (1985). Visual half-field presentations of incongruent color-words reveal mirror-reversal of language lateralization in dextral and sinistral subjects. *Cortex, 21,* 359-374.

Hynd, G., Teeter, A., & Stewart, A. (1980). Acculturation and the lateralization of speech in the bilingual native American. *International Journal of Neuroscience, 11,* 1-7.

Lambert, W. E. (1973). Cognitive and attitudinal consequences of bilingual schooling. *Journal of Educational Psychology, 65,* 141-159.

Mägiste, E. (1979). The competing language systems of the multilingual: A developmental study of decoding and encoding processes. *Journal of Verbal Learning and Verbal Behavior, 18,* 79-89.

Magiste, E. (1980). Memory for numbers in monolinguals and bilinguals. *Acta Psychologica, 46,* 63-68.

Magiste, E. (1984a). Stroop tasks and dichotic translation: The development of interference patterns in bilinguals. *Journal of Experimental Psychology: Learning, Memory, and Cognition, 10,* 304-315.

Magiste, E. (1984b). Learning a third language. *Journal of Multilingual and Multicultural Development, 5,* 415-421.

McGlone, J. (1980). Sex differences in human brain asymmetry: A critical survey. *Behavioral and Brain Sciences, 3,* 215-264.

Oldfield, R. C. (1971). The assessment and analysis of handedness: The Edinburgh inventory. *Neuropsychologia, 9,* 97-113.

Piazza, D., & Zatorre, R. (1981). Right ear advantage for dichotic listening in bilingual children. *Brain and Language, 13,* 389-396.

Ringbom, H. (1985). *Foreign language learning and bilingualism.* Åbo, Sweden: Åbo Akademi.

Ruke-Dravina, V. (1971). Word associations in monolingual and multilingual individuals. *Linguistics, 74,* 66-84.

Schneiderman, E. I. (1986, in press). Leaning to the right: Some thoughts on hemispheric involvement in language acquisition. In J. Vaid (Ed.), *Language processing in bilinguals: Psycholinguistic and neuropsychological perspectives.* Hillsdale, NJ: Lawrence Erlbaum.

Sussman, H., Franklin, P., & Simon, T. (1982). Bilingual speech: Bilateral control? *Brain and Language, 15,* 125-142.

Vaid, J. (1983). Bilingualism and brain lateralization. In S. Segalowitz (Ed.), *Language functions and brain organization* (pp. 315-339). New York: Academic Press.

12

Interethnic Perceptions and Relative Deprivation
British Data

DEEPA PUNETHA   •   *University of Allahabad, India*
HOWARD GILES   •   LOUIS YOUNG   •   *University of Bristol*

This study explores (nonstudent Asian) Sikh-, Hindu-, and Muslim-immigrant and indigenous Britons' perceptions and evaluations of each other (and West Indian immigrants) across a range of character traits as well as sociostructural conditions. All groups perceived Asians favorably and West Indians unfavorably along certain dimensions, while recognizing the superior power/institutional support of White Britons. Nevertheless, the latter preferred to be as distant from West Indians as Asians who, despite some evaluative differences ascribed to their ethnoreligious backgrounds, appeared to be creating a communal, comparative social identity. Those making up the indigenous group were more satisfied with their job opportunities, intragroup relations, and language status than were Asians, who in contrast, were more satisfied with their economic conditions. Although it was argued that more progress was needed to achieve an adequate level of bilateral cultural adaptation, it was concluded that these particular Asians had adapted their social psychological worlds reasonably well to the prevailing interethnic climate. Methodological/ethical issues relating to this study were discussed.

The postwar shortage of labor in Britain encouraged a substantial immigration from the West Indies and the Indian subcontinent, and there exists a large multidisciplinary literature concerning their adaptation as well as the host society's responses to their residency (see, for example, Allen, 1971; Bagley & Verma, 1983; Husband, 1982; Khan, 1979; Mullard, 1973; Watson, 1979). Although British society had experience of immigrants in the past, for example, Irish, Jews, Poles, and Italians, the new "colored immigrants" were more physically distinctive and

AUTHORS' NOTE: *Gratitude is expressed to the Association of Commonwealth Universities in the United Kingdom for funding the senior author for a postdoctoral scholarship at the University of Bristol (1984-85), and to Karen Henwood and Joha Louw for comments on an earlier draft.*

brought quite alien traditions, values, and behaviors to Britain. In fact, "colored immigration" was commonly known as a "problem" and was reported as such in the news media (Husband, 1977; Khan, 1982). These people were considered "outsiders," and their relationship with the mainstream British society was deemed marginal. Banton (1983) argues that, presently, the British attitude toward colored immigrants is one of resentment owing to their ability to compete for scarce jobs and other resources.

South Asian immigrants, in particular, experienced severe problems in adaptation not only due to constraints imposed from without, but also because of their own particular attributes, motivations, and aspirations. In addition to large-scale differences between their home and the host country with respect to climate, culture, language, and religion, many of them tried to maintain their religious and ethnic identities in Britain (Ballard, 1979; James, 1974) to the extent of keeping themselves separate from mainstream Anglo society. Those who resisted intercultural mixing did so for several reasons: They were unable to speak good English, were less educated, were from a rural background, and had a "dream" of returning to their home country (Brooks & Singh, 1979). Moreover, many of those who possess this "myth of return" perceive their own culture in *static* terms and change in it is viewed by them as a possible or inevitable source of danger to the retention of their distinctive value system. In this sense, they entertain no conception of their own home culture and values undergoing modifications in response to a changing and shrinking world. Yet at the same time, many Asian immigrants who are educated professionals become westernized in their behavioral styles and outlook (Nowikowski & Ward, 1979).

Interestingly, and perhaps in part owing to the crucial sensitivities inherent in gauging *adult* interethnic attitudes directly as shall be seen in due course, the vast majority of British empirical research on interethnic perceptions has been based upon child developmental data (Davey, 1983; Milner, 1984). The present study then explores (nonstudent) Asians' and indigenous Britons' (1) perceptions and evaluations of each other and West Indians along a wide range of character traits as well as sociostructural conditions (see Giles, Bourhis, & Taylor, 1977), (2) their comparative feelings of group satisfaction about prevailing societal conditions (so-called "fraternalistic relative deprivation," (see Tripathi & Srivastava, 1981; Walker & Pettigrew, 1984), and (3) their levels of self-esteem (Louden, 1981; Verma & Bagley, 1979). An important and seemingly innovative feature of the present investigation was that potential differences *among* the different Asian communities' perceptions was examined. While migrants from India, Pakistan, and Bangladesh and the children born to them are known as "Asians" in popular as well as in academic literature, they are, of course, from quite different religious backgrounds and constitute a wide variety of regional, ethnic, and linguistic groupings (see, for example, Bowen, 1981 for Hindus; Tomlinson, 1984 for Muslims; Ballard & Ballard, 1979 for Sikhs) having their own distinctive histories and value systems (Puentha, Giles, & Young, submitted). This study then allows us some access into how different Asian immigrants, who are adapting to British multicultural life, perceive themselves and the position of their group vis-à-vis others.

METHOD

Respondents

A total of 167 respondents from Hindu, Muslim, Sikh (Asian), and White British (indigenous) groups from a cross section of cities (11) in mainland Britain (namely, Southern and Northern England, Scotland, and Wales) participated in the study and were predominantly middle class. The mean age of the indigenous group (n = 97, 36 males and 61 females) was 35 years (S.D. = 15.78) and the mean age of the Asian group (n = 70, 33 males and 37 females; 37 Hindus, 20 Muslims, and 13 Sikhs) was 32.7 years (S.D. = 11.87). All Asian respondents were bilingual in their own language and English and noted to be so when interacting with the female Asian multilingual experimenter who talked to them in both their tongues (usually in a not uncharacteristic code-switching between them). They constituted a first generation immigrant group who had been living in Britain, on average, 7 years.

Procedure

The respondents contacted were those who would be likely to cooperate in academic research as suggested by indigenous and Asian associates and community leaders in the different cities. The respondents were told that the purpose of the study was to discover more about people's views about ethnic and linguistic communities in Britain and they were assured that their opinions would be anonymous and individually confidential. The response rate was 30.85% and 38.3% for the Asian and indigenous groups, respectively. It is believed that the extensive nature of the questionnaire was responsible for this very low response rate but, as will become clear later, other more telling sociopolitical factors also contributed for the Asian respondents.

Research Instruments

Three questionnaires (in English) were provided to each respondent. The first of these was an *evaluative* questionnaire of 34 7-point rating scales; respondents were invited to judge certain target ethnic communities in Britain along these. For most indigenous Britons, Asians constitute a *single* group having common characteristics, often being known as "immigrants" (regardless of time and place of birth) and "Black" (a term designated by South Asians themselves for Britons of West Indian origin). Accordingly, and on the additional basis of a pilot study, our White sample was not required to make evaluative assessments among different sections of the Asian community, whereas our Asian respondents were. Hence, for the indigenous group, the targets were "English," "Asian," and "West Indian," whereas for the Asian groups they were "English," "Hindu," Sikh," "Muslim," and "West Indian." The scales so devised were chosen on the basis of the multidisciplinary literature (cited above) relating to these groups and with recourse to informal interviews (10) with members of these groups. The latter were conducted in the context of participating in mixed-ethnic meetings organized by Asian/West Indian communities for discussing educational, linguistic, immigration, and cultural problems and issues. The 34 scales so chosen thereby related to economic, political, cultural, social, moral, educational, and personal characteristics of the groups concerned. Included in this battery were social distance scales after Bogardus (1925).

The second instrument was a measure of "fraternalistic relative deprivation" (FRD), and the particular items were again selected on the basis of the two sources mentioned previously. This consisted of ten, 7-point scales relating to how satisfied they felt their community was vis-à-vis other ethnic communities in matters relating to jobs, policing, education, health and social services, housing facilities, and language and social statuses. The final questionnaire was Rosenberg's (1965) 10-item measure of self-esteem.

RESULTS

Given that the targets rated were different for Asian and indigenous respondents, the results are reported for each group separately for the evaluative questionnaire. The sample sizes for the three Asian groups were modest (see later) and hence it was not possible to explore statistically the effect of respondent sex on social judgments. Informal examination of means across the three instruments, however, did not result in our construing major sex differences to be operating.

The Evaluative Questionnaire

Appropriate ANOVAs with repeated measures were conducted on each of the 34 scales separately for Asian and indigenous respondents with Neumann-Keuls tests applied to locate differences more precisely.

The Asian respondents. Although interactions emerged between the ethnic group being rated and the ethnic group doing the rating, by far the most evaluative differentiation existed for main effects between "Asians" (summated by raters and as targets) versus "English" versus "West Indians." All three groups of Asians as a whole rated that they were the kindest ($F[4, 260] = 6.87, p < .01$), most hardworking ($F = 15.67, p < .01$), best citizens ($F = 12.51, p < .01$) and most conforming to the standards and rules of their own community ($F = 16.25, p < .01$) in relation to the English. On the other hand, Asians considered the English to be the most intelligent ($F = 12.47, p < .01$), have most access to higher education (F = 43.26, p < .01), higher authority (F = 58.48, p < .01), political power (F = 147.45, p < .01) and political talent (F = 20.86, p < .01), most talented for academic activities (F = 15.00, p < .01), successful in their careers (F = 45.98, p < .01, satisfied (F = 14.08, p < .01), historically dominant (F = 16.26, p < .01), have most useful connections (F = 51.3, p < .01) and business control (F = 27.03, p < .01). Asians as a group considered themselves to have equal economic talent with the English (F = 21.35, p < .01), less cultural superiority than they have (F = 12.43, p < .01), but to have more cultural pride (F = 2.55, p < .05) than the English have. West Indians consistently occupied the other less favorable extreme on all the above scales (p$_s$ < .01) but were considered to be more fluent in English than the Asians with, of course, the English most so (F = 14.14, p < .01).

Interaction effects occurred on a number of scales. Hindus considered their own ingroup the most reliable, followed by Muslims. Muslims considered themselves the most reliable, followed by Sikhs. Sikhs considered themselves the most reliable followed by Hindus (F[8, 260] = 2.06, p < .05). Both Hindus and Muslims believe their own ingroup to be the most cultured, followed by Sikhs, whereas the Sikhs considered the English to be the most cultured, followed by themselves (F[2,260] = 2.59, p < .01). All three groups rated the English as the most well-adjusted group with Hindus and Sikhs considering their ingroup to be the next best well-adjusted group whereas the Sikhs considered that it was the Hindus (F[8,260] = 2.79, p < .01). Hindus and Sikhs considered their own group to be morally superior, which is in contrast to Muslims who rated the English highest in this regard (F[1,260] = 2.15, p < .05).

Following an ingroup preference, Muslims preferred to help Hindus and Sikhs more than they did the English and West Indians, and Sikhs preferred to help Hindus more than they did even their own group (F[8,324] = 6.04, p < 01). After their own ethnic group, Hindus respected Sikhs and English more than they did West Indians and Muslims, whereas Muslims and Sikhs respected Hindus most among the other groups (F 7.17, p < .01). For trust, Hindus trusted the English most after themselves, followed by the Sikhs, and Muslims trusted Hindus second most followed by the English (F = 9.39, p < .01). Apart from their own group members, Hindus liked to invite the English into their houses most, but Muslims preferred Hindus and Sikhs, and Sikhs, Hindus (F = 8.45, p < .01). This pattern of preference is repeated for the items: having a friend (F = 9.63, p < .01), marriage (F = 24.56, p < .01) and being a member of a local community (F = 26.07, p < .01). On the 10 interaction effects noted above, West Indians always received the least favorable rating (p < .01).

The indigenous respondents. Interestingly, the indigenous respondents also considered Asians to be the most hardworking (F[2,303] = 20.20, p < .01), to have more talent for economic activities (F = 23.15, p < .01), and to be the most conforming to their own community rules (F = 4.26, p < .05). West Indians were rated least favorably on the above. On the other hand, indigenous respondents considered themselves, relative to Asians, to be more intelligent (F = 4.11, P < .05) and reliable (F = 9.54, p < .01), to have more access to higher education (F = 30.25, p < .01), to have more talent for academic (F = 9.35, p < .05) and political activities (F = 12.03, p < .01), to be culturally more superior (F = 5.32, p < .01) and richer in culture (F = 13.81, p < .01), more well-adjusted (F = 16.07, p < .01) and satisfied (F = 10.9, p < .01), to be more successful in their career (F = 22.79, p < .01), have greater access to higher authorities (F = 15.3, p < .01) and political power (F = 55.14, p < .01), have more useful connections (F = 30.63, p < .01) and business control (F = 94.67, p < .01), and to be historically the most dominant (F = 147.7, p < .01). With the exception of proficiency in English, West Indians occupied the other (more unfavorable) extreme.

The indigenous respondents preferred to invite a member of their own ethnic group into their houses (F[2,333] = 4.8, p < .01), have an ingroup friend (F = 3.48, p < .05), and marry within their own group (F = 39.79, p < .01) as well as remain a member of the indigenous community (F = 91.41, p < .01). For each of these items, there was a marginal (but nonsignificant) preference for Asians over West Indians.

Fraternalistic Relative
Deprivation and Self-Esteem

The data from the three Asian and indigenous groups were examined together using canonical variate analysis. This was undertaken so as to distinguish which items best differentiated the four groups. In fact, one dimension accounted for 81% of the variance and along this dimension the three Asian groups occupied positions quite close together and separate from the indigenous group. The data can be interpreted as the latter being more satisfied with their job opportunities, intragroup relations, and language status, whereas the Asian groups were more satisfied with their economic conditions. Finally, using a one-way ANOVA, it was found that the four groups did not differ in their self-esteem scores.

DISCUSSION

The findings show that the Asian respondents perceived and accepted their minority group status with the indigenous group being considered the dominant group, thereby enjoying most of the available resources and social power. The data do not suggest, however, that Asian immigrants possess a negative social identity. On the contrary, the findings reveal that they consider their own languages, cultural standards and values, and talent in economic pursuits, in a very favorable light. In addition, personal character-istics such as kindness, hard working, and reliability are highly valued and group-ascribed in ways that doubtless contribute to the expression of a positive social identity. Moreover, the social distance they perceive between themselves and the indigenous population on the one hand, and West Indian immigrants on the other, is in line with other reports of their desire to maintain a quite *separate* cultural identity (for example, Khan, 1982; Milner, 1984).

Interestingly, despite their historically conflicting relationships in India (Ghosh & Huq, 1985; Shackle, 1985; Tripathi & Srivastava, 1981) and that the data were collected after the assassination of Prime Minister Ghandi, the findings suggest that Hindus, Muslims and Sikhs perceive themselves to have a communal identity distinctive from that of the other two "outgroups," the "English" and West Indians. At the same time, it appears that Hindus and Sikhs have, at least on our measures, a mutual respect that differentiates them a little from the Muslim group.

The data from the indigenous group suggests a consensus or shared social representation of the personal and social attributes of the groups concerned. They too upgraded themselves on traits relating to socioeconomic success and, of course, recognize the historical institutional support that favors their group. Nevertheless, they also conceded to the Asian group the same positive attributes of working hard and economic talent and denigrated West Indians. At the same time, it could be argued that the Asians express more ingroup favoritism in their own views of themselves being better, ingroup favoritism in their own views of themselves being better citizens, having more cultural pride, and being kinder than was the case with the indigenous community. Regarding social distance items, however, the indigenous group differentiated little between the Asians and West Indians. In general, both sets of immigrant communities are not favored for intimate relationships.

The results from the FRD measure largely reflect the social reality and relationship between Asians and the host society. The prime aim of the former in coming to Britain was to earn more money and enhance their standard of living. Owing to their hard work and business acumen there has been a marked improvement in their economic condition compared with the past. They feel, however, deprived of job opportunities, yet do not depend entirely on them because of their self-employment network. As Asians maintain distance and "separateness" from other groups so as not to contaminate their culture and preserve their group identity, so they become dissatisfied with the relationship with the host society.

In particular, they feel deprived of the status of their ethnic languages. This is an indicator not only of their ethnic identity (see Giles & Johnson, 1981; Gudykunst, 1986; Kim, in press) but it constructs for them a secure social network of ingroup members who share and provide emotional support. This encourages more intragroup interaction (though they are more dissatisfied with this) and avoids intergroup encounters. They derive great satisfaction in watching Indian films and reading magazines and newspapers in their own languages (see Subervi-Velez, 1986). They are concerned to maintain their languages and to this end have organized themselves collectively and are now demanding recognition of these languages in the state schools and media. They have already opened evening classes to teach their tongues to their children and are deeply conscious that loss of their ingroup languages could result in cultural genocide. Their efforts in pursuit of language maintenance receive positive feedback and reinforcement from their relatives in the home country, and it is clear that they derive much strength and support by these means from what is essentially *their* reference group.

Thus this awareness of their cultural distinctiveness in the multicultural world of Britain, together with their economic security and desire to maintain it, leads them to form a positive self- and social image. This is supported by the results obtained from the self-esteem measure. Indeed, it is our guess that the way an individual is perceived and evaluated in their own ingroup is an important determinant of self-esteem. In the case of Asians, they conform to the set standards and rules of their own ethnic group and this is normatively valued. It hardly matters for self-esteem whether they are evaluated positively by the outgroup or not. Hence, personal worth and social acceptance of Asians is determined and constructed by their own group. They would neither expect positive feedback by the outgroup nor be affected by negative feedback.

We have to face squarely implications arising because (hitherto unmentioned) exceedingly strong pressures were placed upon us to curtail *prematurely* this research, which for some Asians was characterized as being in collusion with "White racism." Such individuals felt that questions forcing evaluative comparisons between West Indians and Asians (and among Hindu, Sikh, and Muslim as well) may induce unnecessary rivalry and conflict between them. It was admitted that differences do exist, but in comparison to the dominant White group, they are jointly oppressed and discriminated against. Although it was apparent that more opened-ended questions yielding spontaneous qualitative data would have been more appropriate (see van Dijk, 1984), it was also obvious that methodology was not the real stumbling block. Complementary with the above objection, it was the investigation of interethnic attitudes, cultural adaptation, and immigrant values per se that was *the* issue in that some respondents felt that the community was vulnerable to our data ultimately being used against them. How far it is justified to ask respondents (even though they are a numerical minority) questions with which they feel threatened and that leave them in a state of uneasiness or anger is a moot and challenging one for intercultural research. Paradoxically, the issues raised in the questionnaire were necessarily those which were of direct concern to the Asians as witnessed by our attendance at mixed-community meetings.

Recent research using equivalent methodologies in the Indian subcontinent (for example, Ghosh & Huq, 1985; Tripathi & Srivastava, 1981), where social structure is hierarchical and itself fosters a fixed orientation in categorization, have *not* reported such respondent disaffection with gleaning interethnic attitudes. Whether we can attribute our own data collection problem—and one wonders how many other researchers have done so in the past and how many are not experiencing comparable difficulties—to cross-cultural differences in individualistic orientation seems simplistic. Rather, we feel that a consideration of the historical consequences of academic research for the community studied in the continued context of racism along many dimensions against a changing and enlightened sociopolitical backdrop is more likely the crux of the issue. Informal discussions with other intercultural researchers in Britain suggest that our own experiences are not at all uncommon.

Our experience also implies that very quickly—and particularly so in ethnic communities experiencing racism and enduring negative attitudes to social science—positivistic researchers will need to develop innovative *ethnographic* methods not only to glean real data that does not just scratch the surface, but perhaps in order to acquire data at all from categorization-resistant respondents. Indeed, unless we confront this emergent intercultural communication issue, we may well see many disillusioned, well-trained and good-willed researchers leaving the intercultural arena in certain societies as the everyday angsts become too intense and debilitating for them to continue to research. Having a "Dark Ages" in intercultural research would, of course, be tragic on many counts, not the least of which would be to leave the area fallow for the pickings of government and pressure groups who are uninformed about social science at best and outgroupprejudicial at worst. More optimistically, tapping the whereas, what, and why of intercultural research problems elsewhere (as illustrated in the above) should allow for far greater interdisciplinary sophistication and methodological elitism to combat racism and, therefore, promote the material, physical, and, psychological well-being of our respondents. In tandem, such an enterprise should also enhance theory to the extent that academic research would not be dichotomized from society, as is all too often the case at present, but instead will become a truly dialectical and important part of society.

CONCLUSIONS

The findings showed that Asian immigrants in Britain believed themselves to be in a minority group position vis-à-vis the host community in terms of institutional support and power parameters (see Khan, 1982). Although they considered themselves less favorably on certain competence traits (for example, intelligence), they nonetheless ascribed to themselves many positive characteristics in terms of their cultural pride, being hard working, kind, and reliable. These perceptions were shared largely by indigenous respondents who also conceded some of the favorable Asian characteristics just mentioned; yet we must also be cognizant of the possibility that such similarities might well be based on quite separate *functional* requirements (see Hewstone, 1983; Tajfel, 1981). In addition, it was found that the two groups exhibited no differences in self-esteem and that they both evaluatively denigrated West Indians. Differences between the groups, however, emerged in terms of their feelings of fraternalistic relative deprivation. While Asians were more satisfied with their economic relations, the indigenous group was more relatively satisfied with their job opportunities, intragroup relations, and language status.

During the course of conducting this research, we found that indigenous people were largely oblivious about the differences *among* the different Asian communities. Yet despite this heterogeneity, which was indeed reflected in the modest number of interactive effects reported, it seems that in Britain anyway, a cohesive "Asian" identity might be emerging (or rather is being *created* in this cultural milieu and technological age) that is cutting across traditional ethnoreligious and linguistic lines and is also fulfilling an ethnic differentiation function (Tajfel, 1978). It is also noteworthy that while Asians are far more respected than are their Caribbean counterparts, they are nonetheless just as undesirable to Whites for close contact as are West Indians. Arguably, at certain levels, Black immigrants are "Black immigrants" (Khan, 1982).

The above findings represent quite clear-cut patterns for the admittedly biased sample of middle class respondents surveyed in English. Obviously, other subject population (for example, Caribbean, East African Asians), changing historicopolitical climates (for example, intra-Commonwealth disagreements about economic sanctions against South Africa; further religious turmoils in India), and other dependent measures (such as social attributions), and so forth, need to be considered in future empirical research in the context of the data-gathering experiences discussed above. Yet evidence has accrued suggesting that despite the traumas experienced in the early years of immigration and the frustrations currently felt and reflected through the FRD measures, the Asian social psychological profiles reported herein are not altogether unhealthy ones. Moreover, while recognizing that racism is still endemic in society, the indigenous group has conceded to an apparent consensus regarding certain positive characteristics of the Asian group.

Cultural adaptation is, or should be, a two-way street. At the same time, much has obviously yet to be accomplished not at least of which is a need for the indigenous group to be aware of and educated in the considerable heterogeneities inherent in the Asian communities. An understanding and appreciation of these cultural nuances is a precursor to aiding a reduction in social and communicative distances not only among the cultures, but also to the indigenous community wishing to proclaim Asian traditions as an integral and valued part of contemporary British pluralistic culture *and* institutions. This state of affairs (which must go well beyond tokenism) could then arguably be an important phase near to an optimal level of bilateral adaptation. To promote this level of intercultural communication is a real challenge, especially so in a country where communication studies has hardly any academic disciplinary status. Finally, and perhaps most disturbingly for *multi*lateral cultural adaptation in Britain, are the unfavorable values accorded West Indian attributes by both Asian and indigenous communities (albeit, doubtless, for different reasons and motives). Thus the empirical stage has been set for a much-needed program of intercultural communication research to be initiated in a nation that has been engulfed by waves of interethnic strife in recent years.

REFERENCES

Allen, S. (1971). *New minorities, old conflicts: Asian and West Indian migrants in Britain.* New York: Random House.

Bagley, C., & Verma, G. (1983). *Multicultural childhood.* Hampshire, England: Gower.

Ballard, C. (1979). Conflict, continuity and change: Second generation South Asians. In V. S. Khan (Ed), *Minority families in Britain: Support and stress* (pp. 106-129). London: Macmillan.

Ballard, R., & Ballard, C. (1979). The Sikhs: The development of South Asian settlements in Britain. In J. L. Watson (Ed.), *Between two cultures: Migrants and minorities in Britain* (pp. 21-56, 3rd. ed.). Oxford: Blackwell.

Banton, M. (1983). *Racial and ethnic competition.* Cambridge: Cambridge University Press.

Bogardus, E. S. (1925). Measuring social distances. *Journal of Applied Sociology, 9,* 299-308.

Bowen, D. G. (1981). *Hinduism in England.* Bradford, England: Bradford College Press.

Brooks, D., & Singh, K. (1979). Ethnic commitment versus structural realities: South Asian immigrant workers in Britain. *New Community, 5,* 109-114.

Davey, A. (1983). *Learning to be prejudiced.* London: Arnold.

Ghosh, E.S.K., & Huq, M. M. (1985). A study of social identity in two ethnic groups in India. *Journal of Multilingual & Multicultural Development, 6,* 239-252.

Giles, H., Bourhis, R. Y., & Taylor, D. M. (1977). Towards a theory of language and ethnic group relations. In H. Giles (Ed.), *Language, ethnicity and intergroup relations.* (pp. 307-348). London: Academic Press.

Giles, H., & Johnson, P. (1981). The role of language in ethnic group relations. In J. C. Turner & H. Giles (Eds.), *Intergroup behavior* (pp. 199-243). Chicago: University of Chicago Press.

Gudykunst, W. B. (Ed.) (1986). *Intergroup communication.* London: Arnold.

Hewstone, M. (Ed.), (1983). *Attribution theory: Social and functional extensions.* Oxford: Blackwell.

Husband, C. (1977). News media, language and race relations: A case study in identity maintenance. In H. Gilese (Ed.), *Language, ethnicity and intergroup relations.* (pp. 211-240). London: Academic Press.

Husband, C. (1982). *Race in Britain: Continuity and change.* London: Hutchison.

James, A. G. (1974). *Sikh children in Britain.* London: Oxford University Press.

Khan, V. S. (1979). Migration and social class: Mirpuris in Bradford. In V. S. Khan (Ed.), *Minority families in Britain: Support and stress* (pp. 37-58). London: Macmillan.

Khan, V. S. (1982). The role of the culture of dominance in structuring the experience of ethnic minorities. In C. Husband (Ed.), *Race in Britain: Continuity and change* (pp. 197-215). London: Hutchison.

Kim, Y. (in press). *Communication and cross-cultural adaptation: An interdisciplinary approach.* Clevedon, England: Multilingual Matters.

Louden, D. (1981). A comparative study of self-concepts among minority and majority group adolescents in English multi-racial schools. *Ethnic and Racial Studies, 4,* 153-174.

Milner, D. (1984). The development of ethnic attitudes. In H. Tajfel (Ed.), *The social dimension* (Vol. I, pp. 89-110). Cambridge: Cambridge University Press.

Mullard, C. (1973). *Black Britain.* London: Allen & Unwin.

Nowikowski, S., & Ward, R. (1979). Middle class and British? An analysis of South Asians in suburbia. *New Community, 7,* 1-10.

Punetha, D., Giles, H., & Young, L. *Ethnicity and immigrant values: Religion and language choice.* Manuscript submitted for publication.

Rosenberg, M. (1965). *Society and the adolescent self-image.* Princeton: Princeton University Press.

Shackle, C. (1985). The Sikhs before and after Indian independence. *Asian Affairs, 14,* 183-193.

Subervi-Velez, F. A. (1986). The mass media and ethnic assimilation and pluralism: A review and research proposal with special focus on Hispanics. *Communication Research, 17,* 71-96.

Tajfel, H. (Ed.), (1978). *Differentiation between social groups* London: Academic Press.

Tajfel, H. (1981). Social groups and social stereotypes. In J. C. Turner & H. Giles (Eds.), *Intergroup behavior* (pp. 144-167). Chicago: University of Chicago Press.

Tomlinson, S. (1984). *Home and school in multicultural Britain.* London: Batsford.

Tripathi, R. C., & Srivastava, R. (1981). Relative deprivation and intergroup attitudes. *European Journal of Social Psychology, 11,* 313-318.

van Dijk, T. A. (1984). *Prejudice in discourse.* Amsterdam: Benjamins.

Verma, G., & Bagley, C. (1979). *Race, education and identity.* London: Macmillan.

Walker, I., & Pettigrew, T. F. (1984). Relative deprivation theory: An overview and conceptual critique. *British Journal of Social Psychology, 23,* 301-310.

Watson, J. L. (1979). *Between two cultures: Migrants and minorities in Britain.* Oxford: Blackwell.

13

Common Ethnicity and Separate Identities
Interaction Between Jewish Immigrant Groups

WALTER P. ZENNER • *State University of New York at Albany*

A common phenomenon found in situations of immigrant adjustment is that the newcomers share a common ethnic or religious identity with part of the host population. This segment of the hosts often becomes the most significant reference group for the immigrants. Despite this, the shared ethnicity is interpreted in different ways by the two groups and it becomes an issue in misunderstandings and conflicts between the two groups. In examining such conflicts, the specific historical and cultural context must be considered. Three examples from the Jewish immigrant experience in the United States are presented: East European Ashkenazim and East Mediterranean Sephardim in the early twentieth century, East European Jews and German refugees during the 1930s and 1940s, and in greatest detail, American Jews and Soviet emigrés during the 1970s and 1980s. In each instance, different aspects of Jewish identity were at issue.

INTRODUCTION

A common phenomenon found institutions of immigrant adjustment is that the immigrants often share certain common identities with groups in the host population and with each other, but at the same time such shared features are interpreted by each in ways that make for disagreement and even for rejection. In some instances, this is the outcome of a long history of separate development, as well as adjustment to new circumstances. An example of this was the reaction of the Irish Catholics of Mechanicsville, NY, early in this century, to the near "pagan" celebrations at saints' feasts among the newly arrived Italian immigrants. Both shared the common religion imposed by a

AUTHOR'S NOTE: *This chapter dealing with Soviet Jews is a product of research carried out on behalf of the Albany Jewish Family Services with the assistance of Allan Yasgur, its director in 1981, and Debra Hiller, its resettlement coordinator. The cooperation of Soviet emigrés in Albany made this work possible, as did the aid of Linda Zenner. Gail Landsman read an early version of the chapter and made valuable suggestions.*

centralized hierarchy, yet historical experiences of Irish-American Catholics were forged against the backdrop of being Roman Catholics in iconoclastic Protestant settings, while the Italians had been raised in a setting where Catholics were the over-whelming majority (Kardash, 1975).

In this instance, as in others that will be discussed here, the common religion or descent forms a shared point of reference around which both the new immigrants and the hosts can act. This common point of reference may serve to provide a symbol of family and brotherhood, but it may also serve to focus conflict. The Italians and the Irish in the early 1900s thus could argue over what constituted "true" or "good" Catholicism. Of course, this was more than an understanding or misconstruction of a particular set of doctrines. Interwoven here were issues involved with how the behavior of Italian Catholics would affect the esteem with which White Protestant Americans would hold all adherents of the Church of Rome and the way in which the veteran American hierarchy, dominated by Irish old-timers, could control and mobilize these alien Catholics so as to strengthen their own power. The mingling of cultural and political issues in such intrasectarian and intraethnic disputes will be exemplified in several cases in this chapter.

SHARING A COMMON IDENTITY

This chapter will deal with the interaction of members of groups who claim a common identity. Immigrants often seek out help from groups already resident in the new society and who share a common identity with them. Such a group is not necessarily the dominant ethnic group in the host society. Still, because of its putative and historical relationship with the immigrant group, whether on account of descent, religion, or language, it is the group that the immigrants are most likely to emulate, and elements of the majority culture are often filtered through the institutions of this veteran group.

While the new immigrant and veteran groups share a common identity and partake of a common heritage at a variety of levels, the different settings and experiences that each has had gives each a different form of the common identity. Since the groups come into contact with differing perceptions, the assumed common identity, in fact, becomes a focus of conflict and misinterpretation as well as of comedy. The disappointments that result from such flaws in communication sharpen the conflict that may emerge, but it may also cause the immigrants or the veterans to modify their culture so as to conform to the definitions held by the other.

Ethnicity and Identity

In discussing such identities, we use words that are near-synonyms, as in the use of the word ethnicity, which is opposed to identity in the title. "Ethnicity" implies that a sense of common destiny is shared on the basis of descent, whether factual or fictional. Ethnicity implies a boundary based on such a sense of shared identity, descent, and destiny. Whether the term applies to the larger grouping or the smaller one is irrelevant. For the most part; neither the literatures on ethnicity nor acculturation have yielded any grand theory, though valuable empirical generalizations abound.

In this chapter, the subjects will be Jewish groups, but as indicated above, similar problems in communication arise with regard to others, such as Catholics, Chinese, Poles, and Blacks. This chapter will deal with a number of situations of interaction: between East European Ashkenazic Jews and Eastern Mediterranean Sephardic Jews in the early twentieth century, between American Jews of East European origin and German Jewish refugees during the 1930s and 1940s, and finally between American Jews of East European origin and recent Soviet Jewish emigrés.[1] Each instance involves different aspects of the discrepancies in the identification. The most recent case, that of Soviet immigrants coming to the United States between 1973 and 1981, will be dealt with in greater detail than will the other examples.

Recognition of a Common Jewishness: "Funny, You No Look Jewish!"

Jews in the United States, where many are behaviorally assimilated, often signal their common identity to each other. For instance, two academics who meet may test each other out by using a slightly Yiddish turn of phrase or intonation to see if the other will return the signal. Or, a young woman in a community center locker room may be speaking with an older woman who is unsure if the younger woman is Jewish. The younger woman, realizing this, may signal her Jewishness by referring to her grandmother as *Boba,* the Yiddish term (Plotnicov & Silverman, 1978).

Such signals work however, only when a common linguistic base is shared. In this case, it was the East European Ashkenazic background. The East European Ashkenazim formed the largest block of Jews in the world during the nineteenth and twentieth centuries. They constituted the vast majority of European Jewry in Russia, Poland, and other East and Central European countries, as well as the overwhelming majority of the Jews of the United States and other Western lands. In Eastern Europe, they spoke their own language, the Eastern dialects of Yiddish, a Germanic language, and they were concentrated in towns where they were often the majority. More than any other Jewish group, they formed a solid cultural-ethnic unit. This very size made them feel that their form of Jewishness defined Jewishness.

In the United States, "Jewish food" is generally that of the East European Ashkenazim (such as rye bread, corned beef, chicken soup with matzo dumplings or noodles, chopped liver, bagels, and gefilte fish). The traditional domestic language of these Jews is Yiddish or "Jewish." Even in Israel, where the variety of different Jewish ways is recognized, one can find media statements about a traditional Sabbath meal beginning with chicken soup and gefilte fish. Thus when East European Ashkenazim have encountered Jews who do not share their language or ways, they have often questioned their Jewishness or else their faithfulness to Jewish identity.

SEPHARDIC-ASHKENAZIC COMMUNICATION

Early in the twentieth century, when Eastern Mediterranean Sephardic Jews immigrated to the United States, at the height of the great East European wave of immigration, they found that they were often not recognized as Jews. Even when the Sephardim and Ashkenazim recognize their common Jewishness, they often have found their differing interpretations quite alien. Despite nearly identical Hebrew prayers, the two groups pronounced the Hebrew so that it is almost unintelligible to the others, and different gestures accompany the prayers (Sutton, 1979, p. 23). In such circumstances, one might even have doubts about a fellow worshiper as Joseph A. D. Sutton writes:

> During a mid-week prayer service in an East European synagogue, my father ritually clothed in *taleet*, a prayer shawl, and *tefileen*, phylacteries, was approached by an Ashkenazic congregant. Since he did not understand what was being said to him in "plain Yiddish," the man who had spoken to him asked in evident amazement, *"Bist du a Yid?" ('Are you a Jew?')*

Similar experiences were common (Sutton, 1979, p. 23; also see Zenner, 1983, pp. 186-187; Sephardic Archives, 1986, pp. 31-32).

Marc Angel, writing about the "Hispano-Levantine" Sephardim from Turkey and the Balkans, similarly points out their different ways. He stresses their dismay at not finding a chief rabbi or similar organization of Jewish life. In addition, they were set apart by their "strong sense of pride" and resentment at accepting charity. Like the Arabic speakers, they did not speak Yiddish, yet they also had a strong attachment to their domestic mother tongue. Instead of gefilte fish, they ate *pescado con tomat* (fish in a sweet-sour tomato sauce) or *pescado con huevas y limon* (fish in egg-lemon sauce) on the Sabbath eve. In Seattle, Ashkenazim taunted the Sephardim by calling them *mazola,* because the latter used vegetable oils rather than chicken fat, while the Sephardim retorted by calling the Ashkenazim *shmaltz* (chicken fat).

In this interaction between the Levantine Sephardim and the Ashkenazim, there was the often unspecified norm that Jews should treat each other in a more personal manner than that with which they deal with non-Jews, and that one is given charity on the basis of one's Jewishness. Both the Ashkenazim from Eastern Europe and the Sephardim came from communities where this was the norm, even though there were some exceptions. There were, however, also reasons for maintaining one's distance from the other group of Jews. Various groups of immigrants were stigmatized in several ways. Each group feared that the other might be insufficiently Jewish and there are stories about Askhenazim forbidding marriage with Sepharadim and vice versa.

In some cases the smaller Sephardic group, with Italian or Hispanic surnames and Mediterranean appearances, were not recognized as Jewish by the larger Ashkenazic groups. Individuals tell stories of proving that they were more Jewish than were the Ashkenazic parents of their dates (Stern, 1977, pp. 98-99). Doubts about Jewishness might, however, be expressed in a more fundamental way as when some Syrian Jews question the Jewish ancestry of Ashkenazic neighbors. There were also reflections of the prejudices of "Old" Americans against Turks, Jews, and Syrians. Stern writes (1977, p. 98):

> Prejudice played a significant role in inhibiting a Jewish identity and Sephardic Jews were often reluctant to admit their Jewishness. . . . The hiding of one's Jewish identity and its subsequent revelation is a common motif in immigrant experiences. It was perhaps easier for the Sephardic Jew who could pass for a Greek, Turk, Italian or Frenchman to conceal his identity than it was for Ashkenazi.

The use of the term *Jew* in an unmarked fashion for an Ashkenazi East European assisted the Sephardim in this. It is significant that the self-appellation is generally Sephardi, or some variant, such as SY, while East European Jews are tagged Jew, Yid, and so on (Plotnik, 1958; Sutton, 1979, p. 151; Zenner, 1983). It would fit the effort to dissociate oneself from the more stigmatized group.

Despite these problems in mutual recognition, Sephardic Jews in the United States did not dissociate themselves from the Ashkenazim. Representatives of both groups made efforts to maintain relations. During the period of mass immigration, in fact, the main centers of the new Levantine Sephardic immigrants in New York City, whether Ladino-, Greek- or Arabic-speakers, were on the Jewish Lower East Side. From the earliest period on, Sephardic Jews built "parallel ethnic institutions" (Broom & Kitsuse, 1955; Zenner, 1983). Such parallel institutions include synagogues, but also secular organizations. The models were not just American, but Jewish. Some were branches of other Jewish and general organizations such as B'nai Brith, Girl Scouts, and the like. Others were modeled clearly on those of American Jews and other Americans, such as the Oriental Jewish Maccabee Organization, the Young Men's Sephardic Association, and the later Magen David and Sephardic Community Centers (Angel, 1982; Zenner, 1983). As these examples show, the Sephardim have seen themselves as Jews and have striven to maintain their identity in the new American environment. While they saw the Ashkenazim as somewhat strange, they were also a primary reference group with whom they compared themselves and who served as models.

The interaction of Central European Ashkenzaim with East European Ashkenazim is more complex, since there is a gradient, rather than a clear boundary, separating these two groups, even if we go back in time. First, the East European Ashkenazim are, for the most part, descended from migrants from Germany; their language and rites certainly originated in medieval Germanic lands. As their numbers grew to exceed those of the Jews of the Germanic lands, many found their way back to Germany and the interaction between the two communities was often difficult. This was especially true during the late nineteenth and early twentieth centuries, when the more affluent German Jews received their East European cousins as poor immigrants who also reminded their neighbors of the Jewish exoticism that the former sought to shed. Both in Europe and America, the more acculturated German Jews felt that their own precarious status was endangered by the "Jewishness" of the Jews from Russia and Poland. While the German Jews resented the cultural attributes of the *Ostjuden,* the latter could often not abide the exclusiveness, the condescension and the assimilationism of the *deutsches yehudim.* This mutual repulsion is still vivid in the memory of the older East European generation today, although its significance has diminished.

A symbol of the differences between the two groups was the Yiddish language. While Yiddish has a Germanic base, it also uses Hebrew words and has borrowed such Slavic words as *boba,* the word for grandmother. German Jews formerly used a Yiddish dialect (which is called Western Yiddish by scholars), as their domestic language and continued to use Yiddish-Hebrew words of their own. Still, by the 1930s, many Jews in Germany no longer spoke a dialect of Yiddish, but rather used standard German, though they might use some special Jewish expressions.

As a result of the advent of Hitler in Germany, large numbers of German Jews became refugees. Now they came to communities where they, rather than the East Europeans, were the greenhorns and the recipients of charity. This reversed the relationship between East European and German Jews that had prevailed during the previous half-century. One refugee woman was asked by an American Jewish neighbor, born in Eastern Europe, a question in Yiddish. When she replied that she did not speak that language, the East European woman refused to believe her and suggested that she merely denied knowing Yiddish.

Among those German and Central European Jews who were Orthodox, there was a group who learned Yiddish in America, partly in order to validate their Jewishness and to be able to communicate with other traditionalist Jews. The communication with other traditionalists was not for commercial reasons, since the veteran East Europeans and the refugees both had learned English, nor was Yiddish the language of prayer; rather, it was that Yiddish retained its place as the language that marked Jew from non-Jew and provided both groups of Ashkenazim a private language. (Heilman, 1976, p. 229-230; Lowenstein, 1985, p. 252).

Among those German Jews who were not Orthodox and who remained outside that orbit, there was less need to learn Yiddish, though many picked up the kind of Yiddish expressions that were common among Jews and other urbanites in the United States. There, the need for a common private language was less intense.

A cultural distinction occurred among immigrants of different lengths of stay in the new land, as well as on the basis of an earlier ethnic/cultural division. Recently, Isaac Bashevis Singer wrote an essay in which he expressed this distinction between the East European old-timers and the greenhorns from Poland. He describes the trauma he felt on his arrival in America. This was especially keen, since he was a writer, but he is also describing a more universal experience of immigrants:

In my case, not only was I cut off from my language but I also felt my way of thinking, my notions and my concepts, had been distorted. There was no place for demons in Manhattan or Coney

Island . . . I could no longer recognize my people by their speech patterns, their dress, their gestures and mannerisms. . . . I am not exaggerating when I say that it took me years to get over this crisis. (Singer, 1985)

If one looks at Singer's immigration in 1935, one realizes that he has come to a city in which approximately two million Jews of recent East European origin live. He has arrived about 11 years after the cessation of the great migration and many of those whom he encountered were either first or second generation immigrants. To most Americans, New York Jews are a quite distinctive group, marked by East European mannerisms. Yet they are as foreign to the Jewish greenhorn as to the midwestern Gentile.

THE RECENT SOVIET JEWISH
IMMIGRATION TO THE UNITED STATES[2]

The small wave of Soviet Jewish immigrants between 1974 and 1980 exemplifies the alienation many feel to their own people in a different land. It also illustrates how institutional arrangements may be unsuited for different groups. Even though most of the immigrants who left the Soviet Union in that period were Ashkenazim, descended from Yiddish-speakers in the old Pale of Settlement, which contained most of the Jews in Tsarist Russia, they had been separated from the East European Askhenazim in North America by 60-odd years of the Soviet regime.[3] Both the North Americans and the Soviets had undergone considerable and rapid cultural change. The Yiddish language had ceased to be the main domestic language for both and traditional Judaism has been replaced in both countries, although in quite different ways. The far-reaching effects of the divergent development of these two branches of the eastern Ashkenazim have emerged as members of the Soviet community were thrown into the American Jewish community.

In the United States, Jews asserted their identity, often stressing the religious, rather than the ethnic or national, aspect, although there was always room for expression of the latter ones. Although a great deal of conformity to Anglo-American ways was encouraged and enforced, the individualism of American society allowed for the maintenance and persistence of Jewish expression through voluntary associations. In fact, the degree of voluntarism in the American setting is much greater than it was in the traditional Jewish communities of Europe and the Middle East and is its hallmark. Jewish identity in the United States may be asserted, but it is not legally defined, even for census purposes (Zenner, 1985).

Jewishness in the U.S.S.R.

The situation in the Soviet Union was quite different. While the Jews were recognized as a nationality or people, there was no Jewish republic or autonomous region. Hebrew was suppressed early on because of its connection with religion and Zionism. While Yiddish was recognized, Yiddish literary expression was restricted first by the Soviet attitude that while forms might be national, content should conform to "socialist" ideology. Then in the period between 1948-1952, major Jewish literary figures were purged and liquidated. Just a few synagogues in major cities remain open, so one literary organ remains as a showpiece of toleration. For most Jews in the Soviet Union, Russian was the language of preference, rather than Yiddish or other local languages. The Jews of Georgia are a notable exception to this.

In many ways, being a Jew meant membership in a stigmatized people. One immigrant told the interviewer about his feelings about being Jewish. He stated that in the Soviet Union, Slavs were at the top of the social hierarchy while Jews and Gypsies were on the lowest steps. Then he said:

> You were asking me if I'm proud to be a Jew. I cannot answer . . . you because to say if I am proud to be a Jew, it will not be true. But it will be true if I say to you, I never intended to change my religion . . . it will not be true if I say I'm Jewish and I'm proud, because I feel so many hardships, so many difficulties, it's not a ground to say I'm proud.

It was not easy, though not entirely impossible, to change one's nationality. Jews were recognized on account of family names and patronymics, as well as their nationality on the passport, which all residents of the U.S.S.R. must carry, plus their physiognomy. The same immigrant who came from Moldavia suggested that it is possible to change one's nationality, however. One way is to convert to the Russian Orthodox Church, which despite the atheistic nature of the Soviet state, allows one to escape the stigma of Jewishness. Another is simply to rip up your internal passport and apply for a new one as a Russian. This interviewee suggested that one can change one's name, such as changing the Jewish "Chaim" to the Russian "Efim." Despite its dubious illegalities, he said it is fairly easy for effecting certain nationality changes, so that Moldavians in Moscow can become "Russians" by adopting Slavic names.

This attitude contrasts sharply with that current in the United States today (though not in the recent past). Bearing a Jewish name or asserting Jewish identity is not a particular stigma here today. Even individuals who are fairly assimilated and have little interest in Judaism make no attempts to hide their origins. Articles on Jewish culture appear in newspapers and even such elite food magazines as *Gourmet*. The volunteers and professionals who help Soviet Jewish immigrants to acculturate include individuals who are particularly assertive in expressing their ethnic identity (Markowitz, 1985).

Since religious activity has been discouraged and formal voluntary associations do not exist in the Soviet Union, Jewish cultural transmission has been severely limited. Government-supported Yiddish schools disappeared under Stalin. Jewish cultural transmission after World War II was, in effect, confined to the family and informal groupings.

In Albany, as well as in other places, it was found that many Soviet Jews had been rarely in a synagogue. Those who spoke about Jewish matters had learned about them from outside the Soviet Union. While some would say that they had attended Seders (the ceremonial meal marking the celebration of Passover), the content of such Sedarim was not given. In addition, many Soviet Jewish males are uncircumcised, and weddings in the Soviet Union are civil, not religious.

The lack of formal ritual, however, may lead one to believe that the Soviet Union has reduced behavioral differences among ethnic groups to the point of disappearance. Yet there is evidence from Soviet social scientific sources that considerable variability persists in courtship, family size, and wedding customs, especially in western and central Asia (Gantskaja & Terent'eva, 1978). The maintenance of some separate custom by Jews is likely, especially where there are large concentrations as in Odessa. There are indications that in the Soviet Union, Jews have mainly other Jews as close friends (Gilison, 1981, pp. 46-48). The subculture of these informal "invisible" networks remains to be studied.[4]

In going into some detail about the nature of Jewishness in the Soviet Union, I must note that this parallels the sharp division between an official "command" economy and the unofficial, informal sector of the economy, usually called the "black market." The lack of experience with religious and ethnic voluntary organizations, and having their own administrative structure, mirrors the lack of experience with licensed private enterprise. In addition, the official and informal stigmatization of Jewishness in the Soviet Union makes the freer expression of Jewish identity in the United States seem foreign. Thus despite common roots, the recent Soviet immigrants and the predominantly East European Ashkenazic Jews of the United States have diverged quite radically. Because of the radical transformation induced by both Soviet and American cultures, the interpretation of Jewishness in the two countries is farther apart than it is in the other cases cited here.

"Re-Judaization" Programs and Soviet Emigrés

In coming to America, the Soviet Jews faced a change of identity, which Markowitz (1985) has summarized in the phrase "Jew in the Soviet Union, Russian in America." This kind of marking has been found among the other groups considered. Yet the nature of the Jewishness that was questioned was different in the other cases. The Sephardim were unquestionably Judaic with regard to religion, and the German refugees who were liberal or nonreligious fit in with the varieties of Judaism found in the United States. These other groups arrived in America with their own rabbis or imported them after they established congregations. This could not occur with the "de-Judaized" Soviet emigrés. For the first time in American Jewish history, American Jewish agencies were concerned with the "Judaization" of an immigrant

Jewish group, as well as with its Americanization.

Such "Judaization" efforts in the Albany area included offering scholarships to Jewish day schools and day camps, free tickets to High Holiday services,[5] and invitations to Seders. Volunteers in resettlement programs were encouraged to accompany Russian immigrants to the synagogue and to invite them to their homes for the Sabbath or holidays. Such efforts were desultory. The Jewish family agency was in charge of the resettlement program and it was interested primarily in economic integration. For both agency and immigrant, jobs, apartments, and medical care took precedence over acculturation and "Judaization." To the agency social workers, "Judaization" was a goal secondary to assisting people in their personal adjustment (also see Gold, 1985, pp. 189-191). Still, mutual expectations based on the recognition of Jewish identity affected the relationships between American and Russian Jews.

Decisions relating to housing, for instance, had an important effect on other aspects of the program. Many immigrants were housed in a development in which most other tenants were Black or Vietnamese. This development was in a part of Albany far from the neighborhoods where most other Jews live. There were good reasons for settling the Russians there, but it made them feel excluded from the middle-class Jewish community. They felt that they had been treated poorly. This also inhibited "Judaization" since they were far from the Jewish Community Center and provision of transportation to the Jewish day school and synagogues was difficult, especially since most did not have cars (Zenner & Hiller, 1983).

The American Jews in Albany were ambivalent in their attitudes toward the Soviet Jews in the period of immigration. First of all, some wondered why these immigrants had come to the United States, rather than to Israel. Second, many cited the indifference toward synagogues or the Jewish community as a reason for not giving further aid to the Soviet Jews.

The immigrants in Albany had a quite different perception. One said, in retrospect, that many immigrants had unrealistic expectations that American Jews would raise them to their own economic level. They felt that they should and would be given employment by other Jews. When this did not happen, they were disappointed. The issue of employment was a special sore point in Albany, as elsewhere. While the number of immigrants in Albany was small, an impersonal bureaucratic attitude permeated relations between immigrants and the social service agencies, as occurred elsewhere (Markowitz, 1985; Zenner & Hiller, 1983).

The immigrants felt that American Jews looked on them as aliens, "animals in the zoo," or "poor relations." They felt the effects of being both newcomers and strangers. One recalled being turned away from a synagogue on the High Holy Days because he had no ticket, not realizing that a free ticket awaited him. Another observed that while the American Jews greet each other as old friends and seem to know everyone in the synagogue, they, themselves, did not have friends there.

Other feelings may have come into play. Markowitz (1985) has noted that the very act of applying for emigration requires courage in the Soviet Union. Therefore the Soviet emigré sees herself or himself as a hero, while the American Jew does not understand this or reward it. Schneller (1980) points out that many new immigrants may have feelings of grief and guilt over having abandoned family members in the Old Country, which are quite sharp during the period immediately after arrival.

The Soviet emigrés felt particularly uncomfortable because of an economic disparity between themselves and the old community. While they had been given free memberships and scholarships during the first years after immigration, there was pressure to withdraw such advantages unless need were proven. If children were in school with American Jewish children, the latter had more material possessions and expected to go away to college, which many of the new immigrants were unable to do. All of this added to a sense of alienation and deprivation.

The different perceptions of significant Jewish symbols has been a bone of contention. Many Soviet immigrants have withdrawn their children from Jewish day schools because these schools were seen as parochial in outlook. Many Soviet Jews have no inhibition about eating pork, while Americans active in helping to integrate them were often Jews who saw such behavior as "un-Jewish." In the Brooklyn area where many Soviet Jews have settled and established small businesses, the dominant Jewish organizations are Orthodox. The Soviet Jews shocked their American neighbors a few years ago when they kept their businesses open on the Jewish New Year and Day of Atonement, when Jewish businesses are closed. When the Soviet emigrés realized the shock that this had caused, they conformed the following year. In the Brooklyn context, many have taken to wearing outward symbols of Jewish identity as a Star of David to stress their Jewish identity (Markowitz, 1985).

The stress on Jewishness, however, is only one possible reaction to pressure on the part of the American Jewish community. There are some who desire to transcend the stigmatized Jewish identity and, out of resentment of Jewish pressure or spiritual longings, turn to Christianity or assimilation through ignoring religion. Some assert their Russianness through affiliation with the Russian Orthodox Church (Howe, 1986).

In general, ambivalence in the relationship remains. Religious Conservative and Orthodox Jews find it hard to reconcile themselves to the often nonreligious Russians, while the Russian Jews find the religious practices of the Americans strange and obsolete. At the same time, they have found their treatment by the latter cold and not deserved by relations. Yet within the content, they have more relationships with them than they do with other groups in American society.

CONCLUSION

Immigration to a large and complex society often means that the immigrants must seek special relationships with one or another group already resident in that society. Those who share a common ethnic or religious identity provide the immigrants with assistance and with models for adjustment. The behavior of the two groups toward each other may be explained on the basis of a general sociological concept such as "reference group." In addition, general propositions concerning ethnocentrism show that much prejudice is directed against those outgroups who are close to the ingroup spatially and through culture, since they represent the stranger (LeVine & Campbell, 1972; pp. 60-71; Merton, 1957; pp. 281-386). The general propositions, however, give us only the outline of the communications that take place among these different groups.

In examining the various Jewish groups, it is clear that any assertion of a common ethnicity was contradicted by various behavioral characteristics and differing symbols of that common identity. For each set of groups, the issues of the contradiction were different. For the Ashkenazim and Sephardim, there was no question about sharing a common religion, but the "world-as-taken-for-granted" surrounding that religion was not the same. The East European immigrants, in particular, found it difficult to understand that Jews might exist who did not speak Yiddish or eat gefilte fish. The interaction between the Americanized Eastern Ashkenazim and German refugees was colored by a long history of charity and social distance in both Europe and America as well as the consequences of Americanization. The most recent immigrants from the Soviet Union face a different set of "culture shocks." Along with "Americanization," their coethnics wish to "re-Judaize" them, a difficult process following several generations of atheistic propaganda and stigmatization as Jews.

Those who study other ethnic categories and groups can profit from these studies of Jewish immigrant groups, even if they must set these into the particular cultural and historical context of that entity. For instance, the interactions between Irish Catholics and others, especially Eastern-Rite Catholics in the early 1900s, was marked by attempts to assert power and autonomy, and by differences in worldview comparable to that of Ashkenazim and Sephardim (see Brux, 1923). The separation of East and West Germans dates back a mere 40 years, yet it has resulted in suspicion and misunderstanding (Gill, 1986).

Americans in general are more conscious of the British than are Yiddish-speakers of their Arabic-speaking coreligionists. Yet a young Briton reported the following exchange. An elderly American woman asked him "What is your mother tongue?" She looked at me with astonishment when I replied, It's English. After she had recovered her composure, she drawled grudgingly, "Well, I guess they can speak it over there, too." (Van Buren, 1986).

Although not stressed explicitly, the "occupational subcultures" of those who come in contact is as significant as the historical backgrounds of the groups as a whole (Social Science Research Council Memorandum, 1954). Leichter and Mitchell

(1967, pp. 209-258) have demonstrated the contrasting kinship values of Jewish clients and of Jewish social workers in New York City. Similarly, Jews have often stressed different aspects of American Jewish culture (also see Gold, 1985, pp. 171-202). Certainly managers, priests, and others in positions of authority often select symbols from their culture as a means of coercing the newcomers. This may be a means for asserting their own power.

Ethnic markers often appear in subtle factors, which verbally oriented social scientists ignore, as in the *mazola/shmaltz* distinction. The odors produced by spices, cooking oils, and drinks are among these and require attention (see Largey & Watson, 1971).

These general propositions about intergroup relations could apply to almost any set of human groups. To understand the particular content of such encounters, one must turn to the special culture and history of the groups being studied. There is no shortcut.

NOTES

1. In this discussion, I confine myself to what are Rabbinite Jews from Europe and the Middle East, and their descendants. Most Jews in the world are "Rabbinite," that is, adherents of the Pharasaic-Rabbinic brand of Judaism, derived from the Talmud. Even those who have broken from this tradition through secularization still bear its mark. What Rabbinite Jews share are common rules for various aspects of life, including dietary laws, such as the separation of milk and meat, which is based on one alternative interpretation of Biblical laws; the lighting of Sabbath candles; and the use of certain warmed foods that can be eaten on the Sabbath when cooking is not allowed. The prayer services of all Rabbinite Jews follow a common order, even when they have been altered as among Reform Jews. For a discussion of the problems encountered by non-Rabbinite Jews of various types, see Roshwald (1973) and Sumi Colligan (1985). The term *Ashkenazic* refers to Jews who trace their/ origin to Germanic and Slavic lands and whose recent ancestors spoke Yiddish. *Sephardic* refers to Jews who trace their origins to Spain, although, by extension, the term today is used for most Jews from Mediterranean and Middle-Eastern lands.

2. In this section, a variety of materials will be used, including a study of the smaller number of Soviet Jews who arrived in the Albany, NY area between 1973 and 1981 (Zenner & Hiller, 1983).

3. There are some non-Ashkenazic Jews in the Soviet Union, especially in the Georgian, Tadjik and Uzbek republics. We are not considering them here, however.

4. Abner Cohen (1974, pp. 64-118) has demonstrated the importance of "invisible organizations" in maintaining ethnic identity. Such invisible organizations are probably

even more invisible in the Soviet Union than they are in such countries as Sierra Leone, the United Kingdom, and Israel, in which Cohen has found examples.

5. Since synagogues do not take collections on holidays and Sabbaths, their revenues are generally based on membership fees. Without paying dues, one cannot usually gain admittance to synagogue services on the Jewish New Year and the Day of Atonement, the times of the year when most Jews wish to go to services.

REFERENCES

Angel, M. (1982). *La America: The Sephardic experience in the United States.* Philadelphia: Jewish Publication Society.

Bromley, Y. V. (1978). On the typology of ethnic communities. In R. E. Holloman & S. Arutiunov (Eds.), *Perspectives on ethnicity* (pp. 15-22), The Hague: Mouton.

Broom, L. & Kitsuse, J. I. (1955). The validation of acculturation: A condition of ethnic assimilation. *American Anthropologist, 57* (1), 44-48.

Brux, A. A. (1923). A collection of Arab letters. Unpublished doctoral dissertation, University of Chicago, Chicago.

Cantskaja, O. A., & Terent'eva, L. N. (1978). Ethnicity and family in the Soviet Union. In R. E. Holloman & S. Arutiunov (Eds.), *Perspectives on ethnicity* (pp. 147-156). The Hague: Mouton.

Cohen, A. (1974). *Two dimensional man.* Berkeley, CA: University of California Press.

Colligan, S. (1985, December). *On the importance of being a Karaite Jew in Israel: Identifying identity in a multi-ideological society.* Paper presented at the annual meeting of the American Anthropological Association, Washington, DC.

Gilison, J. M. (1981). The resettlement of Soviet Jewish emigrés: Results of a survey in Baltimore. In D. J. Jacobs & E. F. Paul (Eds.), *Studies of the third wave* (pp. 29-56). Boulder, CO: Westview.

Gill, E. (1986, February 16). Foreigners in their own land. *New York Times Magazine,* pp. 16, 46-47, 55, 62, 64-65.

Gold, S. (1985). *Refugee communities: Soviet Jews and Vietnamese in the San Francisco Bay area.* Unpublished doctoral dissertation, University of California, Berkeley.

Heilman, S. (1976). *Synagogue life.* Chicago: University of Chicago Press.

Howe, M. (1986, January 5). The plow has slowed from the old country. *New York Times,* p. 6E.

Jacobs, D. N., & Paul, E. F. (1981). *Studies of the third wave: Recent migration of Soviet Jews to the United States.* Boulder, CO: Westview.

Kardash, P. (1975). *Irish and Italians in Mechanicville, N. Y.* Unpublished research paper, State University of New York at Albany, Department of Anthropology.

Largey, G. P., & Watson, D. R. (1971). The sociology of odors. *American Journal of Sociology, 77,* 1021-1034.

Leichter, H., & Mitchell, W. (1967). *Kinship and case work.* New York: Russell Sage Foundation.

LeVine, R. A. & Campbell, D. T. (1972). *Ethnocentrism: Theories of conflict, ethnic attitudes and group behavior.* New York: Wiley.

Markowitz, F. (1985, December). *Jewish in the USSR, Russian in the U.S.A.: Social context and ethnic identity*. Paper delivered at the annual meeting of the American Anthropological Association, Washington, DC.

Merton, R. K. (1957). *Social theory and social structure* (2nd ed.). Glencoe, IL: Free Press.

Plotnicov, L. & Silverman, M. (1978). Ethnic signalling: Social bonding among Jews in contemporary American society. *Ethnology, 17,* 407-423.

Plotnik, L. (1958). The Sephardim of New Lots. *Commentary, 25,* 28-35.

Roshwald, M. (1973). Marginal Jewish sects in Israel. *International Journal of Middle Eastern Studies, 4,* 219-237, 328-354.

Schneller, D. P. (1980). *The immigrant's challenge: Mourning the loss of homeland and adapting to the New World*. Unpublished masters thesis, Smith College School for Social Work, Northampton, MA.

Sephardic Archives. (1986). *The spirit of Aleppo: Syrian Jewish immigrant life in New York 1890-1939*. Brooklyn, NY: Sephardic Community Center.

Singer, I. B. (1985). Greenhorn in Sea Gate. *New York Times Magazine,* Part 2: The World of New York, p. 106.

Social Science Research Council. (1954). Acculturation: An exploratory formulation. *American Anthropologist, 56*(6), 973-1002.

Stern, S. (1977). *The Sephardic community of Los Angeles: A study in folklore and ethnic identity*. Unpublished doctoral dissertation, Indiana University.

Sutton, J.A.D. (1979). *Magic carpet: Aleppo-in-Flatbush*. Brooklyn, NY: Thayer-Jacoby.

Van Buren, A. (1986, March 19). Dear Abby. *Albany Times-Union,* p. C-2.

Zenner, W. P. (1983). Syrian Jews in New York twenty years ago. In V. Sanua (Ed.), *Fields of offerings: Studies in honor of Raphael Patai,* New York: Herzl Press.

Zenner, W. P. (1985). Jewish in America; Ascription and choice. In R. D. Alba (Ed.), *Ethnicity and race in the U.S.A.: Toward the twenty-first century* (pp. 117-133). London: Routledge, Kegan Paul.

Zenner, W. P., & Hiller, D. (1983). *The adjustment of Soviet Jewish immigrants in the Albany (N. Y.) area: A research report*. Albany, NY: Albany Jewish Family Services (ERIC Microfilm-ED 244019; UD 23-555).

14

Refugee Resource Acquisition
The Invisible Communication System

CAROL A. MORTLAND   ●   *Refugee Assistance Program, Ithaca,*
  New York
JUDY LEDGERWOOD   ●   *Cornell University*

The adaptation of Southeast Asian refugees in the United States is related in an essential way to a refugee patronage system invisible to American service providers, although it reaches into service agencies through bilingual workers. The refugee communication network works in conjunction with the patronage system, as refugee patrons control the flow of information and resources among Americans, including service agencies, and the refugee population. The impact of this refugee patronage and communication system on refugee clients, American service providers, and bilingual agency staff is enormous yet it remains largely invisible to most Americans.

INTRODUCTION

The adaptation of immigrants and refugees in new cultural situations has been of interest to scholars for some time and much has been written on this fascinating and complex topic, particularly since the massive movements of people during and after the Second World War. Now the discussion of cultural adaptation has been joined by those who are involved in the provision of services to refugees to the United States in the past decade. The discussion of adaptation has flowed from the academic to the social service arena, as policy makers and direct service providers struggle to implement relevant and effective assistance to new, undoubtedly permanent, residents of this country.

Since 1975, over 830,000 refugees from Southeast Asia have been resettled in the United States by voluntary resettlement agencies (Refugee Reports, 1987). They have been aided in this effort through services and resources provided by public and private agencies and by numerous individuals. These American efforts have been hampered, however, by communication difficulties of which they are very much aware, and to which they have devoted various strategies of solution. Their efforts have been hampered also by processes of refugee communication that involve refugee strategies of solution, the nature of which they do not understand.

In order to better comprehend the adaptation processes of people thrust into new ways of living, this chapter explores the relevance of the refugee communication network to the delivery and reception of refugee services that have been provided for the resettlement of Southeast Asian refugees since 1975. To do so, we will describe the different perceptions of and procedures for service provision and the different assumptions and attitudes that accompany service provision to refugees, in regard to American service providers, on the one hand, and refugees on the other. We suspect that the processes of adaptation among Southeast Asian refugees in the United States exist to some extent among other immigrant and refugee groups. Thus we hope our discussion will lead to a better understanding of not only Southeast Asian refugee adaptation in one country, but immigrant and refugee adaptation in general.

THE AMERICAN CONTEXT[1]

American Refugee Resettlement

Those who assist Southeast Asian refugees in the United States must deal first with the language difference: Not only do most refugees have difficulty speaking English, many are illiterate in their own language. The characteristic of illiteracy has as its greatest impact the concomitant lack of classroom experience. Thus, not only are many of the refugees unable to speak English, they find studying a new language a challenge that is outside their previous experience. Their unfamiliarity with classroom procedures and student discipline ill prepared them for a country that not only demands that they learn to speak and comprehend another language, but usually requires in addition that they learn to read and write. Besides trying to learn a new language, adult refugees struggle to learn employment skills that become more difficult to acquire with age. These difficulties are compounded by the very limited time given refugees to receive support for language study and job training.

This is the communication reality understood by American service providers, and they have taken steps to deal with it. The formal system of public assistance has been made available to refugees: Government agencies provide cash assistance, medical assistance, and food stamps to refugees to assist them while they gain the necessary skills to attain self-sufficiency. Both public agencies and private, nonprofit agencies (for example, local community centers, religious service agencies) provide other services with the same goal, such as English language classes, employment and vocational training, and interpretation and translation.

Ironically, the inability of refugees to speak English hampers the provision of services designed to help them overcome that and other difficulties. Most American service providers do not speak the languages of the refugee groups and, since most refugees continue to struggle to speak English for a number of years, a communication barrier between those needing services and those willing to offer services continues to separate, more or less effectively, the two groups. Refugees often do not have accurate information on what services are available at what agencies, let alone know the processes through which they can gain access to those services. Vivid illustration of this separation is given repeatedly in program reports, needs assessments, and funding proposals that describe, on the one hand, the meager use of available services by refugees, and on the other, the continuing needs of refugees in those same areas.

Resettlement and service providers throughout the United States have attempted to overcome the communication barrier by hiring refugee staff. The difficulty of communication between agency personnel and refugees usually results in English-speaking ability being the first criterion sought in selecting bilingual staff; it is almost always the most important criterion used in actual selection. Since the ability to learn a second language is generally in inverse relationship to age, younger refugees are better able to gain employment when English is a major prerequisite. For a variety of reasons, most bilinguals do not have previous social service training or experience comparable to that of the Americans with whom they work. In addition, the ability of bilinguals to comprehend, to speak articulately, and to read and write English remains inferior to the abilities of the Americans with whom they work. Consequently, their youth, lack of training and experience, inferior (or at the least, different) English, and recentness of employment places these bilingual intermediaries on the bottom rung of the American refugee service network. Yet these individuals are the *key link* in the communication network and the actual use of services by the refugee population.

American Philosophy of Assistance

The American system of social service provision to refugees is based on a particular attitude toward problem solving and "helping" others. Americans tend to look for causes of problems, and then to apply mechanistic procedures for solving these problems. Finding the solution to a problem involves diagnosing the exact problem, specifying the cause, and determining the remedy. Because Americans tend to view problems as solvable and not necessarily personally caused, it is culturally appropriate to seek assistance for a wide variety of difficulties; consequently, an enormous and complex system of "helping" exists to furnish that assistance (Gourash, 1978).

Often such assistance takes the form of providing the client with information on the options available (for example, these three training courses have available space; or this employer hires on Tuesdays at 10 A.M.). Armed with the information, individuals may then make their own decisions regarding the appropriate path to freedom from public assistance. The goal in this American model is one of independence. This assistance can be provided for needs such as employment, vocational training, language training, and interpretation. It can also be applied to psychological problems—which Americans refer to as "personal" problems—and is often offered without fee for people unable to pay. A vital element in this helping system is the existence of salaried professionals whose educational background and experience has qualified (or certified) them to assist with other people's problems.

Actors Within the American System

The communication difficulties inherent in the relations between American service providers and refugee clients have been immediately and abundantly experienced by both authors while working with Southeast Asian refugees. From early 1981 to late 1983, Mortland, an anthropologist, directed a resettlement office in a large city in the Pacific Northwest. Ledgerwood worked in the same office from mid-1982 to mid-1984 as volunteer coordinator, job developer, and then director. Office responsibilities include providing resettlement assistance to hundreds of arrivals each year and to their sponsors, most of whom were relatives or fellow countrymen. We developed training programs, referred clients to a variety of services and resources, used federal funds to begin a refugee-owned business, assisted in emergencies, and worked closely with American volunteers, agencies, and refugee self-help groups.

This agency, as did others in the area, employed bilingual workers to assist in the multiple day-to-day contacts with refugees and Americans. In addition, an extraordinary degree of conflict (or so we thought at the time) between and among refugee and American individuals and groups in 1983 and 1984 led to unusually detailed and open revelations by numerous refugee coworkers, acquaintances, and friends on the difficulties involved in dealing with American agencies, as bilinguals or as clients.

Our *participation* as agency personnel with other service providers and bilinguals as colleagues and with refugees as clients increased our interest in and *observation* of the patterns of relationship between Americans and refugees and the processes by which refugees were acquiring resources. Using an anthropological "participant observation" approach, we supplemented the work hours already being spent with refugee and American colleagues and clients through conversations and interviews with those same people and with other refugees. When we were not working as service providers, we were listening to refugees talk about the realities of resettlement. In addition, we have reviewed refugee adjustment and Southeast Asia literature, visited a number of refugee service agencies, and talked with numerous bilingual workers in other cities. Additional research has accompanied Mortland's direction of a refugee assistance program in New York State for the past two years, and membership in the New York State Refugee Program Advisory Council since 1985. Ledgerwood has continued research with refugees while completing graduate studies in anthropology, Khmer language, and Southeast Asian studies at Cornell University.

Our conversations and interviews were transcribed as fieldnotes. Additional information on particular topics was collected spontaneously (that is, as refugees and Americans commented on particular subjects in informal conversations), and in more formal conversations when informants were responding to our questions. When patterns seemed to be emerging, we gained additional information from a number of different informants in order to evaluate the generality of our information. In this ongoing process of listening, taking notes, suspecting patterns of action and reactions, participating, observing, questioning, and refining our conclusions, we gradually came to recognize certain patterns in refugee communication and service. In gaining an understanding of the communication realities of refugees, we needed to familiarize ourselves with their attitudes toward problems and "helping," and with the way Southeast Asian attitudes differ from those of Americans; we turn to that now.

SOUTHEAST ASIAN CONTEXT

Southeast Asian Philosophy of Assistance

It is of great importance to recognize that the American network of professionals, who offer their assistance to strangers and get paid primarily for being helpers, has virtually no counterpart in the Southeast Asian countries from which refugees have come: Vietnam, Cambodia, and Laos. The attitude of Southeast Asians toward problems and solutions is also different from that of most Americans. They are more willing to accept the problems that come to them, viewing them as natural consequences of their previous acts. There is a more limited range of causes for Asians than there is for Americans, and many of those causes relate to the violation of regulations: Problems are personally caused and must be personally endured.

The services by paid professionals in the United States are offered in Southeast Asian countries by a traditional, highly personal, system of assistance. Assistance is first sought from those closest to the individual, primarily kinsmen, who are most obligated to furnish assistance and most assured of reciprocal assistance in their time of need. Second, assistance is sought from specialists whose primary occupation relates not to "helping" but to other activities. Thus Southeast Asians look for help with their problems from religious personnel, civil servants, and school-teachers. These local specialists are expected to assist in areas outside their specialty; for example, one's doctor might be asked for a loan, a local administrative official or teacher might be asked to mediate in a marital dispute.

The Patronage System

The form that the system of resource and service distribution takes in this context is patronage; and without an understanding of the patronage model, we cannot comprehend the ways refugees in America acquire services and communicate with one another. Patronage is a reciprocal exchange between a patron who disperses services to clients in exchange for other services. Patronage involves an asymmetrical relationship between patron and client, a relationship that Scott (1977) accurately describes as an "imbalance in exchange between the two partners which expresses and reflects the disparity in their relative wealth, power, and status." While both patrons and clients provide services to each other, patrons possess power and influence superior to that of their clients, allowing them to assist and protect clients; in return, clients contribute loyalty and personal assistance to increase the patron's power (see Saller, 1982; Scott, 1977; Gellner & Waterbury, 1977).

The patron-client relationship is characterized by face-to-face contact between the parties. Patrons and clients know one another personally; while this may lead to reciprocal affection, it does not necessarily do so. One implication of face-to-face contact between patron and client is that the number of clients of a particular patron is limited, and if he overextends himself in committing resources, he risks losing a portion of his clientele. The personal contact also implies a flexible relationship in which the services delivered by the patron can vary widely, temporally and in type.

The patron role often includes the role of broker, in which the patron is influential in having delivered to his clients resources and services not directly under his control. If the holders of those resources view the broker as merely an inconsequential cog influencing, in a mild way, the delivery of those resources, the clients do not at all see it in that light. For them, the resources are *virtually unavailable* without the intervention of the broker. In this sense, the brokerage done by a patron is seen by his clients as additional resources over which their patron has control. In a patronage system, patronage is viewed as normal and proper; it has a public face because it is used by the entire population and it is the most effective way for citizens to relate to their state and to gain necessary services and resources in their society.

The patron-client relationship can be viewed in contrast to the relationships that exist between provider and client in a modern bureaucracy. In a centralized bureaucracy, each individual member of the state is able to gain resources from the state directly. In such a state, centralized authority results in a system of administration, or bureaucracy, in which services, resources, and protection are provided to the citizenry on the basis of universal and impersonal criteria (Saller, 1982). In contrast is the patronage state, in which services, resources, and protection are best obtained from the state through a patron. It is only this personal patron-client relationship that allows citizens access to the state's resources, since many segments of the population have no direct contact with the state (for example, in a decentralized state, there is usually no formal administration at the local level). In the United States, the centralized bureaucratic model of resource distribution is the ideal that is taught to bureaucratic workers at all levels.

Changes in the relationship between the state and the citizenry have occurred throughout history, among them a philosophical shift away from the idea that the state exists to serve only its leader and some of its members, toward a view of the state as the servant of all its members, who should be served equally. In this view, the rights of individuals to have their needs met by the state become of major importance, thus encouraging the development of an ideal system of state administration in which the citizens of the state are served equally and efficiently and the employees of the state are chosen equitably by a system of meritocracy.

Patronage is a pervasive element in modern life in Southeast Asia: Scott (1977) suggests that the basic pattern of patron-client relationships is an important part of the structure of Southeast Asian politics and that the informal networks of patronage are crucial and omnipresent in modern Southeast Asian institutions. Certainly attempts by human beings to tie others to themselves in hierarchical relationships of obligation are not unique to Southeast Asia,[2] but it is important to understand the extent to which these ties of obligation do exist there and do impinge on every aspect of everyday life.

Most specifically, we can see the system of patronage at work in a country from which a number of refugees have come: Cambodia.[3] Cambodian leadership has been based on a master-servant relationship; one's master might shift with changing times and circumstances, but always, one was obligated to obey (Vickery points out that the Khmer word for servant does not mean "one who serves or helps" but "one who is told"). The Cambodian language and rules of etiquette reinforce the societal roles, thus demonstrating, in an everyday arena, people's places and obligations. In Chandler's (1973, p. 39) words, "The rectitude of these intransitive, graded relationships has been drummed into everyone from birth. Cambodian proverbs and didactic literature are filled with references to the helplessness of the individual and to the importance fo accepting power relationships as they are."

Thion (1983) also sees patronage as the "backbone" of traditional Cambodian political structure that has survived in the politics of post-independence Cambodia; and Thompson and Adloff (1955) and Osborne (1976) link post World War II Cambodian politics with a patronage system that connects people to their leaders in a hierarchical system of linear loyalty, which has survived even the dramatically different regimes of Sihanouk and Pol Pot (Chandler, 1979). While writers might disagree on the nature and extent of hierarchy in historical Cambodia, most will agree that Cambodian society has been built, from top to bottom, on a system of patronage. Similar documentation could also be given for the existence of patronage in Laos and Vietnam.

SOUTHEAST ASIANS IN AMERICA

The Patronage Systems in the New World

Cambodians, Laotians, and Vietnamese refugees in America, accordingly, act on their cultural upbringing, use the model of service provision with which they are familiar, and thus look for and find patrons in America.[4] Through these patrons, refugee clients are able to find the resources and services they need in an unfamiliar environment. In a similar way, other refugees—operating on the same cultural assumptions—are eager to serve as patrons in the new world, for in so doing they demonstrate their success to their fellow countrymen in a new world. Their rewards are: power over others, money for services rendered, increased contact with Americans—who are themselves valuable for patronage reasons—and a restatement of identity and status that has been so desperately battered during flight, refugee camps, and resettlement. It is this system of refugee, patron, and client relationships and obligations that functions as the communication network that enables refugees in the United States to acquire the services they need.

Refugee patrons control, or appear to control,[5] information, services and resources desired by refugees. Patrons are financially independent,[6] speak English, and exhibit personal possessions or achievements that are desired by other refugees (for example, attractive cars, houses, entertainment equipment, positions of leadership). They promise to assist their clients in obtaining similar acquisitions and achievements, a promise that has meaning for clients since patrons have demonstrated their abilities to become successful in the new world. In the ways that they can demonstrate these abilities, they attract clients to them: clients who either wish to have similar possessions or achievements or who want the services and resources under the control of the patron.

The higher the refugee's level of education, social standing, and economic situation in his country of birth, and the higher his economic, social and political achievements in the country of resettlement, the greater are his chances of acting as a patron.[7] Most important, the greater a refugee's English language abilities, the greater is the potential to be an effective patron in the United States. Patrons are almost always literate men, both in their first language and in English. The potency of this factor may not be recognized by observers who lack an understanding of the unique political power of men able to read and write in a society that is primarily illiterate and traditional (Anderson, 1972); but it is recognized by illiterate or barely literate (in the language of birth and/or English) refugees in America. Anderson attributes the potency of literacy to its esoteric character and its ability to facilitate rapid and incomprehensible communication, to spread new ideas, and preserve old and secret knowledge. For refugees in America, whether illiterate in their own language, functionally illiterate in English, or continuing to struggle with English, a patron who can actually communicate and produce actions with his English words is a powerful and wonderful man indeed.

The Bilingual Worker as Patron

Since refugee service agencies are also looking for effective bilinguals, it is not surprising that bilingual agency staff and patrons are usually one and the same. Qualifications for both roles are similar: focused on the refugee's comprehension of American knowledge, communication and systems of action. And the duties of both roles are similar: focused on the delivery of that knowledge, communication, and action to refugees. Refugee staff are in a position to deliver those services, both formally as bilinguals, and informally as patrons. In addition, they are in a position, literally as well as figuratively, to increase their comprehension of American ways and thus become more effective bilinguals and more powerful patrons.

While an agency evaluates a potential bilingual staff person primarily on English language abilities, a patron or refugee seeking to become a patron evaluates a bilingual position on the basis of the quality and quantity of the resources the agency controls. Employment in government offices that control the delivery of cash, medical assistance, and food stamps, in offices that control information about and facilitate access to jobs, and in nonprofit agencies that deliver a variety of resources (such as employment assistance, interpretation and translation, sponsorship information and assistance, and material goods such as food, furniture, clothing, gifts, and financial assistance) will be particularly valuable to a patron, and a person in such a position will be especially valued as a patron. These agency personnel will be more likely to develop clientele than will the personnel of agencies and offices dealing in only one commodity, such as health services.

The longer a refugee is employed in an agency position, the greater is his standing as a patron and the greater is his ability to control his clients. The continued and increasing status as a patron is dependent on maintaining the position of employment— thus keeping happy the Americans over him—and supplying his clients with sufficient resources to keep them from turning to other patrons. In addition, patrons legitimize their position through ties with other refugees, such as influential businessmen, former political or royal leaders, or current guerrilla officers. One refugee leader reinforced his position by identifying himself with a nationally recognized Buddhist monk, although he acknowledged that he had never served an apprenticeship as a monk and had never thought much of Buddhist ideas. In addition, he talked of influential Cambodians he knew in the centers of Khmer power in America: Washington, D.C., New England, and Long Beach, CA. He also displayed photographs of himself taken with the former prince of Cambodia and other well known Khmer.

A patron/bilingual worker may first meet a client when the client seeks a service at the worker's office. If the service is provided to the client's satisfaction, the client will ask for further services, which the patron will provide through his office, through his knowledge of America (either at his office or on his own time), or by obtaining the service (if it is not immediately under his own control) through another office, or through American or refugee contact. Because the patron's English and information is superior to that of the client, the client is best served by remaining with that patron, and he will do so unless he is dissatisfied with the patron or finds a better patron.

Each client is also a type of patron to a number of others, usually family members, who lack even the client's ability to contact the patron/bilingual worker (for example, drive a car, locate the office, know what questions to ask). Each client also brings additional arrivals into the patron's network: relatives sponsored from Southeast Asian refugee camps, migrants from other localities, even friends who are clients of another, possibly less satisfactory, patron. In this way, each patron/bilingual worker becomes responsible for and to a widening circle of clients and those others whom each client represents.

For example, one month after he was hired as a bilingual worker, Anh sponsored a large family to the area. The head of that household, Bonh, was a young man who quickly learned English, purchased a car, and began volunteering as an interpreter in Anh's office. Much of his work involved providing information and services to families sponsored by Anh. Within six months, both Anh and Bonh had sponsored a number of new families, using the resources of the office and working evenings and on weekends. When able, new arrivals, in turn, furnished services to yet newer arrivals, always on Bonh's immediate instructions under Anh's ultimate direction. This pyramiding structure of assistance and responsibility continued with little visibility (to the Americans) and with few difficulties until charges were made by some refugees in the community that Anh was stealing money from the people he sponsored. This contributed to an eventual break between Anh and Bonh, but the pyramid on sponsorship, allocation of duties by the patron, client responsibilities to the patron, and flow of information between patron and clients continued, now with two competing patrons.

The patron-client relationship works because of the responsibilities each has to the other.[8] The patron must supply services of sufficient quality and quantity in order to retain a client; the client must render services as required by the patron. The less the authority of the patron, the greater his regard for the needs of his clients, the opinions and rules of the community, and "nurturance" of the clients (Muecke, 1983). As the clients' destinies rest on the destiny of the patron (Anderson, 1972), so the patron's destiny rests, in part, on retaining client loyalty. For example, the American supervisor of an important patron working as an agency bilingual began receiving a rash of invitations to refugee homes, at which time complaints were made against her bilingual worker: that he was getting too arrogant, joining with other refugee leaders, and acting "like he was better than other refugees." When the worker heard this, he began spending his evenings visiting his clients, drinking and talking, as he had done in the early days of his patronage. The complaints quickly ceased as his responsiveness to clients increased.

The mutual obligations between patron and client are reflected in the language of address and reference used by refugees in America: the language of kinsmen. For example, "close" kin terms used by Cambodian refugees reflect ties between patrons and clients and reflect the importance of their exchanged services to each party and their mutual dependency and expenditure of time, energy, and resources. These kinship terms are reflective, not necessarily of affection, as Scott (1977) suggests, but of the reciprocal, necessary obligations of kinsmen. Thus Cambodian patrons are addressed by their terms for "grandfather" (*taa*), "older brother" (*bong*) and "teacher" (*krou*), depending on the age, sex, and occupation (in Cambodia) of the clients. Patrons, in turn, address clients in kinship terms dependent primarily on the age and sex of the addressee: thus "younger brother" (*baowng bro*) and "younger sister" (*baowng srey*).

One adjustment in the kinship terminology used between patrons and clients reflects a major difference between patronage in Southeast Asia and patronage in America. In America, clients often use terms of respect, such as those of "grandfather" and "older brother," for patrons who are similar in age to them, or even younger. This is so because patrons in America are generally younger than are patrons in Southeast Asia; this is a result of the qualifications necessary to operate in an American environment as a patron and a bilingual worker, the most important of which is English-speaking ability, which is more easily gained by younger refugees. This is a major cause of conflict in the refugee community, since younger men are less experienced in the obligations of being a patron and clients are less familiar with depending on and giving allegiance to young patrons.

Consequently, clients charge that patrons give less than they are obliged to give, that they disregard clients' needs, that they act "too important" for their position, that "back in Vietnam" (or Cambodia, or Laos) the man would never be a patron. Patrons complain about excessive demands by their clients and about their ignorance of American customs and procedures. These difficulties are often minimized by cooperative arrangements between younger patron/bilingual workers and older community members. In one New York town, for example, the college-educated bilingual worker confers on a regular basis with several elders in his community; in fact, his selection as the bilingual staff person was suggested by the older people of his ethnic community. In any event, patron/bilingual workers quickly learn that criticism from their community is a constant element of their work, whether or not it is justified.[9]

Each specific patron-client relationship will depend primarily on the degree of dependence of the client on his patron. For example, patrons lose their mediation role when other links to resources and services become available to clients (Silverman, 1965), through other patrons, for example, or when clients become more able to directly seek agency services. Thus we frequently see patron/bilingual staff competing for clients with bilingual staff from other agencies and encouraging or threatening clients to continue their use of the patron's and agency's services. This often has a effect contrary to that desired by the agency as, for example, when bilinguals employed by government welfare offices encourage refugees to refuse employment that would remove them from the rolls, and eventually, remove the bilingual from his position. The loss of the bilingual position would then affect his role as patron by restricting the services over which he had control and, possibly more important, by showing him to be vulnerable to the vicissitudes of life—in this case, unemployment.

The above examples demonstrate ways in which the nature of the patron-client role affects how bilinguals perform work. Similarly, the priorities of refugee employees guide their activities and objectives within the agency, whether or not those activities and objectives are priorities with the agency. Because refugee staff are usually the most recently hired and their initial employment is directly related to local refugee population size, an increase in the population of their language group may benefit their employment situation by increasing their responsibilities and thus, probably, their salary and status in the agency, whereas a decrease in that population almost certainly would be detrimental to their situation. Without bilinguals who speak their language, bilingual staff are, by definition, unnecessary. It may be expected, then, to see bilingual refugee staff active in those endeavors that would be likely to increase local refugee population size.

INVISIBLE SYSTEMS

Patron-client relationships are mutually beneficial transactions with political implications (Lemarchand & Legg, 1972). One of the most important of these is that Americans do not see the patron-client relationship as existing; when they do catch a glimpse of it, they do not realize its mutual benefit to both partners, and they certainly are not aware of the political ramifications of the system.

One reason that Americans do not perceive this system is the "invisibility" (Errington, 1977) of the obligations of the client to the patron. Since the contributions clients make in a patron-client relationship are, by definition, of less value and importance than are those of the patrons, a client's services to his patron are small and generally spread over time. In America, these client obligations to patrons include labor; goods and support (such as giving money); appearing at meetings, demonstrations, or parties; voting when and as the bilingual desires; and contributing food, beverages, gifts, handicrafts, or entertainment for public events or for the patron's private parties. Other people, even other clients, may not be aware of the client services being provided or of the extent of delivery. However, the contributions of a patron to his clients are usually highly visible to the clients and especially to potential clients as the patron attempts to increase clientele by displaying the benefits of partaking in patronage with him. Thus clients see their patron obtaining jobs, training opportunities, and rental units for refugees, and they see the patron associating with Americans, who in turn offer additional services to refugees.

Patronage is kept invisible from the Americans by patron middlemen, in part so that patrons can then pass off client contributions as their own. For example, a refugee patron may give a party for an important American, frequently the boss, presenting for the guests' enjoyment, food, drink, and gifts that have been provided by clients. We have attended parties where many different dishes of food, large quantities of beer, wine, and soft drinks, and numerous bottles of cognac were displayed on the table. All had been prepared or purchased by the refugee host's clients; in fact, at one party the bilingual's house had been cleaned by a refugee's wife prior to the party. Most of these clients were not in attendance, however, either because they did not speak sufficient English to converse with the American guests or because they were not sufficiently important or visible in the community. The refugee guests included other clients or potential clients of the refugee patron/host whose English, importance, and presentability could keep the American guests comfortable and entertained.

Patron/bilingual workers also work to keep their patron-client relationships invisible because they have sufficient grasp of the bureaucratic structure to know that some of their acts would be prohibited by the Americans for whom they work. American social workers do not usually know what is occurring in another language in their offices. We knew American resettlement workers in one office who were shocked to find that for two years their bilingual colleague had regularly advanced services to some agency "clients"[10] and refused services to others because of their association with rival patrons in the community. Although the bilingual worker knew office procedures and goals, he did not consider them as important as advancing his patron position in the community.

Just as the patronage system is invisible to the American social service provider, the bureaucratic system is obscure to the refugees, a system that social service workers see as functioning to provide services to refugees. The goals within the American setting focus on mechanical problem solving: By providing clients with information and allowing them to make independent decisions, the clients, in theory, move toward independence. Yet the opposite—dependence—is the key to the success of the patron-client model—as the patron well knows.

CONCLUSION

The key to the successful coexistence of the American social service system and the refugee patron-client system lies in the patterns of information flow. All communication runs through the patron/bilingual workers to a pyramiding network of clients. The refugees coming to ask for assistance see a broker with whom they deal in a face-to-face patron-client pattern. The patron controls the flow of information, as through the narrow channel of an hourglass, from the agency to the client and from the client to the agency. In this process, patrons may alter the information in order to serve their own purposes and what they perceive to be the purposes of their clients. Were the clients to gain the ability to make decisions, or acquire access to resources on their own, the system would collapse. Since the perception of the system as *the* only system is that it is mutually beneficial, neither the client nor the patron/bilingual worker want it to cease.

Thus, an understanding of the realities of refugee communication is the key to understanding how services actually are provided to Southeast Asian refugees in America, and not "communication" as it is commonly perceived. Most Americans think primarily of gaining proficiency in the English language (a task well nigh impossible for many adult refugees) when they consider refugees adapting to their lives in America. For most refugees, the more relevant perspective is to consider the level of the communication network, which works in conjunction with the patronage system. By viewing the realities of communication on this level, by studying the flow of information through a recognizable system, the observer may better understand the process through which refugees acquire the services designed to assist them in their adaptation to life in America.

By understanding that there is a functioning communications network among refugees, Americans can avoid some common errors in refugee assistance. Americans frequently state that refugees do not understand and do not properly work with and through American service agencies in service distribution. These complaints apply to refugees who are *receiving* services, who will not or cannot follow established procedures in applying for and receiving services. The reason for their actions become clearer if one realizes that the completion of forms or sitting through the required hours of intake sessions are often meaningless to clients. They know what they must do in order to be referred to the job or training program: Act to make the patron happy so that he will intercede in English with the Americans for the clients.

Understanding this system also allows Americans to be aware of some of the ramifications of their position within it, in that they themselves may act as patrons or the patron of patrons in the view of refugees. Refugees who bring gifts to Americans or invite them to dinner may be viewed as friends or as grateful people trying to pay back kindnesses; the Americans seldom realize that their acceptance of such gratuities is seen by the refugees as obligating them to provide future services. Americans see themselves as paid to do a job, and not as patrons, which, in the eyes of the refugees, they often are.

In addition, understanding this system can help in addressing the concerns of American social service agencies regarding the bilingual staff *providing* services to other refugees. American social providers are often baffled when these intermediaries do not seem to be "playing the game" correctly. American explanations for the patron/bilingual worker's actions, which do not recognize the patron-client system outlined above, often label refugees as irrational or ignorant, as helpless victims floundering in their new environment. Or should Americans catch a glimpse of the patronage system at work—for example, a job being offered to a bilingual worker's brother-in-law rather than to a more qualified applicant—they interpret it as corrupt.

Refugee clients, on the other hand, may view the patronage system as legitimate rather than as exploitive because it allows them access they would not otherwise have and because it is familiar to them. Some *may* view it as exploitative. How clients evaluate the patronage system will depend not only on the proportion of received services to given services (Scott, 1977), but on other factors such as the view clients hold of patronage in their homeland, the knowledge and expectations they have of the American bureaucratic system and their ability to gain access directly to the American system.

As time goes on and refugees and their children grow more familiar with the American social service system, they will—as have immigrants and their children before them—more often use American systems directly and independently, and will abandon the traditional patronage system. At the same time, the invisible communication network now flowing through patron/bilingual workers to clients will fade as refugees increase their abilities to communicate with and receive information through American individuals and systems. Consequently, one can anticipate that the prevailing refugee patron/bilingual worker and client network and the coexisting communication network will collapse. In the meantime, the refugee patron-client communication system is a rational, highly effective, and often mutually satisfactory system—even though it is invisible.

NOTES

1. In this chapter, we use the term "American" in contrast to "refugee" for ease in reference. However, we need to note that refugees are gaining American citizenship as they become eligible, thus the term "American" in fact now applies to "Vietnamese-Americans," "Laotian-Americans," and "Cambodian-Americans."

2. See Bledsoe (1980) for recent ethnographic examples.

3. For example, Vickery (1984).

4. See Scott (1982) and Van Esterik (1981).

5. In other words, they become "brokers" or intermediaries between those who actually control resources and those who want them.

6. Most are employed, but some are supported by wives, by invisible sources, or by government stipends. In any event, patrons have money coming in.

7. Our use of the term "he" is deliberate; it is in fact an accurate reflection of refugee realities in the United States. The great majority of refugee patrons are male, for which there are many reasons. First, it conforms with Southeast Asian patterns of male and female roles, in which men usually fill public and political positions. Second, education in Southeast Asia has been biased toward males; if a refugee has previous English language schooling, that refugee is probably a male. Third, women find their child care and household responsibilities continuing in the new world while men face new challenges in finding ways to support their families. This support may come from employment as a bilingual staff member or from payment for services as a patron. While a number of bilingual staff members are female, they are less likely than are males to combine that role with the patron role, and it is in the combination of these roles that we find the key to much of the communication networking and acquisition of services that operate among the refugees.

8. As one reviewer of this chapter noted, there are psychological benefits for participants of ethnic networks, including the patron-client network; such relationships may continue, in part, because of the emotional and linguistic comfort gained from following traditional models of social relations, with their complex of privileges and obligations. See, for example, Baskauskas (1977); Choldin (1981); and Freedman (1960).

9. This is frequently a handicap to their superiors in judging which criticisms from the community are legitimate concerns with which the agency must deal, and which are unfounded and flung indiscriminately at any young bilingual patron employed to serve the refugee community.

10. As they are known in both systems.

REFERENCES

Anderson, B.R.O'G. (1972). The idea of power in Javanese culture. In C. Holt (Ed.), *Culture and politics in Indonesia* (pp. 1-69). Ithaca, NY: Cornell University Press.

Baskauskas, L. (1977). Multiple identities: Adjusted Lithuanian refugees in Los Angeles. *Urban Anthropology, 6,*(9), 141-154.

Bledsoe, C. H. (1980). *Women and marriage in Kpelle society.* Palo Alto, CA: Stanford University Press.

Chandler, D. P. (1973). *Cambodia before the French: Politics in a tributary kingdom.* Ph. D. Dissertation, University of Michigan, Ann Arbor.

Chandler, D. P. (1979). The tragedy of Cambodian history. *Pacific Affairs, 52,* (1), 410-419.

Choldin, H. M. (1981). Kinship networks in the migration process. *International Migration Review, 7* (2), 163-175.

Errington, S. (1977). Order and power in Karavar. In R. D. Fogelson & R. N. Adams (Eds.), *The anthropology of power* (pp. 23-43). New York: Academic Press.

Freedman, M. (1960). Immigrants and associations: Chinese in nineteenth-century Singapore. *Comparative Studies in Society and History, 3,* (1), 25-48.

Gellner, E., & Waterbury, J. (Eds.). (1977). *Patrons and clients in Mediterranean societies.* London: Duckworth.

Gourash, M. (1978). Help-seeking: A review of the literature. *American Journal of Community Psychology, 6,* (5), 413-423.

Lemarchand, R., & Legg, K. (1972). Political clientism and development: A preliminary analysis. *Comparative Politics, 4,* 149-178.

Meucke, M. A. (1983). Thai conjugal family relationships and the Hsu hypothesis. *Journal of the Siam Society, 7,* 25-41.

Osborne, M. E. (1976). Reflections on the Cambodian tragedy. *Asia-Pacific Community, 8* (1), 1-13.

Refugee Reports (1987). Statistics. *American Council for Nationalities Service, 8,* (7), 16.

Saller, R. P. (1982). *Personal patronage under the early empire.* Cambridge: Cambridge University Press.

Scott, G. M., Jr. (1982). The Hmong refugee community in San Diego: Theoretical and practical implications of its continuing ethnic solidarity. *Anthropology Quarterly, 55,* 146-160.

Scott, J. C. (1977). Patron-client politics and political change in Southeast Asia. In S. W. Schmidt et al. (Eds.), *Friends, followers, and factions. A reader in political clientism* (pp. 123-146). Berkeley, CA: University of California Press.

Silverman, S. F. (1965). Patronage and community—nation relationships in central Italy. *Ethnology, 4,* (2), 172-189.

Thion, S. (1983). The Cambodian idea of revolution. In D. P. Chandler & B. Kieran (Eds.), *Revolution and its aftermath in Kampuchea: Eight essays* (pp. 10-33). New Haven, CT: Yale University Southeast Asia Studies.

Thompson, V., & Adloff, R. (1955). *Minority problems in Southeast Asia.* Palo Alto, CA: Stanford University Press.

Van Esterik, P. (1981). In-home sponsorship for Southeast Asian refugees. *Journal of Refugee Resettlement, 1,* (2), 18-26.

Vickery, M. (1984). *Cambodia: 1975—1982.* Boston, MA: Southend.

Name Index

Subject Index

About the Authors

JOHN W. BERRY was born and raised in Montréal, Canada, and attended university there and in Scotland. His work has ranged from the study of ecological and cultural factors in development in Africa, Australia, and the Arctic among hunter-gatherers, to research on how individuals in these areas adapt to culture contact and change. Current research extends these interests to adaptive phenomena in plural societies. He is past president of the International Association for Cross-Cultural Psychology.

PAWEL BOSKI was born and raised in Poland and attended university there. During seven years teaching at the University of Jos, Nigeria, he developed a novel approach to the study of culture-group contact and relations, using the concepts of schema and prototype. Since arriving in Canada in 1985, he has been a Visiting Professor at Queen's University, working on Polish immigrant adaptation and self-identity.

ADRIAN FURNHAM was born and grew up in Africa, then emigrated to England at the age of 21. He has various degrees including an MSc from London University (LSE) and a doctorate (DPhil) from Oxford University. He has published six books and over 150 papers in scientific journals. His primary academic interests lie in applied, cross-cultural, economic, personality, and social psychology. He lives and works in central London.

HOWARD GILES obtained his Ph.D. from the University of Bristol, England, in 1971. In 1984 he succeeded the late Henri Tajfel as Professor of Social Psychology in the same institution. In 1982, he became the founding editor of the *Journal of Language and Social Psychology,* and in 1985 co-organized the First International Conference on Social Psychology, Language and Ethnic Relations in Australia. He has published widely in the interface of bilingualism, intergroup relations, and cultural identity, with much of this in the context of his birthplace of Wales. He is currently engaged in establishing an international and interdisciplinary Centre for the Study of Communication and Social Relations at Bristol, part of which will be concerned with the relationships between ethnicity, communication, aging, and health.

WILLIAM B. GUDYKUNST is Professor of Communication at Arizona State University. His research focuses on uncertainty reduction processes across cultures and between people from different cultures. His most recent book is *Intergroup Communication,* published by Edward Arnold. Currently, he is writing *Culture and Interpersonal Communication* (with S. Ting-Toomey and E. Chua for Sage) and *Strangeness and Similarity: A Theory of Interpersonal and Intergroup Communication* (for Multilingual Matters), as well as coediting *The Handbook of Intercultural Communication* (second edition, with M. Asante for Sage) and *Theorizing Intercultural Communication* (with Y. Kim for Sage).

MITCHELL R. HAMMER (Ph.D., University of Minnesota, 1982) is Assistant Professor of Communication in the Department of Communication at the University of Wisconsin—Milwaukee. His research interests include intercultural communication effectiveness, cross-cultural training, and organizational communication and development. His work has appeared in *International Journal of Intercultural Relations, Journal of Black Studies*, and *Communication Yearbook,* among others.

ANDRES INN (Ph.D., University of Illinois, Champaign-Urbana) is Research Director for the Institute of Comparative Social and Cultural Studies (Bethesda, Maryland). He recently completed an appointment with the Graduate School of Business Administration at the Chinese University of Hong Kong. He is an industrial/organizational psychologist with international experience in management and research. He has published in *Journal of Applied Psychology, Journal of Applied Social Psychology,* and *Journal of Urban Analysis.*

KYUNG-WHA KANG is Lecturer in the Department of Mass Communication at Yonsei University, Korea, and news writer and newscaster for the Korean Broadcasting System. She received her graduate degrees from the Department of Communication at the University of Massachusetts, Amherst. Her research interests focus on the communicative strategies employed by persons confronting a novel culture. She is coauthor of a new book, *Communication and the Human Condition* scheduled for publication in 1987 by Southern Illinois University Press.

UICHOL KIM was born in Korea and emigrated to Canada as a youth. He attended the University of Toronto, working in cross-cultural social psychology, and is now a doctoral student at Queen's University. His doctoral research is on Korean immigrant adaptation to Canada. He is presently conducting research on cultural differences in individualism/collectivism, and on indigenous psychologies.

YOUNG YUN KIM (Ph.D., Northwestern) is Professor of Communication at Governors State University (University Park, IL). Her research interests include the role of communication in cross-cultural adaptation, the process of psychic and behavioral transformation of individuals in a new or changing cultural environment, and cognitive information processing and communication competence. She has published *Communicating with Strangers* (with W.B. Gudykunst), *Communication and Cross-Cultural Adaptation, Methods for Intercultural Communication Research* (with W.B. Gudykunst), and *Interethnic Communication: Current Perspectives.*

JUDY LEDGERWOOD is a graduate student in the Department of Anthropology and Southeast Asia Program at Cornell University and a third year student in Khmer language studies. From 1982 to 1984, she was on the staff and later director of a refugee resettlement program in Washington.

EDITH MÄGISTE (Ph.D., Stockholm) is Professor of Psychology at the University of Uppsala, Sweden. She teaches in cognitive psychology, and has conducted research on the psychological effects of bilingualism. She has written a number of book chapters including one in *Language Processing in Bilinguals* (Erlbaum, 1986), and has published articles in *Journal of Experimental Psychology, Journal of Verbal Learning and Verbal Behavior, Acta Psychologica,* and *Scandinavian Journal of Psychology,* among others.

STEVEN McDERMOTT (Ph.D., Michigan State University) is Assistant Professor of Speech Communication at the University of Georgia. His intercultural research has focused on socialization processes, especially in children. In 1983, he received a "Top Three" award from the Intercultural Division of the International Communication Association for his research on communication correlates of Black children's esteem.

MICHAEL McGUIRE (Ph.D., University of Iowa, 1975), is Associate Professor of Speech Communication at the University of Georgia. He has lectured and taught in West Germany and Austria. He is a past recipient of the Ralph Cooley Award for intercultural and international communication research (1983).

CAROL A. MORTLAND (Ph.D. Anthropology, University of Oregon) has served recently as director of a refugee-resettlement program in Washington, D.C. and as director of a refugee assistance program in New York. She was president of the Pierce County Refugee Forum in 1983, and currently is a member of the Advisory Council for the New York State Refugee/Entrant Assistance Program.

W. BARNETT PEARCE is Professor and Chair of the Department of Communication at the University of Massachusetts, Amherst. He received his graduate degrees from the School of Interpersonal Communication at Ohio University. His current research interests include the description of forms of discourse and the methods of intervening in communication to cause a change from one pattern of discourse to another. His most recent book is with Uma Narula, *Development as Communication: A Perspective on India* (Carbondale: Southern Illinois University Press, 1986).

DEEPA PUNETHA is Lecturer in Psychology at the University of Allahabad, India, where she obtained her Ph.D. in 1983. She is interested in ethnic socialization and aggression as well as the interrelations between values, language, and culture.

LORAND B. SZALAY is a psychologist with advanced degrees and training in modern languages (1950), psychology and cultural anthropology (Vienna, 1961), and psycholinguistics (University of Illinois, 1962). He is director of the Institute of Comparative Social and Cultural Studies (Bethesda, MD). He has conducted comparative studies of American, Latin American, Middle Eastern, and Far Eastern cultures. His articles appear in *Journal of Personality and Social Psychology, Current Anthropology, The American Political Science Review, Journal of Communication,* and *The American Anthropologist.*

RONALD TAFT (Ph.D., University of California) is Emeritus Professor of Monash University in Melbourne, Australia, formerly Professor of Social Psychology in the Faculty of Education. After working on social cognition, personality assessment, and creativity in the 1950s, in more recent years he has been involved primarily in studies on ethnic factors in behavior, covering such topics as the assimilation process, the adjustment of immigrants, ethnic relations, ethnic identity, bilingualism, and language competence. His publications include *From Stranger to Citizen* and many book chapters and articles on the above topics in ethnic psychology.

INGEMAR TORBIORN (Ph.D. in psychology, University of Stockholm, 1977; B.Sc. of Economics, The Stockholm School of Economics, 1967) is Associate Professor of Psychology, Department of Psychology, University of Stockholm. His main research interests are in the field of psychology of intercultural relations at the individual and organizational levels. His work includes *Living Abroad: Personal Adjustment and Personnel Policy in the Overseas Setting* (Wiley), and articles in *International Studies of Management* and *International Journal of Intercultural Relations.*

MUNEO JAY YOSHIKAWA (Associate Professor of Japanese at the University of Hawaii) obtained his Ph.D. in American studies. His research areas include Japanese and American modes of communication, Japanese language and culture, and the development of a dialogical theory for intercultural communication. He is coauthor of *Japanese Language and Culture for Business,* and has published articles in *Handbook of Japanese Popular Culture, Communication Theory: Eastern and Western Perspectives, Communication and Cognition,* and *Modern Language Journal,* among others.

LOUIS YOUNG is Research Associate in Social Psychology at the University of Bristol, where he obtained his Ph.D. in 1983. His interests incude cross-cultural studies of values, perceptions of the social structure and change, and group performance.

JUNE O. YUM (Ph.D., Annenberg School of Communications, University of Southern California) is Assistant Professor of Communication at State University of New York at Albany. Her primary research interests are in intercultural communication and interethnic relations, stereotyping, and Asian perspectives of communication. She has published articles in *Human Communication Research, Communication Yearbook, Human Organizations,* and *International Journal of Intercultural Relations,* among others.

WALTER P. ZENNER (Ph.D., Columbia) is Professor of Anthropology at State University of New York at Albany. He teaches courses in cultural anthropology. His main research area has been the ramifications of immigration and ethnicity, especially in the Middle East and North America. He has conducted research on the relationship of commercial specialization to culture among Syrian Jews in New York and Jerusalem, Arabs in the Galilee, and Soviet Jewish immigrants in Albany, New York. He is coeditor of *Urban Life: Readings in Urban Anthropology* and *Jewish Societies in the Middle East.*